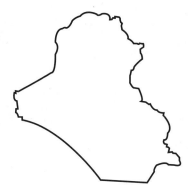

WHAT AFTER IRAQ?

Donald M. Snow

PEARSON
Longman

New York   San Francisco   Boston
London   Toronto   Sydney   Tokyo   Singapore   Madrid
Mexico City   Munich   Paris   Cape Town   Hong Kong   Montreal

Acquisitions Editor: Vikram Mukhija
Associate Marketing Manager: Sasha Anderson-Smith
Supplements Editor: Brian Belardi
Project Coordination, Text Design, and Page Makeup:
    Grapevine Publishing Services, Inc.
Cover Designer: Ian Crowther
Manufacturing Buyer: Roy Pickering
Printer and Binder: R.R. Donnelley / Harrisonburg
Cover Printer: R.R. Donnelley / Harrisonburg

What After Iraq? by Donald M. Snow.

ISBN: 0-205-64284-5; ISBN-13: 978-0-205-64284-7

1 2 3 4 5 6 7 8 9 10—DOH—11 10 09 08

CONTENTS

Introduction

Ending Another Trauma

The Iraq War is now the third-longest war in American history, measured in terms of active combat. Vietnam, the longest war, was active American combat participation which spanned eight years, followed by the American Revolution, which lasted six years—from Lexington and Concord to Yorktown (for a discussion, *see* Snow and Drew). The United States invaded Iraq on March 20, 2003, active combat spans more than five years, and it continues. Present projections by military and administration officials suggest the war could easily surpass Vietnam in terms of length, and even Democratic presidential candidates Barak Obama and Hillary Clinton have said they can imagine American combat forces there in 2013, although both have hedged those positions. Involvement may not end when the fighting ends; there are plans (*see* Chapter 7) for an "enduring," postwar American presence that has only recently been widely publicized in the presidential campaign.

American public opinion has turned on the war, and most Americans now believe it was a mistake to launch it and an even bigger mistake to continue it. Yet, the war continues, and there is no indication that the end is in sight. Indeed, in his final State of the Union address on January 28, 2008, President Bush warned that there was a long road ahead for Americans in Iraq. Although many voters took the 2006 Congressional elections to be a referendum on ending the war, troop levels are higher than they were before that election. Beyond talk of an enduring presence after all combat troops are withdrawn, the United States is establishing permanent bases in Iraq, and Secretary of Defense Robert Gates has drawn the analogy between American continuing presence in Iraq and the American record in South Korea, where U.S. troops are still stationed, fifty-five years after the end of the Korean War. On January 15, 2008, Abdul Wadir, the Iraqi defense minister, was quoted in the *New York Times*, opining that Iraq would be incapable of self-defense "until 2018 to 2020." Is this what the American public had in mind?

It is a virtual axiom that political democracies do not like long wars, especially if those involvements seem indeterminate in length, and ambiguous in terms of the virtue of their conduct and probable outcomes. The United

States is no exception to this rule, and yet the current administration continues the Iraq War as if its prosecution was so obviously compelling that public dissatisfaction should be ignored. In important ways, the dynamics of Vietnam seem to be repeating themselves, including the growing and predictable unpopularity of the endeavor.

During the Vietnam War, the presidential election of 1968 was largely contested over whether Richard M. Nixon or Hubert H. Humphrey would most quickly end the Vietnam War. Nixon won, and withdrawal took five years—longer than the American conduct of the war when the policy of Vietnamization was engaged. In 2006, the American public voted overwhelmingly in favor of candidates dedicated to ending American involvement in Iraq, and a key issue in the 2008 election is the future of American involvement there. Like Vietnam, everyone agrees that ending the war is a priority; they disagree on how quickly and under what circumstances withdrawal will occur.

Two-thirds of the American public (give or take a few percentage points, depending on when the poll is taken) favor ending the war in Iraq. At the strictly rhetorical level, most political figures have adopted the idea of war termination that the 2006 election results seemed to mandate, but American troop strength actually increased during 2007 from 138,000 to 168,000 due to the administration's "surge," intended to help quell Iraqi violence (a parallel to Vietnam's maximum troop levels reached in 1969—after Nixon's inauguration). Those numbers are returning roughly to pre-surge levels due to troop rotations, but the physical commitment has not lessened. Since November 2006, the apparent will of the people has gone unheeded for nearly two years, and it is not clear whether, or how rapidly, that preference will be implemented, regardless of who wins the presidential election. Why?

The reasons that the public "referendum" on Iraq in 2006 has not translated into an effective, undeniable public demand for withdrawal from Iraq are numerous and complex. For the moment, it is possible to look at four dynamics that will help frame the question of why the United States remains in Iraq. It will also help to answer this book's other, more fundamental question, which is what the national security equation will look like after the Iraq War. The two questions are clearly interactive, since an assessment of what Iraq will become, based on different scenarios of American withdrawal, clearly affects the kind of withdrawal, and timing one favors. The four dynamics are the framework in which proponents have cast the debate, questions about the consequences of disengagement, the lack of direct involvement of Americans in the war, and the slow-building nature of the Iraq trauma.

The first dynamic is how the war has been depicted. The Bush administration has framed the war as a national security crusade, vital to the country's security. Support of the war effort toward whatever successful conclusion the president deems necessary, a point of some ambiguity in practice, thus becomes a moral and patriotic imperative. Conversely, opposition is a sign not only of lack of resolve, but also a feckless abrogation of the patriotic entreaty to defend the country against those who would do it harm. Continued financial support for the troops, at whatever levels and for whatever purposes the administration deems necessary, is part of this framing of the question. This argumentation rests on the debatable assumptions that prosecuting war against Iraq is, in fact, necessary for the country's security, and that the absence of that effort would place the country in danger. Proponents have, in effect, succeeded in wrapping the American flag tightly around this position. Opponents have been unsuccessful in rebutting this typecast; to do so would require that the public be persuaded that continuing the war does not further the national interest and that withdrawal is the patriotic course.

The second dynamic is related: People have serious, unresolved questions about the consequences of implementing policies that result in withdrawal from Iraq. These questions congregate around two poles. One is whether continuing American involvement will change the outcome. If the United States leaves soon and rapidly, will that action contribute to victory, or defeat, or will "staying the course" produce a more satisfactory outcome for Americans? Proponents clearly believe that continuation will leave Iraq a place of which the United States can be prouder than the Iraq a precipitous withdrawal would leave behind. This "better" Iraq may be either a model democracy for the region (the publicly stated U.S. objective), or, more minimally, an Iraq that does not devolve into chaotic violence. Opponents argue the opposite: It does not matter when the United States leaves, that the results will be the same regardless of the departure date. Another of these unresolved questions is what kind of Iraq will be left behind. Americans, by and large, accept Colin Powell's "Pottery Barn rule" analogy ("You break it, you own it."). Since the United States "broke" Iraq, the United States "owns it" and must fix it. The question is, would a continuing U.S. presence help fix the problem, or simply defer the process of working things out, or would that continuing presence actually makes things worse? The answer is not as simple as advocates on either side suggest.

The third dynamic is more controversial: A major reason the American public has allowed Iraq to fester for so long is because it does not represent a clear, compelling, and personal problem for most Americans. The only Americans who have been fundamentally affected by the Iraq War are those who have volunteered for military service and the loved ones of these service members. Since there is no current application of the selective service (conscription) laws, no one is compelled to serve. Were there the Damoclean sword of involuntary draft, amounting to placement into harm's way for all Americans in the eligible demographic categories, there would almost certainly be a greater urgency to bring the war to completion than in the absence of such a threat.

Fourth and finally, the Iraq War has been a slow-developing trauma. The war, after all, was proposed in the shadow of the terrorist attacks of September 11, 2001, as a major theater of the global war on terror (GWOT) declared on September 12. Saddam Hussein's alleged possession of weapons of mass destruction (WMD), and the possibility he might share these with terrorists, was the heart of the Bush administration's call for a regime change in Iraq. At the time, the long shadow of the GWOT connection overwhelmed any skepticism of the rationale. Kenneth Pollack, former Clinton administration official, captured this rationale in *The Threatening Storm*, his prewar advocacy of invasion. "Saddam's pursuit of nuclear weapons is the real reason for invading," he argues, and "those who argue for deterrence for fear of the costs of an invasion, and particularly, fear of Iraqi WMD, are setting a very dangerous precedent." In the early invasion and conquest phases of the war, the results seemed stunningly successful. This was encapsulated by President Bush's May 1, 2003 declaration of the liberation of Iraq, while standing on the deck of the battleship *USS Abraham Lincoln*, a banner declaring "Mission Accomplished" waving behind him. That the occupation, called Phase IV operations, would become a disaster was only hinted at by initial scenes of looting and chaos in Iraq. Administration officials like then-Secretary of Defense Donald Rumsfeld predicted the war would be easy and quick and that almost all American forces would be out of Iraq by the end of summer 2003. Gordon and Trainor quote his February 14, 2003 speech aboard the *USS Intrepid*: "The war should be a win-win situation. The United States could oust a dictator . . . without America committing itself to [a] lengthy, costly, and arduous peacekeeping effort." Gordon and Trainor add that the administration was so confident in this assessment that President Bush convened a White House meeting on April 15, 2003 "to consider the plan for withdrawing U.S. forces from Iraq." In addition, the war would not be costly, since Iraqi oil revenues would help defray costs (*see* Packer). Although these depictions were uniformly false, the depiction of Iraq as part of the "long war against terrorism" effectively muted criticism through the presidential election year of 2004. Only as these falsehoods became increasingly evident during 2005 and 2006 did criticism mount.

These factors suppressed criticism of the war, but they did not extinguish it. Political officials may seem curiously out of step with the public sentiment to disengage from Iraq, but criticism has mounted and will become more and more irresistible with time. At this juncture, it is impossible to project with certainty what kind of withdrawal timetable will be adopted, or when the process will be completed. To a great degree, how soon American involvement in the Iraq War will end and what, if any, residual involvement will remain has not been decided, and will be influenced by the level and quality of public opinion. Projecting past the 2008 election risks moving from Rumsfeld's realm of "knowing what we don't know" to his more ethereal realm of "not knowing what we don't know." The further into the future the projection goes, in other words, the more unforeseeable vicissitudes will intervene. There are, however, some fairly safe assumptions that can be made about how this process will unfold and what the likely outcomes will be (typifying them as "fairly safe" is a caveat—they could be wrong). With that rejoinder in mind, these assumptions will help frame the discussion in the rest of the book.

The first assumption is that there will be no clear, definitive outcome to this war. The war (or at least the American part in it) will not end with some decisive action or set of events that represents a "victory" for one side or the other. Apologists for the war have been unable to present a coherent definition of what victory is or which side should prevail, which is part of the problem. The other part of the problem is that victory, in any traditional military sense, is virtually unattainable in this kind of war, and it is equally unclear which of Iraq's factions the United States wants to see victorious; one of the inevitable consequences of invading a highly fractionalized state. If victory is to be declared, it will have to be of the kind the late Senator Claude Aiken (R-VT) proposed for the Vietnam War: Simply declare victory, leave, and let others decide what victory means.

The American withdrawal, rather than being the result of some honest climactic event, will instead be slow, gradual, and indecisive. That indecision will be of two sorts: There will be ambiguity about whether sufficient progress has been made to allow disengagement, and there will be ambiguity about what the results of disengagement are. It will, in other words, be hard to distinguish the change from the day the last American combat troops leave Iraq from the day before. Iraq will end with a whimper, not a bang. Withdrawal and leaving may not be the same thing. As noted, in June 2007, Secretary Gates told a military group that he could imagine a "long continuing presence" that he analogized to Korea (*see* Seale). Protecting American access to Iraqi oil could be the reason for this.

The second assumption is that regardless of how the war ends, there will be a spirited, recriminatory national debate about the ending. That debate has already begun, and it has two aspects. One is over how and why the United States got involved and why so many Americans—including elected officials—supported a decision that many now decry. But as Dobbins put it in a recent *Foreign Affairs* article, "There is more than enough blame to go around. The United States went into Iraq with a higher level of domestic support than almost any time in its history." This problem is particularly acute for those who initially supported the war but have recanted—why were they wrong? The other aspect of the debate is whether the United States will in effect "sell out" those Iraqis whom it has supported by the conditions of withdrawal that are adopted. The opposite poles of this debate are a more-or-less either immediate withdrawal (former Democratic presidential candidate George McGovern's view that "the quicker we get out, the better") or "stay the course" (Col. H. R. McMaster, quoted in *Mother Jones,* "I believe that certainly [the strategy] does have a strong chance of succeeding if we have the will to see it through"). This debate, like its equivalent regarding Vietnam, will long outlast the war itself.

The third assumption is that there will be an "Iraq hangover" in the form of resistance to the use of military force in the years following the end of the Iraq War. Mueller calls this an Iraq "syndrome," which he defines as a "strong aversion to embarking on such ventures again." Much of this argument will be military in content. Partly, it will involve an examination of the military's role in promoting, or not vigorously opposing, involvement in a war many knew could not be won, what Lt. Col. Paul Yingling refers to as "a failure of generalship" in a seminal 2007 article. Retired Lt. General Gregg Newbold is more blunt: "We must never again stand quietly by while those ignorant of and casual about war lead us into another one and then mismanage the conduct of it." A related consideration is whether the United States should have anticipated the kind of asymmetrical war it became in Iraq, and what the Iraq experience means for the future. Mueller believes that "among the casualties of the Iraq syndrome could be the Bush doctrine, unilateralism, preemption, preventive war, and indispensable nationhood." The likelihood of the hangover/syndrome may provide some comfort to those Americans concerned about the Bush administration's apparently aggressive intentions toward Iran.

The fourth assumption is that, regardless of the circumstances of American disengagement from Iraq, there will be negative consequences that will affect the American recollection of the war. Within Iraq, there will almost certainly be instability as the various factions create a new, post-American reality for their country, and that likely includes recriminations against those Iraqis who have supported the American presence. Dreyfuss quotes Zbigniew Brzezinski in *Mother Jones* on this point: "The only Iraqis who want the United States to stay are the ones who will have to leave when we leave." Likewise, the conditions after the withdrawal will affect the view others have of the United States. There will be mixed reactions, depending on whether countries or groups supported the effort in the first place. Much of this concern surrounds access to Iraqi oil, a theme developed throughout the text. Support for, or opposition to, the war's ending may also become part of the partisan divide within the United States, if support for the outcome becomes a sign of patriotism.

The fifth assumption is that the post-Iraq War debate will have an important impact on how the United States uses force in the future. In some important ways, this is the most important outcome of the Iraq War. This war has undeniably stressed the American military system well beyond initial expectations, and no one welcomes the prospect of a repeat performance. Whether this situation could or should have been anticipated is debatable. However, in the future, enemies of the United States are certainly going to analyze the impact of this war and conclude that the asymmetrical campaign mounted by Iraqi insurgents is an effective way to negate American military prowess. Ironically, General Petraeus, the commanding general of the multi-national force in Iraq, has been a leading proponent of this interpretation. Exactly what adjustments the United States will make after this experience—the lessons learned—will be arguably the most important outcome of the war.

Several emphases distinguish this book from other works on Iraq. It attempts to look beyond the Iraq War and to address the consequences for the United States. It argues, for instance, that there will be effects similar to those after the Vietnam War: An Iraq hangover that will impede American military adventurism for a period of time, for example. It also explores issues such as the need to rebuild the badly stressed American military system following the Iraq War, and likely domestic attitudes toward future uses of the military. It examines the reasons the United States became involved in Iraq, why it was deemed necessary (see Lewis and Reading-Smith), and why some feel that U.S. troops must stay. In particular, it presents the viewpoint that access to or control of Iraqi oil reserves—which have largely been ignored in policy statements and most analyses—cannot be underestimated and must be included in assessing the situation. It argues that the American policy of withdrawal from Iraq is in place, and it follows the process of Vietnamization of a generation ago. President Bush outlined this policy of "Iraqification," a term the administration avoids, in his 2008 State of the Union address, sounding like Vietnam redux: the goals are stabilization of the ongoing situation (including helping prepare the Iraqis), a gradual turnover of responsibility to the Iraqis as the Americans leave, and progress toward political settlement. Next, the book considers the matter of "enduring presence," a policy emphasis that has been largely obscured from an American public likely to disapprove of the concept. Do Americans really want U.S. troops in Iraq and beyond (or in bases "over the horizon" in neighboring countries, so they could rapidly be reinserted into Iraq)?

The organization of the rest of the book elaborates these introductory remarks. There are two sequential parts. Part I, "The Context," consists of four chapters that define the Iraq experience. Chapter 1, "Kuwait City to Baghdad," looks at the process leading to the decision to invade Iraq, revealing that advocacy far precedes the events of 9/11, that President Bush and many others in the Bush administration had resolved to invade Iraq prior to 9/11 and that 9/11 served more as pretext than the cause of the war. Chapter 2, "A Tale of Two Wars," compares the Iraq and Vietnam War experiences. It presents the argument that there are more similarities than differences, and that the post-Vietnam environment thus provides beguiling clues to what the post-Iraq environment will be. Chapter 3, "On the Domestic Front," brings the discussion to the present, with an emphasis on how the Iraq War is both affecting, and being affected by, domestic political concerns, and on how the 2008 election might influence the Iraq War's impact on American politics. Chapter 4, "Iraqification," posits that the process of disengagement, Iraqification, will resemble the process of Vietnamization a generation ago, and then assesses the likely impact of various scenarios of U.S. withdrawal.

Part II, "The Consequences," has three chapters aimed at predicting the impact of the Iraq War on the American security future. Chapter 5, "No More Iraqs," focuses on two aspects of the post-Iraq War environment: "lessons learned" by the military and political leadership to guide orientations toward future similar situations, and the direct impact of the Iraq experience on how the United States faces security threats in the years immediately after Iraq. Chapter 6, "Repairing American Military Power," examines one of the most glaring problems arising from the Iraq War, the question of adequate military manpower for this and future situations. In the process, it assesses possible alternative ways to man the future force, including a return to conscript forces and the increased privatization of elements and functions of the force via instruments such as Blackwater and other "private security" entities. Finally, Chapter 7, "Forecasting American Security," looks at the Iraq War's impact on how the U.S. handles security threats in the future. The post-Vietnam period witnessed a drawing back from commitments with military implications, and this chapter delves into whether there will be a similar reaction post-Iraq, particularly in a world where America's enemies will have learned from Iraq how to confront the United States in ways that it has yet to successfully counteract. Hopefully, the totality will provide some answers and insights to the question, "What After Iraq?"

The analyses included in these pages are largely my own. I have been studying the problem of Iraq for over 30 years, especially when Iraq has been prominent in American policy. I first opposed the idea of invading Iraq in 1990, when, on the heels of Saddam Hussein's invasion of Kuwait, I took part in a seminar at the U.S. Army War College, analyzing possible American responses to the invasion. We concluded that invading Iraq was a bad idea for reasons that have become evident since 2003. That judgment holds today. As the process leading to invasion began to build in 2002, I met with graduate students from at the University of Alabama to discussed the prospects, and reached the same conclusion. A number of these students, including Jeff Taylor and Saskia Bunting, investigated the primary proponents on the war, the neoconservatives, and some of their findings are included. I thank these more or less willing contributors for some ideas contained in these pages, but accept full personal responsibility for any errors there might be. Moreover, the subject continues to evolve, and new developments will be included in the blog that accompanies the book.

SELECTED BIBLIOGRAPHY

Bush, George W. "President Bush Delivers the State of the Union Address." Washington, DC: The White House, January 28, 2008.

Dobbins, James. "Who Lost Iraq? Lessons from the Debacle." *Foreign Affairs* 86, 5 (September/October 2007), 61–74.

Dreyfuss, Robert. "The Bad, the Worse, and the Ugly." *Mother Jones* 32, 6 (November/December 2007), 42–43.

Goldberg, Jeffrey. "After Iraq." *The Atlantic* 301, 1 (January/February 2008), 68–79.

Gordon, Michael R. and General Bernard E. Trainor. *Cobra II: The Inside Story of the Invasion and Occupation of Iraq.* New York: Pantheon Books, 2006.

Lewis, Charles, and Mark Reading-Smith. "False Pretenses: Iraq: The War Card." Washington, DC: Center for Public Integrity, January 2008.

Mueller, John. "The Iraq Syndrome." *Foreign Affairs* 84, 6 (November/December 2006), 44–54.

Newbold, Lt. Gen. (Ret.) Gregg. "Why Iraq Was a Mistake." *Time* (online edition), April 9, 2006.

Packer, George. *The Assassin's Gate: America in Iraq*. New York: Farrar, Straus, and Giroux, 2005.

Pollack, Kenneth M. *The Threatening Storm: The Case for Invading Iraq* (A Council on Foreign Relations Book). New York: Random House, 2002.

Seale, Patrick. "US Is Building Base in Iraq." *Gulfnews.com* (online). June 4, 2007.

Shank, Thom. "Minister Sees Need for U.S. Help in Iraq Until 2018." *New York Times* (online edition), January 15, 2008.

Simon, Steven N. *After the Surge: The Case for U.S. Military Disengagement from Iraq*. New York: CSR 23, Council on Foreign Relations, February 2007.

Snow, Donald M. and Dennis M. Drew. *From Lexington to Desert Storm and Beyond: War and Politics in the American Experience*. Armonk, NY: M. E. Sharpe, 2000.

Yingling, Lt. Col. Paul. "A Failure in Generalship." *Armed Forces Journal* (online edition), May, 2007.

PART

I

THE CONTEXT

Chapter 1

Kuwait City to Baghdad

The determination of those who advocated and made the decision to invade and conquer Iraq did not result from the terrorist attacks of September 11, 2001, nor from President George W. Bush's declaration of an American war on terror the following day. The roots of the Iraq War go back much further, to the wake of the Gulf War of 1990–1991 and, in the case of many of the most prominent neoconservative advocates of the action, the desire to overthrow Saddam Hussein goes back at least to the 1980s. Indeed, some of those who had counseled attacking Iraq well before 9/11 became prominent national security officials in the Bush administration in January 2001 and suggested, presciently, that Iraq should be the *first* regime change in a process that would include Iran, Syria, and Saudi Arabia.

That making war on Iraq was a long-held policy goal of many who entered public office or positions of influence in 2001 was not a closely guarded secret. The advocates had hinted at, or openly proposed, such a course with growing vehemence during the 1990s, but very few Americans paid much attention to them. Many had left office with the defeat of George H.W. Bush in 1992 (most were mid-level officials who did not enjoy inner circle status). During most of the 1990s, George W. Bush expressed few foreign policy positions of any kind, although he did endorse his father's decision not to have invaded Iraq in 1991—a position he would reverse by the end of the decade. The point is that the desire to make war against Iraq was not a byproduct of the period surrounding September 11, 2001; its roots are far earlier and quite independent of the terrorist attacks that provided the public explanation for attacking Iraq.

Is it an important aspect of, or a diversion from, a central focus on Iraq's future to dredge up the origins of the decision to start the war in the first place? Apologists for the war argue that it is irrelevant and counterproductive to raise these concerns now. They maintain that regardless of whether or why the decisions were made, they have, in fact, been made and cannot be undone. The pottery has indeed been broken (as then-Secretary of State

Colin Powell stated often in his analogy), and the United States does "own" the broken pot that Iraq represents. Thus, looking backward is a diversion from what must be done now. A retrospective orientation can only sap vital energies needed for looking forward.

The other side of this argument is that the decision process and motivation for invading Iraq are highly relevant in determining whether the United States should have invaded, what it sought to accomplish and what it can accomplish, and thus, whether prolonging the war makes accomplishing those goals more likely. "The Pottery Barn rule" (as *New York Times* columnist Thomas L. Friedman dubbed it) analogy certainly does provide some of the context for determining the parameters of the future, but it is not the entire rationale for continuation. Part of the post-mortem on the Iraq experience, the lessons learned, is necessarily an examination of what got the United States where it is. Without examining that question, one cannot assess whether the country should act in the same way or a different way when, or if, similar conditions recur.

To the extent they have developed positions on the reasons for going into Iraq, most Americans believe the genesis is related to 9/11, which is certainly the way proponents portray it (Iraq as a theater of the war on terror). But is that belief accurate? Would initial American support for the invasion of Iraq have been as great if the public had not believed there was a 9/11 connection? Would, for instance, the response have been as positive if instead the administration maintained that the real reason was to buttress Israeli security or to gain control of Iraqi oil (both alternative explanations of U.S. motivations)?

THE CONCEPTUAL ROAD TO WAR

Advocacy of overthrowing Saddam Hussein predates both the Gulf War and 9/11. One of the earliest and most vocal advocates was (and still is) Richard Perle, a Reagan administration official and charter neoconservative with close connections to the George W. Bush administration. Perle is a leading spokesman for the neoconservatives who have been prominent in the Bush administration and who were among the most vocal proponents of overthrowing Saddam Hussein.

The basic neoconservative position on Iraq is that Saddam Hussein's regime was a menace to the region and had to go. Perle, for instance, is on the public record as far back as at least 1987 on this point, arguing, "Saddam Hussein's Iraq is ruled by one of the most brutally repressive regimes in the world." As Operation Desert Storm was being organized in September 1990, he made this position more explicit, arguing, "Our objective must be disman-tling or destroying Saddam Hussein's military power. Nothing less will suf-fice." During the Kuwait crisis of 1990, Perle warned in a *Wall Street Journal* opinion piece that "if this crisis ends with Iraq's nascent nuclear capabilities and chemical-weapons production facilities and stockpiles intact, the Western world will have made a mistake of historic proportions" that, among other things, will "threaten to destroy Israel." This article is typical of neo-conservative thought at the time (for a summary, see the Snow online paper). The methods for attaining this end were spelled out in a 1992 draft Defense Planning Guidance (DPG) written by neoconservative Paul D. Wolfowitz (who would serve as a close foreign policy advisor to George W. Bush in 2000) and endorsed by his then-supervisor, Defense Secretary Richard Cheney. The document proposed the essential ideas of what would become the Bush Doctrine (unilateralism, preventive war, overwhelming military strength). The first President Bush vetoed the draft, and it lay fallow until his son took office (*see* Armstrong).

The positions that would provide the justification for the invasion were refined during the early years of the Clinton administration and resurfaced in the 1990s. In a November 4, 1997 *Washington Post* op-ed article, which he co-authored with former U.S. Ambassador to Iraq and current Ambassador to the U.N. Zalmay Khalilzad, Wolfowitz wrote, "The United States should instead consider a comprehensive new strategy aimed at promoting a *change of regime* in Baghdad," (emphasis added). On January 26, 1998, a group of neoconservatives wrote an open letter to President Bill Clinton warning that "if Saddam does acquire the capability to deliver weapons of mass destruction, as he is almost certain to do if we continue along the present course, the safe-ty of American troops in the region, of our friends and allies like Israel and the moderate Arab states, and a significant portion of the world's supply of oil will all be put at hazard." The signatories to the letter were a virtual who's who of George W. Bush officials and apologists: Elliott Abrams, Richard Armitage, William J. Bennett, John Bolton, Robert Kagan, Khalilizad, William Kristol, Perle, Donald Rumsfeld, Wolfowitz, R. James Woolsey, and Robert B. Zoellick, among others. The letter is one of the few occurrences of oil being linked to possible U.S. actions in Iraq.

This letter was the opening gambit in a renewed campaign to bring pressure on the government to engage in "regime change" in Iraq. Two weeks later, on February 8, 1998, Perle carried the advocacy a step further in an op-ed article published in the *Washington Post*: "The United States— *alone if necessary*—with our friends if possible, should encourage, recognize, help finance, and protect with air power a new provisional government broadly representative of all the people of Iraq," (emphasis added). Following the August 7, 1998 Al Qaeda attacks on the American embassies in Dar es Salaam, Tanzania and Nairobi, Kenya, and Clinton's signing of the Iraq Liberation Act of 1998, the *Weekly Standard,* a recognized neoconservative journal, published an editorial entitled "How to Attack Iraq." It endorsed a plan that had been proposed by Wolfowitz to create a "liberated zone" in Shiite southern Iraq. In September 2000, the Project for a New American Century (PNAC), a Washington-based neoconservative think tank, produced a report titled "Rebuilding America's Forces" that endorsed and reiterated many of the arguments in the rejected 1992 draft DPG, also written by Wolfowitz.

This selective history suggests that the desirability and rationale for attacking Iraq were in place well before the 2000 election or the terrorist attacks of 2001. From the vantage points of leading neoconservative thinkers like Perle and Wolfowitz, there were two major underlying reasons to oppose Saddam Hussein and to advocate his overthrow. One was the danger he posed to the region, the most obvious manifestation of which was his actual and potential possession of WMD. This concern was certainly not groundless; the Iraqi dictator had, in fact, used chemical weapons against Iran during the latter stages of the Iran-Iraq War during the 1980s, and also against indigenous Kurdish opponents in 1987. Ascertaining whether he retained such capabilities, or was attempting to expand them, was more problematic.

The other theme is that the Hussein regime posed a particular menace to the security of Israel. Basic to the neoconservative philosophy going back to the 1950s is that American and Israeli security interests in the Middle East are tightly interwoven (if not essentially inextricable), meaning that a threat to Israeli interests in the region is a threat to American interests as well. Indeed, a number of neoconservative leaders—Perle being a notable example—have close relations with Israeli organizations and think tanks, like the Jewish Institute for National Security Affairs (JINSA) and the Institute for Advanced Strategic and Political Studies (which has centers both in Washington and Jerusalem). American neoconservative redoubts include the American Enterprise Institute (where President Bush gave a major speech in 2003, outlining his war policy, and where he has subsequently given other speeches), the Center for Strategic Policy (CSP), and PNAC.

Although the current discussion only provides snapshots of the beginning and end of the period, the failed 1992 draft DPG and the 2000 PNAC report provide the policy rationale for taking aggressive action against Iraq (in contravention to the Geneva Conventions on War and provisions of the U.N. Charter prohibiting military aggression). Thus, all the pieces were in place to carry out regime change in Iraq by 2000. The central problem for the neocon-servatives during the 1990s was finding a political candidate to sponsor their reentry into government and thus enable them to implement their Iraq strat-egy. If someone who was sympathetic to their cause could not recapture the White House, their agenda would remain fallow and their goals unfulfilled. Thus, the search for a sympathetic figure who could also be a viable presiden-tial candidate was a major endeavor during the waning part of the Clinton administration. They found such a sympathizer, ironically, in the son of the president who had rebuked them in 1992 by rejecting the draft DPG. In George W. Bush, they found a candidate who both could win and who could be molded to accept the neoconservative position. In his vice presidential choice, Richard Cheney, they had one of their own.

The Courtship and Conversion of George W. Bush

At first glance, George W. Bush seemed an unlikely champion for the neo-conservative cause of overthrowing Saddam Hussein. His father had rejected the advocacy of doing so in 1991 as the Iraqis collapsed in Kuwait, and he had rebuked the aggressive security policy stance formulated by Wolfowitz and Cheney in the 1992 draft DPG. The generally liberal internationalist senior Bush had surrounded himself with advisors like Brent Scowcroft, who reject-ed the neoconservative position as utopian. On those occasions during the 1990s when the subject came up, the younger Bush supported his father's decision not to invade and conquer Iraq in 1991. In a 1997 interview with the *San Antonio Express*, he said, "I think my father conducted himself bril-liantly during Desert Storm and understands the situation pretty clearly." He added that "to ferret out" Saddam in 1991 would have changed the Gulf War into an unpopular "guerrilla war." In a November 22, 1999 interview with *Newsweek*, he added that overthrowing the Iraqi regime "would have expand-ed the mission." Moreover, Bob Woodward reported in his book, *Bush at War* that George W. Bush had told Condoleezza Rice "before the 2000 campaign" that his position on Iraq had not changed.

Bush and the neoconservatives are an odd personality fit as well. Many of the core neoconservatives are hard-driving conservative Jewish intellectuals (Perle and Wolfowitz are prime examples) who are infused with enormous zeal for their missions. They are, in Clintonian terms, "policy wonks" who stand, as personalities, in stark contrast to Michael Lind's depiction of Bush as "the macho, swaggering, Southern, born-again Protestant son, a genuine cultural Texan" who, according to critic Molly Ivins, "said he doesn't like to read long books, especially books on policy."

There were, of course, countervailing influences. Although previously Bush held what turned out to be a very prescient view of what a war in Iraq could become, he also harbored a deep resentment and hatred for Saddam Hussein, apparently from his reaction to reports that Saddam had commissioned an attempt to assassinate the senior Bush during a 1993 visit to Kuwait. In addition, there was some basic philosophical agreement between Bush and neoconservatives on the aggressive, unilateral stance on foreign policy in the 1992 DPG draft. Lind explains this affinity in terms of the Texas influence on Bush: "The Wolfowitz-Bush doctrine of unilateral militarism, influenced by the unilateralism of the Israeli government, was easily identified with the preferred foreign policy tradition of the American South, dating back to the early days of the Republic" and including "a hostility toward diplomacy and international organizations rooted in both Southern militarism and Southern fundamentalism." When Rice assembled a group of advisors to help form the Bush positions on foreign policy for the 2000 election campaign (the so-called Vulcans, as described by James Mann in his book, *Rise of the Vulcans*), Wolfowitz shared top billing with the future National Security Advisor and Secretary of State, and several other neoconservatives (Stephen Hadley, for instance) were members of the team.

Despite his feelings on the wisdom of restraint in the Gulf War, the outlines of what would become Bush's decision to go to war with Iraq became evident by 1999. In a speech entitled "A Period of Consequences," given at the Citadel in Charleston, South Carolina on September 23, 1999, he declared that "it will require firmness with regimes like North Korea and Iraq," and that, if they threaten the United States with WMD, they "must know, if they sponsor such attacks, our response will be devastating." A few sentences later, he added, "I will put high priority on detecting and responding to terrorism on our soil. The federal government will take this threat seriously." Less than two months later, he gave a major speech at the Ronald Reagan Presidential Library in Simi Valley, California, outlining his views on national security. This November 19, 1999 speech, titled "A Distinctly American Internationalism," outlined many of the principles in the 1992 DPG that became the basis for the Bush doctrine justifying the war in Iraq. To his concern with Iraq, he added the neoconservative position on Israeli security, arguing that an American president should "advance peace in the Middle East based on a secure Israel."

These signs of early determination to engage in war with Iraq are arguably oblique and indirect, but before the end of 1999, candidate Bush created a minor flap about his intentions toward Saddam Hussein in an early December 1999 debate among Republican candidates in Bedford, New Hampshire. Asked by FOX broadcaster and host Brit Hume what he would do about

Hussein, Bush declared, "If I found out in any way, shape, or form that he was developing weapons of mass destruction, I'd take him out." He added, "I'm surprised he's still there. I think a lot of other people are as well." Hume then asked for a clarification of what Bush meant by "take him out," to which Bush replied "take out the weapons of mass destruction." The *New York Times* account of the event suggested that Bush had slurred his reference so that it could be interpreted either as "take 'em out" (the weapons) or "take him out" (Hussein). The next day, however, Bush was asked again about what he meant—to "take out" the WMD or Saddam himself. Bush replied, "That's up for Saddam Hussein to figure out. He doesn't need to be building them. . . . He just needs to know I'll take them out. It's important for a future commander in chief to state our intentions and the means will be evident to him."

Thus, before the 2000 election campaign formally began, Bush had apparently taken both sides on whether the United States should act to overthrow Saddam Hussein. In supporting the wisdom of his father's demurral from marching to Baghdad in 1991 because it would result in a civil war (a particularly insightful prediction that apparently was lost to him between 1997 and 2003), he seemed to argue against the idea. His words at the Citadel, at the Reagan Library, and in Bedford, New Hampshire, all provided hints that he had changed his mind on the subject and had adopted at least part of the neoconservative stance on the Middle East, including the desire to overthrow the Iraqi regime. Patching together the intellectual odyssey which Bush went through personally is difficult, because prior to the 2000 campaign, he had very little to say on foreign policy subjects or the Middle East. His views on the region and on Iraq may have been long and deeply held, but he had not directly stated them previously in any comprehensive way.

What is clear, however, is that advocacies of overthrowing Saddam Hussein had been a prominent part of the political positions of the neoconservatives for a decade or more by 2000. By the time Bush began his quest for the presidency in earnest in 2000, he had adopted some of those positions, and he had surrounded himself with advisors who shared this view. From the public record, it is not clear how committed Bush was to attacking Iraq at this point—over three and a half years before the invasion and a year and a half or more before 9/11. It is, however, clear that the seeds for the decision to invade Iraq had been sown well before the terrorist attacks of September 11.

The Impact of 9/11

What role did the American reaction to the terrorist attacks of September 11, 2001 have on the decision to make war on Iraq? In popular constructions, the

Al Qaeda attacks are part of a causal chain from 9/11 forward through the American military anti-terrorist effort in Afghanistan to the decision to invade Iraq. But does that interpretation accurately describe the decision process that caused the Bush administration to choose the course of war? Or was it a rationale by the administration to explain a decision it reached at least partly independently of the 9/11 shock? Put more simply, was 9/11 the cause (or part of the cause) of the Iraq war decision, or was it a pretext to justify a decision that would have been made quite independently of 9/11?

The evidence is not unambiguous. Certainly, there is a linkage between the events. Both occurred as the result of events in the same part of the world (specifically the gestation and sanctuary of Al Qaeda in neighboring Afghanistan). Both Al Qaeda and Iraq were worrisome to both the United States and Israel, and the general hysteria that emerged from 9/11 and the "war on terror" created great anxiety within the public and elites about the Persian Gulf region. Knowledge about the nature of Al Qaeda, the depth of its penetration of the region, and its interrelationships with other forces in the region were not well understood (at least outside the expert community). Moreover, the first American response in the Global War on Terrorism (GWOT)—the campaign in Afghanistan—was at that point an apparent success, validating the efficacy of using American military force to bring about retribution against the terrorist threat.

The preceding discussion, however, raises some questions about the causal linkage. What is clear is that the predilection to invade Iraq and overthrow the government of Saddam Hussein predates 9/11 by well over a decade. It had been articulated prior to, during, and after the Persian Gulf War of 1990–1991. Many of those who argued for attacking Iraq after 9/11 had been arguing the same thing for years, including a number of people who had been part of the George H.W. Bush administration that had been rebuffed by the failure of the United States to move into Iraq in 1991. Somewhat ironically, then-Secretary of Defense Richard Cheney was among those who wanted to "finish the job" against Saddam Hussein in 1991, whereas George W. Bush (who publicly voiced no opinion at the time) later opined that his father had done the right thing by restraining American forces. Meanwhile, the neoconservatives, who by and large occupied second-tier positions in the first Bush administration, waited for the inauguration of the second Bush in 2001 to provide the platform to do what they had wanted to do for years.

The case that the neoconservatives made for invading Iraq neither included nor required, in their minds, the events of 9/11. The argument before 9/11 rested on both an assessment of why Saddam should be overthrown and a methodology for doing so. The assessment was that Saddam was a dangerous dictator who possessed WMD and had shown the willingness to use those substances against his enemies, and that he was likely not only to continue to pose a threat but that, in defiance of U.N. sanctions on his WMD program enacted after the Persian Gulf War, he would likely expand that threat, probably to include nuclear weapons. This specter raised particular dangers for Israel and destabilized the rest of the region as well. Among the dynamics that Saddam endangered was the free flow of petroleum from the region, a point made almost in passing at the time, but arguably central to the effort.

The question was whether these dangers posed enough of a threat to the United States to engage in war, and the case before 9/11 was not conclusive. The Clinton administration had responded to the threat by signing legislation to sponsor alternatives to the Iraqi regime, but had stopped far short of endorsing the strong action the neoconservatives coveted. Prior to 9/11, it is not unfair to suggest that the public, by and large, was mostly unaware of an Iraq "threat" or of any plans to invade that country.

One way to think about the impact of 9/11 is that it created an enabling condition for the desire to invade Iraq. The method for doing so was to tie Iraq to the 9/11 events. Not unsurprisingly, Perle, in an article in the *San Diego Union-Tribune* on December 16, 2001, made the case: "So the question in my mind is this: Do we wait for Saddam and hope for the best, do we wait and hope he doesn't do what we know he is capable of doing, which is distributing weapons of mass destruction to anonymous terrorists, or do we take preemptive action?" Thus, the Saddam threat was merged into the GWOT.

In the same article, Perle also provides a rationale for why taking down the Iraqi regime would serve the broader purpose of stabilizing the Middle Eastern region (and, not coincidentally, reinforcing Israeli security). As noted earlier, the list of potential candidates for regime change extends across the region to include Iran, Syria, and Saudi Arabia at a minimum, and one can reasonably ask whether the United States has the wherewithal to complete all these actions with force. The Perle answer is that Iraq would serve as an example that would likely not have to be repeated: "When I recite this list (of potential foes), people typically say, 'Well, are we going to go to war against a dozen countries?' And I think the answer is that, if we do it right with regard to one or two, we've got a reasonable chance of persuading the others that they should get out of the business of supporting terrorism. . . . We could deliver a short message, a two-word message: 'You're next.'" Thus, military action against Iraq serves both the goals argued before 9/11 and the goals of the GWOT. A connection between Iraq and 9/11 is thus asserted.

ASSESSING THE REASONS FOR GOING TO WAR

When Congress passed the Authorization for the Use of Force against Iraq Resolution of October 2002, followed by the President's State of the Union address of January 2003 and a series of other speeches made by the president before the war was launched on March 20, 2003, three of the arguments that had arisen previously were used to justify the effort. They were the threat posed by Saddam Hussein's WMD program and intransigence in allowing U.N. inspections of dismantling that program, the alleged ties of the Iraqi regime to international terrorism, and the promotion of freedom and self-determination for the Iraqi people (the advocacy of a "model democracy" in the country). The first two arguments were tied together in the prospect that the Iraqi regime might provide WMD to terrorists potentially for use against the United States, and accomplishment of the third would both stabilize the region (thereby making it safer for Israel, among other things) and make Iraq a peaceful and responsible member of the international community, rather than a troublesome rogue.

In retrospect, of course, most of the stated reasons for invading Iraq have either been decisively disproven or have yet to be proven, depending on one's view of the war. No WMD has been found in Iraq, and even those who most fervently believed they existed in 2003 have by and large given up hope of finding any. Similarly, alleged ties to terrorism, and especially Al Qaeda, have not been substantiated, and critics point out that the only connection might be that the U.S. occupation of Iraq spawned an Al Qaeda presence in that country in the form of Masub al-Zarqawi's resistance group, formed in 2004 to oppose the occupation. Spreading democracy has long been a staple part of the Wilsonian idealism of the neoconservatives (although Woodrow Wilson did not endorse the idea of imposing democracy by military force), including the use of American military power as the instrument of that process. Kristol and Kagan articulated this principle in a 1996 *Foreign Affairs* article: "American hegemony is the only reliable defense against a breakdown of peace and international order. The appropriate goal of American foreign policy, therefore, is to preserve that hegemony as far into the future as possible . . . (through) military supremacy and moral confidence." The attainability of democracy (aside from its desirability) and the efficacy and possibility of American "hegemonism" remains debatable.

What is to be made of these rationales for going to war? All of them were justified directly or indirectly in terms of the GWOT, even if their real intent was to remove Saddam Hussein, a goal that far preceded the GWOT. Iraq's possession of WMD was important both because it established Saddam as a reprehensible tyrant in need of replacement (a pre-9/11 argument) and more importantly because he might provide safe haven and even WMD to terrorists. A post-Saddam democratic government was desirable because it would remove a source of destabilization in the region (thus promoting Israeli stability, also a pre-9/11 goal) and because, if democracy spread throughout the region (a neoconservative goal), it would make the area more stable, and thus, less vulnerable to terrorist appeals. A post-Saddam government might also be less hostile to U.S. oil companies.

These goals were not broadly questioned in the post-9/11 atmosphere of late 2002 and early 2003, when the decisions were reached and implemented to invade Iraq. Thus, assessing them now, one runs the risk of being criticized for ex post facto, "Monday morning quarterbacking." At the same time, since the most telling public justifications have proven false, it is necessary to question these goals as preface to assessing "lessons learned" later on in the text. Moreover, if the primary division between the "policy class" and the general public is partly over whether the war should have occurred in the first place, then assessing the adequacy of the reasons for the war is important to the public's preference for a rapid withdrawal.

The purpose of war, according to the late British strategist Sir Basil Liddell-Hart, is the "better state of the peace," the postwar political situation that was previously intolerable and is to be remedied by acts of war (*see* Snow and Drew for a full discussion). The *political objective* of war frames why or whether one goes to war. Among the major questions that must be asked are whether the objective(s) are important enough to engage in war, and whether the goals are attainable. These two aspects are, of course, related, in that part of attainability is the cost of reaching the goal (if it can be reached).

The objectives in Iraq can be understood in these terms. The major political objective in Iraq was to overthrow the Saddam Hussein government and replace it with some more compatible alternative, one that has consistently been described as democratic. In terms of attainability, the first part of that objective, overturning the Saddam Hussein regime, proved to be easily attainable, as the invasion and conquest phase of the war demonstrated. Replacing that regime with a democratic successor that meets U.S. policy objectives has, however, proven much less attainable and more costly. The first part of the objective was accomplished in less than six weeks; the second has taken over five years and continues with no "victorious" end state in view.

Whether that goal was born in pre-9/11 determinations (an evil Saddam) or because of post-9/11 concerns (a terrorist-supporting Saddam or, according to a new biography of Bush by Weisberg, the fear arising from the anthrax attacks of late 2001) is an open question.

Two questions can be, and have been, raised about the political objective. First, was it adequate to justify war? In the traditional realist view of the world that dominated American thinking before the rise of the neoconservatives, the use of force was limited to situations where *vital interests* of the country are at stake. In *National Security for a New Era* (third edition), the author has conventionally defined these as "properties and conditions on which states will not willingly compromise" and which "are too important to be submitted to any superior authority." The neoconservatives reject this limitation on using force as too restrictive (one neoconservative serving in the Pentagon once reportedly replied to a question about whether a response comported with realism by saying "We make our own reality"), arguing for a more expansive set of circumstances for using force—less than tolerable situations.

How does the decision to overthrow Saddam Hussein stand up in these circumstances? The answer to this second question is mixed. If Saddam possessed WMD and was prepared to share them with terrorists who would use them against the United States, then a strong case could be made that removing the source of that problem represented a vital interest for the United States. Thus, framing the case in those terms, as the Bush administration consistently and frequently did (*see* Lewis and Reading-Smith), made the most unassailable case for getting rid of the Iraqi regime.

The problem, of course, is that the administration's reasons proved false, and it is now difficult to argue that the continuation of the Saddam Hussein government in power violated either of these sources of challenge to vital American interests. If these reasons are stripped away, one is left with the desirability of removing Saddam because he was a destabilizing tyrant whose removal would pave the way for a more stable, Israel-friendly region (the pre-9/11 reasons).

In the absence of the WMD/terrorism connection, was removing Saddam a justification for war? The neoconservatives who signed the 1998 letter to President Clinton thought so, but before the stimulus provided by the 9/11 tragedy, their arguments did not have adequate public appeal to allow implementation. There is some indication that people in the administration found 9/11 potentially enabling; Richard Clarke, for instance, reports in his book, *Against All Enemies*, that one of the first things Bush wanted to know about 9/11 was whether there was an Iraqi connection (a position reinforced by Bob Woodward in *State of Denial*). Adding the events of 9/11 provided gravitas to the case for attacking Iraq, and it may be the only real connection between the terrorist tragedy and the war.

Determining whether Iraq was worth attacking in the absence of a GWOT connection is much more problematical. One aspect of the question is whether it was important enough to justify war (were vital interests involved?), a matter of continuing disagreement. Seen in this light, the question of cost and attainability take on added importance. The war has obviously proven more expensive, open-ended and inconclusive by orders of magnitude than when Rumsfeld argued that troop strength could be reduced to 6,000 by the end of summer 2003. The assertions that the war would be easy and cheap (among other things, Iraqi oil revenues would pay for most of it) were true if the goal was simply to overthrow Saddam Hussein; they were wildly false if the goal included replacing the tyrant's regime with the neoconservative dream of a model democracy that would help stabilize the region and act as a model for other Middle Eastern countries to follow. At the time, there was ample evidence that achieving the second task would be extremely difficult, or even impossible (*see* Chapter 5), but it was ignored or suppressed at the time. Had there been a comprehensive national debate in 2002–2003 in which the 9/11 connections were stripped from the calculus of invasion, and the rationale been reduced to the neoconservative goal (with its resulting costs), would the decision have been as easy or, possibly more importantly, acceptable, to the American people and their elected representatives?

The gist of looking at the road to war through these conceptual lenses is to cloud the vision of whether that process led to the conclusions and consequences the country has faced for over five years of war. The desire for war was not a new impulse in 2003, nor was its basis the attacks of September 11. Rather, those attacks provided a pretext for a decision that many had advocated for some time before the decision was publicly made. Among those who had made this determination well before 9/11 appears to have been President George W. Bush. The GWOT-based case was compelling only if one accepts the GWOT connection. With that connection effectively severed, however, one is left with the pre-9/11 case that did not make the case for invasion before and without an alleged 9/11 connection. Was it enough?

There is another justification for the war that is seldom raised but stands as the "800-pound gorilla" in assessing whether war should have been waged. That justification is oil: was the "real" reason the United States has invaded and conquered Iraq to gain control of its vast oil resources? Through that control, the argument goes, the United States will potentially make itself oil-independent during the next decades, when access to oil will be an increasing source of international competition and discord, which in turn will put the United States in an advantageous geopolitical position in its relations with other oil competitors, including producers like Russia, Iran, and Saudi Arabia and consumers with growing petroleum appetites, like China.

This argument is very rarely mentioned by official or unofficial sources supporting the war. It is mentioned in passing in the 1998 open letter to President Clinton, and occasionally there are references to the Carter Doctrine of 1980, which declared continuing access to Persian Gulf oil to be a vital interest of the United States. During the period when the justification of Iraq was being formulated and presented by the Bush administration, the President never publicly mentioned oil in pronouncements, although Iraq's status as an oil-rich country was hard to ignore.

Somewhat ironically, the argument that control of oil is the American political objective comes from outside sources. One source is Iraqis themselves: As Jeffrey Record puts it, "In the minds of many Iraqis and other Arabs, the real purpose of the U.S. invasion of Iraq was to steal Iraq's oil." The other source, ironically, is liberal opponents of the administration. As Jim Lobe argued in a January 20, 2003 online article for Inter Press Service, "To most of the left, oil seems entirely persuasive, particularly when . . . you assert the fact that the United States is quickly running out of oil and that Iraq sits on the world's second largest oil reserves." Morgan and Ottoway applied this idea to a potential war in a September 15, 2002 article in the *Washington Post:* "A U.S.-led ouster of Iraqi President Saddam Hussein could open a bonanza for American oil companies *long banished from Iraq,* scuttling oil deals between Baghdad and Russia, France, and other countries, and reshuffling world petroleum markets," (emphasis added). Former chairman of the Federal Reserve Board Alan Greenspan, hardly a liberal, supports the importance of oil in his memoir: "I am saddened that it is politically inconvenient to acknowledge what everyone knows: the Iraq war is largely about oil."

One can only speculate about why the Bush administration is reluctant to adopt the capture of Iraqi oil assets as a goal of the invasion. There is certainly a natural connection for Bush and his father and Vice President Cheney, each of whom has considerable experience and connections with the petroleum industry. At the same time, the political objective of attempting to achieve petroleum energy independence in a competitive world meets much more clearly the realist standard of a vital interest, and one already established through the Carter Doctrine. Because the petroleum argument is less publicized but still plausible, it merits some more detailed examination. This more detailed look does not imply an endorsement of the position.

The argument begins with America's need for Persian Gulf oil. Record summarizes the situation: "Simply put, hostile control or massive disruption of the Persian Gulf's oil wealth would threaten U.S. capacity. . . . The United States is, and for the foreseeable future will remain, critically dependent on Persian Gulf oil." That recognition exists in the context of a very politically volatile Persian Gulf region that, among other things, conflicts with the neo-conservative vision of peace in the region. Saudi Arabia and Iran are high on the list for regime change after Iraq, but such action is hardly feasible as long as the United States remains dependent on oil from those very regimes it may want to change. If it could control a large source like Iraqi oil, these kinds of concerns would largely disappear.

This problem gains particular meaning in the larger geopolitics of world petroleum dynamics for the future. Michael T. Klare, who has studied the petroleum situation for some time, raised the problem starkly in a recent *Nation* article. Global output of petroleum in 2005 stood at about 84 million barrels of oil equivalent (mboe) against a global demand of about 83 mboe. Energy Department figures cited by Klare suggest that supply will rise to about 117.7 mboe by 2030, with anticipated demand at 117.6 mboe. Moreover, this projection appears to be at the upper limit of likely production because, as Klare points out, "most oil geologists believe we have already reached the midway point in the depletion of the world's original petroleum inheritance and so are nearing the peak in global output; the real debate is over how close we have come to that point."

Two factors exacerbate these projections. One is growing demand, especially by countries like China and India that have not historically been large oil consumers. The other is that added demand comes at a time when part of the problem of increasing output involves replenishing the supplies from old oil sources that are becoming depleted in addition to servicing new demand. Klare cites the example that an increased current demand for two mboe actually requires five mboe of new oil: three mboe to "make up for decline in older fields" in addition to the two mboe in new demand.

The result of these dynamics is to make the competition for access to petroleum even more important than it was before. The rush is clearly on to see what countries can gain influence, access, or control over those parts of the world where existing reserves still exist and have not been entirely exploited. One of the prizes in this competition is Iraq.

Iraq has an estimated 115 billion barrels of known oil reserves, the second largest untapped reserve in the world, and a Council on Foreign Relations (CFR) study suggested there may be as much as 200 billion barrels yet to be discovered. Holt points out the level to which this potential remains untapped, particularly when compared to the United States: "A mere two thousand wells have been drilled across the entire country; in Texas alone there are more than a million." For the world's largest petroleum consumer (the United States uses about one-quarter of world oil), this is a tempting prize: guaranteed access to, or control over, Iraqi oil could go a long way toward lifting the United States above the increasingly cut-throat competition for oil, as well as guaranteeing continuing large profits for American oil companies.

The problem has been that under the Iraqi government of Saddam Hussein, "American oil companies have been banished from direct involvement in Iraq" since the 1970s, according to Morgan and Ottaway, while a dozen other countries, "including France, Russia, China, India, Italy, Vietnam, and Algeria have either reached or sought to reach agreements in principle to develop Iraqi oil fields." As long as Saddam Hussein remained in power, that situation was unlikely to change. Access to Iraqi oil reserves required regime change in Baghdad.

Record argues that gaining oil access was part of the neoconservative agenda for the region: "For neoconservatives Operation Iraqi Freedom promised the United States an opportunity to groom a new Persian Gulf strategic partner as an insurance policy against the political uncertainties surrounding the future U.S.-Saudi relationship as well as free the United States to take a less tolerant and more demanding attitude toward the House of Saud." Iraqi oil, in other words, could substitute for Saudi oil and thus remove some of the inhibitions toward fomenting regime change in Riyadh. Moreover, American influence over Iraqi oil could also compromise the positions of other countries competing for those reserves, a geopolitical advantage for the United States. The result might not be energy independence for the United States— which an October 2006 CFR report calls a "chimera"—but it would certainly be advantageous to the country.

None of this was possible without the removal of Saddam Hussein, and its realization requires a government willing to grant favorable oil leases to American interests (oil companies) and an assurance that those leases will be honored and the oil flow secured. Holt, for instance, suggests that the "five self-sufficient super-bases" being built in Iraq by the United States provide the venues to station enough American troops within the country on a long-term basis to insure that the oil flows in directions the Americans want. The much-trumpeted idea of stationing U.S. troops "over the horizon" from Iraq in bases from which they could easily be dispatched to Iraq can also be interpreted as evidence of this intent. Moreover, the recently reduced gap of U.S. Democratic Party aspirants to the 2008 presidential nomination from popular demands for a rapid withdrawal (both Obama and Clinton now favor total withdrawal within a year or so of their inaguration) makes more sense if it is a recognition that there is a *good* reason to maintain that presence: oil.

Is the oil explanation convincing? There is an irony in making an assessment. The oil argument is most appealing to war opponents, for one of two contrasting reasons. For core opponents, it is evidence of the venal cynicism of an administration that would sacrifice American "blood for oil." For those who have opposed the war on realist grounds (Iraq is not important enough to fight over), the oil argument provides a geopolitical justification for the invasion: oil is arguably important enough to fight over (the Carter Doctrine). The irony continues in that the geopolitical argument, while arguably the strongest case that can be made for the war, is very difficult for the administration to adopt. For one thing, it sounds cynical to accept the notion of sacrificing American lives for oil, and the administration would clearly be criticized on that ground if it admitted that underlying cause. The more high-sounding justifications would also be harder to make to Americans and the world at large: Rather than liberating Iraqis, the war instead would be revealed as a campaign to liberate Iraqis from their oil (at the expense of the rest of the world). Moreover, the Bush administration has close ties with the American oil industry at the very top (Bush and Cheney), and admitting to a policy that has the effect of promoting, and especially enriching, oil companies would be a very difficult political sell.

Thus, the question of "how we got there," at least in terms of the reasons for the invasion, remains elusive. The desire to remove Saddam Hussein clearly predates the tragedy of 9/11 to which the war's rationale has been tied. Whether it was to remove a heartless dictator, to stabilize the region and make it safer for Israel, or to regain access to Iraqi oil, there was a clear desire on the part of the neoconservatives to overthrow the Iraqi regime as far back as the 1980s and 1990s. When they joined the Bush administration, their previously rejected arguments gained a friendly ear in high places. The official case for invading Iraq has largely been discredited (WMD and terrorism); the geopolitics of Persian Gulf security and oil remain the alternative justifications. Were they reason enough?

SELECTED BIBLIOGRAPHY

Armstrong, David. "Dick Cheney's Song of America." *Harper's Magazine* 305, 1829 (October 2002), 76–83.

Bush, George W. "A Distinctly American Internationalism." Speech at Ronald W. Reagan Library, November 19, 1999 (http://www.fas.org/news/usa/1999/11/199119-bush-foreignpolicy.htm)

———. "A Period of Consequences. " Speech Delivered at the Citadel, Charleston, S.C. on September 23, 1999 (http://citadel.edu/pao/addresses/pres_bush.html)

Deutch, John, James R. Schlesinger, and David C. Victor. *National Security Consequences of U.S. Oil Dependency*. New York: Council on Foreign Relations Press, 2006.

Greenspan, Alan. *The Age of Turbulence: Adventures in a New World*. New York: Penguin Press, 2007.

Holt, Jim. "It's the Oil." *London Review of Books*, October 18, 2006 (online edition: http://www.truthout.org/docs_2006/101207.shtml)

"How to Attack Iraq." *The Weekly Standard*. November 16, 1998, 17–18.

Ivins, Molly, and Lou Dubose. *Shrub: The Short and Happy Political Life of George W. Bush*. New York: Random House, 2000.

Khalilizad, Zalmay, and Paul D. Wolfowitz. "We Must Lead the Way in Deposing Saddam." *The Washington Post*, November 9, 1997.

Klare, Michael T. "Beyond the Age of Petroleum." *The Nation* 285, 15 (November 12, 2007), 16–20.

Kristol, William, and Lawrence F. Kaplan. *The War over Iraq: Saddam's Tyranny and America's Mission*. New York: Encounter Books, 2003.

———, and Robert Kagan. "Toward a Neo-Reaganite Foreign Policy." *Foreign Affairs* 75, 4 (July/August 1996).

"Letter to the Honorable William J. Clinton." January 28, 1998 (http://newamericancentury.org.clintonletter.htm)

Lewis, Charles, and Mark Reading-Smith. "False Pretenses: Iraq: The War Card," Washington, DC: Center for Public Integrity, 2008.

Lind, Michael. *Made in Texas: George W. Bush and the Southern Takeover of American Politics*. New York: Basic Books, 2003.

Lobe, Jim. "Politics: Why Is the United States Going to War Against Iraq?" Inter Press Service, January 30, 2003.

Mann, James. *Rise of the Vulcans: The History of Bush's War Cabinet*. New York: Viking Press, 2004.

Morgan, Dan, and David B. Ottaway. "In Iraq Scenario, Oil Is Key Issue." *Washington Post* (online edition), September 15, 2002, A01.

Perle, Richard. "Keeping the Bomb from Iraq." *Wall Street Journal*, August 22, 1990, A8.

———. "No More Halfway Measures: Calls Have Grown Larger for the United States to Take Action Against Iraq's Saddam Hussein." *Washington Post*, February 8, 1998.

———. "Should Iraq Be Next?" *San Diego Union-Tribune*, December 16, 2001.

————. "State Sponsors of Terrorism Should Be Wiped Out, Too." *The Daily Telegraph (London)*. August 9, 2002.

————. "The Real Stakes in the Persian Gulf." *U.S. News and World Report*. October 26, 1987.

"Rebuilding America's Defenses: Strategy, Forces, and Resources for a New Century." Washington: The Project for a New American Century, September 2000.

Record, Jeffrey. *Dark Victory: America's Second War Against Iraq*. Annapolis, MD: Naval Institute Press, 2004.

Snow, Donald M. *National Security for a New Era: Globalization and Geopolitics after Iraq*. New York: Pearson Longman, 2009.

————. "The Neoconservative Assault on American National Security Policy, November 2003. (http://bama.ua.edu~dmsnow/neoconservatives.htm)

————, and Dennis M. Drew. *From Lexington to Desert Storm and Beyond: War and Politics in the American Experience*. Armonk, NY: M E Sharpe, 2000.

Weisberg, Jacob. *The Bush Tragedy*. New York: Random House, 2008 (Excerpted from *Newsweek*, January 28, 2008, 30–35).

Woodward, Bob. *Bush at War*. New York: Simon and Schuster, 2002.

Zuckerman, Jill. "On Iraq Question, Bush's Debate Answer May Have Gone Too Far." *Boston Globe*, February 4, 1999, A12.

Chapter 2

A Tale of Two Wars

In some circles, virtually anything one says about the American war in Iraq is controversial at some level. Whether any comparisons can be drawn between the U.S. involvements in Vietnam and Iraq, although a generation apart, is a part of the controversy. There is disagreement over whether the two events are comparable enough to draw any comparisons., However, among those who do find parallels, there is equal disagreement about what comparisons can be drawn and what those comparisons mean.

The basis of this disagreement tends to reflect either support of, or opposition to, the Iraq War effort. Since the Vietnam War was less than a success and is arguably the most traumatic military experience in American history, equating it with the effort in Iraq implicitly suggests an invidious comparison and tarnishes the Iraq War. Sometimes that criticism is valid, and sometimes it is not. Nevertheless, to those making these comparisons, the more the Iraq War resembles what they view as the United States' failure in Vietnam, the more likely they are to conclude that the Iraq effort is, or will be, a failure. The controversy is great enough when comparisons are made between events of both wars—the comparative nature of the anti-U.S. insurgency in each case, for instance—but it is particularly heated when outcomes of Vietnam are extrapolated to likely outcomes in Iraq. Those who support the war effort and believe it can still achieve a positive result necessarily oppose a comparison to Vietnam, where the outcome was unfavorable. Moreover, the claim of comparability of outcome can be viewed as defeatist, creating a self-fulfilling prophecy by which the United States will fail because it is believed that it will fail. Those who argue the validity of the comparison, by contrast, contend that the similarities are sufficient to be heeded, thereby avoiding what they fear would be an unfortunately similar outcome to that of Vietnam. To those who see the Iraq War as a probable failure, the Vietnam analogy is consequently more convincing than to those who see the possibility of success.

The disagreements are both fundamental and persistent. While most Americans believe the Vietnam War represented an unsuccessful application of American force, for instance, there remains disagreement on whether that point is valid. Two recent books, Moyar's *Triumph Forsaken* and Sorley's *A Better War* both argue in essence that the conflict in Indochina was almost won by the French, and later by Ngo Dinh Diem (Moyar), and later by American forces (Sorley), only to have successes reversed by political decisions made far from the scene. This assertion, of course, can easily be extrapolated to the opposition to continuing effort in Iraq, a point that then-presidential contender Rudy Giuliani mentioned in his 2007 *Foreign Affairs* article: "Then, as now, we fought a war with the wrong strategy for several years. And then, as now, we corrected course and began to show real progress . . . But America then withdrew its support." Beyond the intrinsic merit of this argument, it suggests that regardless of the outcome in Iraq, it will continue to be debated for years to come.

Since there is disagreement over the outcome and comparability of the two wars, does it make sense to devote a chapter to discussing comparisons? One reason for doing so is that the comparison is, in fact, made in policymaking and academic circles, and thus deserves to be aired. Another is that there are, at least on the surface, some fairly obvious points of comparison between the various military involvements of the United States in the past half century or so, and, more specifically, between Iraq and Vietnam. Moreover, the existence of the Vietnam analogy also speaks to the question of whether the United States should have become involved in Iraq in the first place: if the analogy is valid, it suggests involvement in Iraq was a bad idea destined for failure. Thus, those who defend the decision to invade Iraq have a vested interest in denying the analogy. At the same time, broad acceptance of the analogy reinforces the underlying general public belief that the United States should get out as quickly as possible, since it suggests the country should never have become involved.

All events are to some extent unique in detail, and it can be said that if any two apparently comparable events are viewed in sufficient detail, differences will be revealed and will negate claims to comparability. On the other hand, as a science, it is the mission of social science to try to determine underlying commonalities among events that form something like scientific laws and theories of behavior. Whether it is possible to generalize or whether uniqueness means individual phenomena can only be examined and understood within their special contexts is a question that divides political scientists and historians, and it has not been resolved. Recognizing that no generalization will be flawless under a microscope, it is nonetheless possible, and of some value, to examine some similarities among the conflicts in which the United States has been involved in the post-World War II era, as a context for comparing Vietnam and Iraq.

Four points of comparison are worth making. The first is that the United States has used—as opposed to deployed—military force exclusively in the developing world since 1945. While the center of American concern, and where its most vital interests were engaged, was in Europe and Northeast Asia, Americans were fighting in the developing, or Third World. The "central battle" of the Cold War, should it have gone hot, would have been Central Europe, but that contingency never occurred. The main reason for this absence of violence was that the potential consequences of war in Europe (or Japan) included escalation to an all-out nuclear war between sides headed by the nuclear superpowers—the United States and the Soviet Union—and everyone would lose. During the Cold War, the "safe" places to fight (safe in the sense of minimizing the likelihood of nuclear engagement) were in the Third World. The closest America came to a "hot war" was probably in Korea, but other involvements, including Vietnam, could be conducted without significantly increasing the chance of direct confrontation between major powers in places like the Dominican Republic or Grenada. The major exception was the threat of escalation of the Cuban missile crisis to direct confrontation. With the Cold War ended, the danger of direct confrontation over those places most important to the United States disappeared, and so the United States has sent forces into other Third World locations from the Balkans (Bosnia and Kosovo) to Africa (Somalia) to the Caribbean (Haiti) to the Middle East (Iraq).

The second point of comparison all these involvements share, is that the issues involved did not clearly or unambiguously involve vital interests—conditions so important that they could not voluntarily be forfeited. Put another way, none of these were situations where the basic security of the United States dictated going to war; rather, they were all what is now called "wars of choice" (situations where conditions do not dictate but allow the country to choose the application of force).

Clearly, some of the conflicts in which the United States has been involved were more important to the country than others. In terms of the unacceptability of an unfavorable outcome, for instance, it is difficult to argue that Americans would have been greatly affected by the resulting outcome in Somalia or Bosnia. At the same time, an argument can be made, and was at the time, that failure to rebuff the North Korean invasion of South Korea in 1950 would have so emboldened the Soviets that they would have moved aggressively elsewhere in a global campaign of conquest, clearly a violation of American interests. A similar argument, the "domino theory," was made about Southeast Asia in order to justify involvement in Vietnam. In this particular case, there remains to this day debate about what the United States lost when its policy in Southeast Asia (keeping it non-Communist) failed and how important that loss was in terms of American interests.

The term "war of choice" has become a shorthand way to describe military conflicts in which vital interests are not engaged (the author first did so in 2000 in *When America Fights*). Within realist circles (where vital interests and adequate motivation to use force are equated), the idea of a war of choice suggests the promiscuous use of American force, and is therefore opposed. Because of its pejorative connotation, those who support the Iraq War are at some pains to convince people that it is instead a "war of necessity," a conflict involving vital interests that cannot be compromised. Historically, wars of necessity have involved direct attacks or the imminence of such attacks; the extension of the GWOT to Iraq is intended to fulfill that function (although, given America's dependency on foreign oil, an explicit acknowledgement of capturing Iraqi oil might qualify in some minds).

A third common characteristic of America's post-1945 military involvements is that none of them had the clear, definitive endings that are associated with earlier wars, such as World War II. In some cases, it is possible to identify the beginning point of these conflicts and American participation in them (Korea, for instance), but in others it is not (which country started the Vietnam conflict dating back to 1946 is a matter of continuing conjecture, for instance). While it might be possible to determine and document when the United States withdrew from a conflict, that is not saying that the conflicts ended and what the outcomes were. There is, for instance, still no peace treaty on the Korean peninsula (although one is likely near—55 years after the fighting ended), and in the cases where no declared war occurred, endings remain elusive in a number of cases. Who won in Somalia, for instance, and how does one know when or how? The same can be said of Bosnia, Kosovo, Grenada, the Dominican Republic, and other minor American applications of force.

The distinction applies when one looks at Vietnam and Iraq as well. In Vietnam, the United States never openly declared hostilities against the Democratic Republic of Vietnam (DRV) or the National Liberation Front and its military arm the Viet Cong (VC), unless the Gulf of Tonkin's 1964 authorization of reprisals constitutes such a declaration, and the last American helicopters leaving the U.S. Embassy in 1975 were not accompanied by any formal admission of DRV victory. The North Vietnamese did formally unite the country in 1975, an act of triumph, but the United States did not formally accept that declaration until July 11, 1995, when the United States and Vietnam extended full diplomatic recognition to one another. In Iraq, it is certainly possible to pinpoint the beginning of the conflict (the

American invasion on March 20, 2003); whether it will be so easy to determine the end of the war is more problematical. If the Vietnam experience offers any lesson, the end of the Iraq War could be some time after the fighting ends and America withdraws, accompanied by acrimonious disagreement about when the war occurred and what it meant. Pinpointing an ending will be particularly difficult if the United States has an enduring presence after combat troops are withdrawn.

A fourth comparison is that each of the post-World War II wars has been unpopular to some extent. One of the reasons for this, as stated in the previous paragraph, has been their somewhat indeterminate outcome; not all Americans agree that the United States won. At the same time, each was conducted for reasons (political objectives) that violated one or more of the criteria of a "good" political objective, a notion discussed in Snow and Drew. In that book, the authors describe four criteria for a good objective—one that will gain and sustain popular support for the war effort, as well as providing adequate guidance for conducting the war toward its preferred end. Three of these are particularly relevant in the present context. First, it must be simple, straightforward, unambiguous, and easy to understand and articulate (preferably reducible to a catch phrase, like "defeat Hitler"). Second, it should be morally and politically lofty. As a moralistic people, Americans like to think they fight for some higher purpose (e.g., making the world safe for democracy). Third, the war must be seen to be in the interests of most Americans. It is much easier to gain and sustain support for wars of necessity than for wars of choice. The fourth criteria—that interests of most Americans are served—applies most clearly to earlier American history, where regional differences were pronounced. The more of these criteria are met, the more popular a war is likely to be; the more that are violated, the less popular involvement is likely to be.

Third World conflicts since 1945 rarely met these criteria. They were difficult to explain in clear language that conveyed a pressing need for American involvement (criteria one and three), and influencing the events in morally convincing terms was often difficult or impossible (criterion two). Stopping North Korean aggression in 1950 seemed to fill the bill, but after the war stalemated and it was no longer clear that the morally wicked aggressors were to be vanquished, opinion turned against the war. There was some moral uplift to ending the suffering of starving Somalis, but it did not extend to determining what faction should eventually rule in that country.

The problem is that, at least in American terms, these conflicts tend to be ambiguous. It is not clear which side is "the side of the angels" and, possibly more important, why or how the United States should align with one side or another, and how American interests are affected one way or the other. Those contemplating or defending involvements during the Cold War could at least argue involvement as part of the global crusade against Communism, but in the post-Cold War world, the GWOT has had to provide a surrogate. The fact that in both Vietnam and Iraq public opinion turned on the enterprises suggests that the objective did not meet the criteria for support. It may be that the reason requires adding another criterion, attainability. The intrusion into Grenada, for instance, did not have a publicly stated compelling justification at the time, but it was successfully completed before anyone could raise the question. Since, as noted earlier, democracies do not like long wars, a political objective must be compelling enough to weather the predictable erosion of support accompanying a long, drawn-out effort. The political objective in Vietnam could not be sustained until success, whatever that meant, could have been achieved. The same is apparently true in Iraq. Critics alleging that America lacks the will to see a conflict through to the end—not to "cut and run"—must accept the fact that the erosion of support is a natural occurrence. Their statement of purpose provided an inadequate conceptual barrier against that erosion.

COMPARING VIETNAM AND IRAQ

The net effect of looking at the various places in which the United States has employed force since the end of World War II is that each was controversial. With the exception of Korea (which, in some ways, was an extension of World War II), the two largest and most spectacular applications of American military force in this period have been in Vietnam and Iraq, and comparisons between them have indeed been drawn. Therefore, it is part of explaining the Iraq War, and thus providing the context for its ending, to consider the differences and similarities between the two.

Dissimilarities

Those who maintain that Iraq and Vietnam are dissimilar tend to argue one or both of two points. Frederick Kagan argues them both in a *Policy Review* article titled, appropriately for his point, "Iraq Is Not Vietnam." On one hand, there is the argument that the two wars do not share enough in common to allow meaningful comparison. Beyond the fact that the United States faced "revolutionaries" in both cases, he maintains, "To make comparisons or to draw lessons beyond that basic point misunderstands not only the particular historical cases, but also the value of studying history to draw lessons for the present." Moreover, historical analogies are of limited value in any case, because "any single historical example . . . will suffer from sharp limits on its power to explain, still less prescribe solutions for, the current conflict. All insurgencies are distinct from one another." In tactical and even strategic detail of how particular conflicts are conducted, this criticism is undoubtedly true; the question of whether the critique is the basis for an honest inability to draw parallels, or an attempt to obscure a valid comparison that may be drawn is a matter for the reader to decide.

For present purposes, the analysis will focus on three basic points of dissimilarity between the two conflicts: the physical nature of the war, including how it began; the physical and demographic differences between Iraq and Vietnam, and the physical scales of the war. Each places some limits on the ability to equate the two experiences.

Nature of the War. In the broadest sense, the nature of the Iraq War is used to support arguments by both those who believe Iraq and Vietnam are similar and by those who believe they are different. For those who support continuing the effort in Iraq, it is important to establish the differences to avoid the implication that Iraq will end the same way Vietnam did, since it is more difficult to argue in favor of sustaining a commitment destined to fail. Conversely, belief in parallels leads to the conclusion that ending involvement as quickly as possible is the only sensible way to cut ongoing losses.

Kagan strongly makes the case that the two wars are dissimilar. "The beginning of the conflict, the nature of the enemy, the enemy's military capabilities, the nature of the current Iraqi government, and the legitimacy of that government are all so widely removed from the circumstances of Vietnam as to make meaningful comparisons almost impossible." Each of these claims bears examining.

The beginnings of the wars clearly differ. In Vietnam, the United States intervened in an ongoing conflict that had begun in the resistance to reimposing French colonial rule and in which concerted fighting had been ongoing for over a decade, as opposed to Iraq, which was the direct result of an American invasion. Because of these differing beginnings, both the nature of the enemy and its military capabilities were indeed different. In Vietnam, two large, well-organized and highly armed forces (the NVA/VC and the Army of the Republic of Vietnam or ARVN) were confronting one another, whereas in Iraq the United States faced and quickly overwhelmed the Iraqi army in a conventional campaign. The Iraqi resistance that rose from the occupation is much smaller than the NVA/VC force, numbering in the hundreds or low thousands of generally uncoordinated fighters. At this level, the wars are clearly different. Colonel H.R. Master, a member of General Patreaus' staff and author of the acclaimed critique of Vietnam, *Dereliction of Duty*, agrees, in effect, by describing elements of American operations in Iraq: breaking the "cycle of sectarian violence," creating conditions for "sustained stability," and "lifting the pall of fear off the people, and then actively engaging the various communities to bring about political accommodation at the local level." (Quoted by Rozen.) Whether the issue of legitimacy of the Iraqi government is a point of positive or negative comparison depends on what constitutes legitimacy in Iraq and who does or does not consider the government to possess legitimacy (a point of arguable sectarian disagreement).

Physical and Demographic Comparisons. The wars are clearly different in terms of the natural environment in which they occurred and in the nature of the societies in which they occurred. The most obvious geographical contrasts are physical: Vietnam (North and South) is a long, narrow country with a 1,400-mile coastline on the east and a ridge of mountains on the west, with a coastal plain. In the south there is the wide, marshy Mekong Delta and areas of mountainous jungle and rain forest as well as grassy plains that dominate the parts of the country where most of the war was fought. Iraq, by contrast, is mostly an arid, alluvial plain including large desert areas bounded by barren mountains. These topographical differences naturally lend to different styles of warfare; the heavily vegetated areas of Vietnam where much of the war occurred encouraged tactics like ambushes and the use of light infantry on foot or transported by helicopter. In contrast, the relatively flat, open territory of Iraq made such tactics difficult, but encouraged the blitzkrieg mobile warfare practiced by the Americans during the invasion and conquest phase of the war. Vietnam has no oil, while Iraq has the world's second-largest known reserves.

The demographics are different as well. Although Iraq is slightly larger than Vietnam (178,754 square miles to Vietnam's 127,244 square miles), Vietnam is, and was then, a more populous country. (According to the 2007 *World Almanac and Book of Facts*, Vietnam's current population is 84,402,966, while Iraq's is 26,783,383.) These differences in population help explain the differences in scale of efforts to affect their conflicts: American forces at their peak in Vietnam were more than three times the size of maximum U.S. forces levels during the "surge" in Iraq. Another salient demographic point is that, with the exception of some small tribal groups largely in the Vietnamese highlands, most of the population of Vietnam is ethnic Vietnamese of differing political persuasions, in contrast to the multi-communal, multi-ethnic composition of Iraq. While Iraq may resemble Vietnam in terms of the dynamics of U.S. involvement, the better analogy with Iraq as a society may be with multi-ethnic and communal societies like Lebanon.

Scale of War. By any measure, the Vietnam War was also a much larger conflict than Iraq has been, or is likely to become. While the American involvement in Iraq may well catch and surpass the American experience in Vietnam and become the country's longest war, it is extremely unlikely to approach the expenditure of blood in Vietnam. Over 58,000 Americans were killed in Vietnam, compared to something over 4,000 in five years of fighting in Iraq. In some ways, this difference points to the vast differences between the physical wars: an ongoing conflict between two well-organized armed forces to which American force was added, as opposed to a military occupation opposed by a loosely organized and shifting opposition. What is more clear is the comparison of monetary costs; estimates are that Vietnam cost over $500 billion (dollar value at that time), whereas the cost of Iraq is roughly $1 trillion and climbing. Both involved sizable deficit spending, which in the case of Vietnam, helped trigger the high inflation of the 1970s. There has been little discussion of the possible inflationary impact of Iraq (*see* Chapter 3). The scale of civilian suffering by the indigenous populations is also on a differing scale; civilian casualties in Iraq, for instance, are generally placed in the high hundreds of thousands, while estimates of combined civilian and military deaths among Vietnamese are conventionally measured in the millions (generally two to three million). Both wars produced sizable refugee populations (largely ethnic Chinese in Vietnam, mostly Sunni in Iraq).

How fundamental are these differences, and do they render comparisons fallacious? They certainly point to major differences in the appearances of the two wars. They are clearly different kinds of wars fought in very different physical and societal places and with very differing levels of intensity and bloodshed. But are these differences fundamental or cosmetic, masking underlying dynamics of similarity that are more important than the differences? The predilection toward one orientation or the other may reflect the basic position one has about the war. Looking at the apparent similarities may facilitate answering the question personally.

Similarities

No one who equates Vietnam and Iraq argues that the wars are identical, but rather, that the underlying dynamics of the two share sufficient similarity that studying the one that has happened, Vietnam, can be instructive in assessing the prospects for the one that is ongoing, Iraq. For those who emphasize the similarities, the question is not whether there are differences between the two, which there clearly are, or whether those differences lead to different conclusions about aspects of the wars. Clearly, for instance, one cannot fight the Iraqi resistance the same way the Viet Cong were confronted. The question is whether there are similar dynamics that can be applied.

There are at least five different points of possible similarity between the two conflicts that can be described. Some are flip sides or nuances of arguments about dissimilarities. They are 1) similarities in the underlying situation in each case between the two, 2) the intractable nature of the opposition, 3) the predictability of outcomes, 4) questions about the positive or negative impact of continuing American presence in resolving the conflicts, and 5) likely impacts of probable outcomes within the United States.

Situational Comparisons. Without pretending the situations in Vietnam and Iraq were identical, they nonetheless shared at least three similarities. The first is that both Iraq and Vietnam were unstable Asian Third World countries recently removed from a European colonial past. France had ruled French Indochina (Vietnam, Cambodia, and Laos) from the middle of the nineteenth century until the end of World War II. Iraq had been part of the Ottoman Empire dissembled by the victorious allies at the end of World War II and had been a British protectorate during the period between the world wars. Both gained independence after World War II, and both were in varying degrees of developing into viable modern states. The problems each faced were different. The Vietnamese, at least the Communists of the North, sought to unify Vietnam into a single entity, as it had been before the French occupation (at least there was a sense of Vietnamese national identity), whereas the basic problem of Iraq was forming a stable multinational state. In both cases, the result was instability and, operationally, the absence of qualified leadership in either country for the people to support.

Because of their locations and internal situations, American interests in both countries were ambiguous. In both cases, intervention was based on a claim of American vital interests justified as part of an application of the dominant foreign policy paradigm of the time. The reason for intervening in the Vietnamese conflict was to prevent the unification of the country under Communist rule during the Cold War, and the justification for Iraq was as a theater of the war on terror.

The problem in both cases has been that the interests served are not unambiguously vital. Vietnam was particularly ironic; the main reason for resisting North Vietnam conquest of the South and unification of the country was the so-called domino theory, which hypothesized that if South

Vietnam fell, so too would the rest of Southeast Asia, and that this result would be intolerable for the United States. The formulation was half right; the domino effect did occur (both Laos and Cambodia did fall to Communism, although the biggest domino, Thailand, did not), but the result turned out hardly to be intolerable for the United States in the long run. In Iraq, the vital interests apparently surrounded the issues of WMD and links to terrorists, but both proved to be erroneous. The importance of remaining in Iraq is now premised on the untoward effects both nationally (a communal bloodbath) and regionally (chaotic regional war). Since either of these eventualities would likely affect the flow of oil from the region, a case for vital interests being involved can be made on those grounds. If the claims are no more valid than the initial claims, then a justification based in vital interests becomes more problematic. A basic comparison may be that unambiguous vital interests are not often present in unstable Third World areas.

Given the fluid, ambiguous nature of the situations, in both cases, the United States chose sides with negative results. In Vietnam, the United States made a conscious choice to support the various South Vietnamese regimes because they opposed a communist takeover, whereas in Iraq the United States has attempted to be neutral in intent but cannot be neutral in terms of the impact of its actions. In Vietnam, the United States supported what turned out to be the losing side, because it joined the side opposing communism and unification of the country, and the people overwhelmingly supported unification. In Iraq, the United States has chosen to support democratic rule, which has had the effect of supporting the faction that will benefit from majority rule, the Shiites. In both cases, the United States ended up taking sides in what was in fact a domestic struggle. In one case, it lost, and the question is whether the same thing will happen the second time.

Intractable Conflicts. In both Vietnam and Iraq, the United States has faced situations and opposition that have proven to be extremely durable and obdurate. It is an important part of the "American way of war" (Weigley's term) that war is an interruption of peace, which is the normal state of affairs. These interruptions are essentially malignancies that are to be excised and healed, so the country can return to the normal condition of peace. Thus, the core of the American way of war is to identify and defeat an opposing transgressor who has broken the peace, to vanquish that foe, and to reassert peace. World War II is the epitome of this approach to warfare.

Third World internal conflicts are not as neat and tidy as this conceptualization, and both Vietnam and Iraq have proven to be particularly resistant to the American preference. In both cases, an American intervention to rectify a situation and return it to peace ended up involving the United States in an open-ended, intractable conflict. The conflicts became intractable for at least two related reasons. One was that the United States became involved in political situations that it either did not or chose not to understand, and thus, became a complicating, rather than a simplifying and clarifying, factor. In Vietnam, for instance, the United States was faced with the alternative of seeing the movement to unify the country by force by Ho Chi Minh's North Vietnamese either as a case of communist expansionism or as an expression of Vietnamese nationalism. The movement contained, of course, elements of both motivations, which Southeast Asian experts like the late Paul Kattenburg pointed out, but were rebuffed. Had Vietnam simply been an instance of communist expansionism opposed by the South Vietnamese, it might have had a chance of succeeding, but opposing unifying Vietnamese nationalism placed the United States in a very difficult position. Similarly, the idea of creating a model political democracy in an Iraq deeply divided along sectarian and ethnic lines has placed the United States in a political situation that is extremely difficult, if not impossible, to realize.

The second source of intractability is military. Although critics like Kagan correctly point out that the way American opponents have confronted the United States is different in the two cases, both sources of opposition fall within the broad category of asymmetrical warfare, an approach rather than a specific method or set of strategies and tactics designed to frustrate the military efforts of a superior American opponent (discussed in detail in Chapter 7). In Vietnam, the North Vietnamese realized after the Ia Drang campaign (portrayed in Moore and Galloway's *We Were Soldiers Once . . . and Young*) that they could not confront the United States in conventional, western-style pitched battle, and so they reverted to Maoist-style guerrilla warfare methods. The Iraqi resistance understood from the beginning that it had no realistic chance of confronting the Americans successfully on the conventional battlefield and thus chose non-conventional tactics for opposing the Americans. The exact methods have indeed been different in the two cases, but the approach is the same: Create a protracted situation which will test the will of the United States to continue a long and increasingly unpopular contest, in the hopes that American public opinion will turn on the war and force withdrawal.

Making the war an intractable affair poses an enormous dilemma for the United States that is reflected in the debate over Iraq. Vietnam demonstrated to many actual and potential American opponents that the way to defeat American military might is to drag the war out past American cost-tolerance. This dynamic causes supporters of the war to add the need for resolution in the face of this tendency to their reasons for staying. If the United States continues to cut and run when wars drag out, enemies will be further emboldened in the future. The dilemma is that a continued American presence may be part of the reason the war drags on. The longer the United States stays, the more it reinforces the internal argument that the Americans must be pushed out or they will never leave. This dynamic is explored in some greater detail in the fourth similarity.

Predictable and Predicted Outcomes. Despite claims made by the Bush administration that the war in Iraq would be a "walkover" that would end quickly and allow a rapid disengagement, there were also dissident voices who suggested that Iraq would be akin to Vietnam in that it would be neither short, tidy, nor successful. These voices came mainly from the academic and expert communities but were, prior to the war, neither heard nor heeded, largely drowned out in a patriotic wave that equated the impending action against Iraq with the events of 9/11. As is so often the case in the rush to war, opponents' patriotism was questioned, and expressions that Iraq would become another Vietnam-style quagmire were dismissed as "ridiculous" (a statement made by a reader, in reaction to an opinion piece by this author suggesting the anti-Iraq case on the eve of the war).

Opposition to American involvement in war is, of course, nothing new. There have been opponents of essentially all American wars, from the American Revolution through the world wars. Generally, however, these objections have been based on whether it was wise for the United States to become involved. Supporters of the British monarchy opposed the American Revolution and many Americans of German descent opposed U.S. participation in the world wars, for instance. What is unique about the predictions surrounding Vietnam and Iraq, however, is that both were grounded primarily in the idea that the United States could not succeed in either case because it misunderstood what it was getting into and that, in both cases, the misunderstandings were parallel.

Although it was largely lost at the time, there were dissenters to the decision to engage in the Vietnam War. One argument was that the United States did not understand the nature of the war and was ending up siding against Vietnamese nationalism, a losing cause. This faction, of which Kattenburg is a strong representative, lost the argument when its recommendation that the United States wash its hands of South Vietnam after the assassination Ngo Dinh Diem was rejected. The other argument was that the United States did not understand the nature of the guerrilla warfare it would face in Vietnam and could not prevail in this form of warfare. Roger

Hilsman, who led guerrilla units in Burma during World War II, made this argument and, like Kattenburg, was pushed out of the decision process for his efforts. As these predictions proved prophetic, those closest to the scene (the military) failed to point to the mounting disaster, which is the heart of the argument by McMaster in *Dereliction of Duty*.

Similar points were made about Iraq. Apologists argued that regime change was necessary and that it was possible. Pollack, for instance contended in 2002, "A full-scale invasion has unfortunately become our best option—or at least our 'least bad' option. . . . We must commit ourselves fully to the effort, employ all the forces necessary *to secure victory quickly* and with the least loss of life, and be ready to lead an international effort to rebuild Iraq," (emphasis added). The other side of the argument, about which most analysts familiar with the region agreed, was that Iraq was a very unstable, artificial state (as a conglomerate of disparate regions with no political history as a unit) that was hardly a candidate for liberalization and democratization, as the proponents suggested. Rather, removing the admittedly reprehensible Saddam Hussein would likely simply open the Pandora's box of ethnic and inter-communal hatreds suppressed by his rule. The likely result was compatible with Colin Powell's Pottery Barn entreaty to Bush: "You *will break it, and it will be yours!*" (emphasis added). George W. Bush's initial assessment that the result of liberating Iraq would be to create a civil war was indeed true. Militarily, it was also predicted that the Iraqis would revert to some form of asymmetrical warfare to oppose the American presence. The military's reluctance to come to grips with this reality is a major part of Yingling's critique in "A Failure of Generalship." As he puts it, "America's general officer corps underestimated the strength of the enemy, overestimated the capabilities of Iraq's government and security forces and failed to provide Congress with an accurate assessment of security conditions in Iraq." In fairness, Yingling believes the surge has addressed some of these problems, but the central point remains that the military problem was initially misunderstood, resulting in faulty assessments about the prospects for success.

The dynamics suggested in this assertion of similarity, if valid, are important for two reasons. First, since these comparisons and their consequences for the Iraq effort were known before the invasion, their wider publicizing might have played a more important role in support for the war in the first place. If it is correct that current opposition in the general public reflects the belief that the United States should never have been in Iraq in the first place, then it follows that support for the march to war would have been modified, if the fact that Iraq was a potential train wreck had been made public. Second, it is at least arguable that Vietnam and Iraq may be models for future Third World involvements for the United States, in which case the lessons may be instructive in dampening enthusiasm for what could become future lost causes.

The Impact of a Protracted American Involvement. Central to the contention that the United States should not withdraw precipitously from Iraq is the assertion that the United States must remain there long enough for the situation to stabilize, thereby reducing or removing the prospect of a bloody civil retribution and even a widening of the instability regionally. The heart of this assertion is that continuing American presence will improve the situation in Iraq, whereas cutting and running will likely result in a less desirable, potentially disastrous outcome.

The Vietnam analogy does not provide particular support for this thesis, another reason defenders of Iraq dislike the Vietnam comparison. The belief that continuing presence will stabilize draws on the idea of state-building, and it has both physical and political aspects. Physically, as the Pottery Barn analogy suggests, the American military campaign indeed broke considerable parts of the Iraqi infrastructure (bridges and electric power grids, for instance), and the United States has an obligation to repair what it destroyed. Politically, the idea is that an American presence provides a security shield that protects the fragile political structure in Iraq and allows it to mature in a way that will result in a self-sustaining, stable political outcome after the United States leaves. More to the point, supporters fear the possible consequences of being wrong and having their worst fears realized.

The Vietnam analogy creates some reasons to question this logic. In Vietnam, the more involved the United States became in the war, and the longer the United States stayed, the more the American stake in the war grew, and the more difficult disengagement became because of the accumulated stake in the outcome. In Iraq, this is most often expressed in terms of implicitly saying that American troops who have died in the war made the ultimate sacrifice for nothing if the United States withdraws without "finishing the job." Part of the problem is that the Iraqi government, like the Vietnamese government of Diem before it, recognizes this American dilemma and concludes from it that regardless of what they do in terms of complying with American directions politically and otherwise, that advice can be ignored. The reason is that the Americans have too much "sunk cost" in the war to make meaningful threats to abandon them if they fail to comply. As this author described it in 1997 in *Distant Thunder*, "the amount of assistance and the degree of influence over the government may be inverse, as the government realizes the extent to which outsider investment makes it harder to cut the government off even if it offers good advice." The idea that degree of commitment and leverage are inversely related helps explain why the Iraqi al-Malaki government has been able to resist or ignore advice from the United States, despite occasional dire warnings about the consequences of doing so. In a July 2007 column, *New York Times* political columnist Thomas L. Friedman takes this dynamic a step further in assessing the continuing American commitment to Iraq: "Staying in means simply containing the Iraq civil war, but at a price of Americans and Iraqis continuing to die, and at a price of the United States having no real leverage on the parties inside or outside of Iraq to negotiate a settlement because everyone knows we're staying so they can dither."

Related to this dilemma of mounting stakes as time passes is the possibility that the continuing American presence in Iraq actually makes the situation worse than it would be if the United States left. Despite whatever other name one gives it, the American armed forces in Iraq are, after all, an occupation force, and occupation forces are rarely—if ever—popular or positive influences. The American occupations of Japan and Germany are often cited as exceptions to this rule (although the occupation of Germany did create some resistance), but these occurred in clearly defeated, developed world countries, consciously being offered great economic incentives to comply and adopt democratic political forms. In these cases, occupation worked, but is this the rule? More often, occupations are, or become, unpopular and spawn resistance, the effectiveness of which depends on the relative strengths of the occupying and resisting forces. For at least some segments of the population that resent foreign occupation, the continuing presence of the occupiers provides a rallying cry for resistance and may even provide a displacement object, allowing the deferral of internal reconciliation or adjustment. In Vietnam, the American occupation of South Vietnam did not alter the outcome that seemed inevitable before intervention occurred (the forceful unification of all of Vietnam), it merely deferred it at great cost in blood and treasure. Is the same true of the situation in Iraq?

Poisonous Outcomes for the United States. This point of comparison is somewhat less concrete, because there is as yet no post-Iraq period, and the poisonous effects of Vietnam on the American polity occurred after the American withdrawal, in the post-Vietnam period. Thus, the comparison must be between what happened in Vietnam and what might happen after the withdrawal from Iraq. The ending of the withdrawal from Vietnam, along with events like the Watergate scandal that ended with Richard Nixon's resignation from the presidency, poisoned the political atmosphere for years and still colors the views of many about Vietnam. Whether the end of American involvement in Iraq will have as corrosive an effect will depend partly on the trauma of that separation and whether it is attended by other unsettling events like Watergate. Because that process will apparently take several years to complete (for reasons discussed in Chapters 3 and 4), the validity of the comparison cannot be immediately established or refuted. With that rejoinder in mind, three possible commonalities stand out between the aftermath of Vietnam and the possible post-Iraq period.

The first possible commonality is that the war will end in a way that at least some Americans will consider to be an unsatisfactory, unsatisfying manner. This unhappiness will likely be different among members of the general public and the policy elite, but it will provoke dissatisfaction among both.

There are, of course, two possible conditions of withdrawal that are supported by various parts of the public and elite: a more-or-less immediate withdrawal (operationally, withdrawal within the next year or so), or the maintenance of American presence until sufficient stabilization occurs in Iraq to permit an orderly withdrawal that leaves behind a stable Iraq (a longer term process that may include an enduring presence). When the public is asked about these outcomes, it favors immediate withdrawal by a majority (in November 2007, the preferences were 53 percent for immediate withdrawal, 40 percent for staying the course) that is smaller than when people are asked if they favor the war (in the same period, polling data showed 65 percent opposed, 34 percent in favor). Although there is not equivalent polling data for members of the elite, it might well reverse those preferences, for reasons which will be discussed in the next chapter. Regardless, the point is that there is a division among Americans about how to withdraw, and if withdrawal occurs, those Americans whose preference was not chosen are almost certain to be dissatisfied by the choice that is implemented.

The second possible commonality is that dissatisfaction is likely to occur regardless of which option is chosen, because it will be ambiguous and will likely include some level of instability and human suffering in Iraq. Although those who argue for staying the course hope and project that doing so will result in a stable post-war Iraq that the United States can view with pride, the fractious nature of Iraqi society is unlikely to yield that result, and it is not clear, as argued earlier, that continued American presence will remedy the situation. Even if Iraq eventually becomes an orderly democracy, it will not be one when the United States leaves, regardless of when that occurs. Even supporters of the war implicitly admit this when they talk about how long it has taken other countries to go through the democratization process. Were it likely that the United States could prevail and make Iraq democratic, then seeing the war through to that outcome would still critics. Since that is unlikely to occur, those who favor immediate withdrawal will contend that the United States should have left sooner than it does and those who favor staying can argue that if the United States had stayed longer, the results would have been better.

Because a neat, determinate outcome is unlikely, there will almost certainly be embarrassing residual violence in Iraq after the Americans leave, regardless of when that happens. The most obvious victims will be those who have cooperated with the Americans, against whom collaborationist retribution seems likely, as in Vietnam, but broader sectarian (Sunnis versus Shiites) or ethnic (Arabs versus Kurds) violence is possible as well. The United States can minimize some of this problem by taking better care of American supporters than it did in Vietnam to avoid a repetition of the terrible scene of the evacuation of the U.S. Embassy in Saigon in 1975, when Vietnamese supporters were literally kicked off the skids of American helicopters rescuing Americans as North Vietnamese forces entered the city. The victims in Iraq are likely to be fearful Sunnis, many of whom have already fled to Syria and Jordan. As of June 30, 2007, only 69 immigration visas for Iraqis to come to the United States had been granted for that year.

The third possible commonality is likely to be an "Iraq hangover" (or Mueller's syndrome, as mentioned in the Introduction). The term itself is borrowed from the "Vietnam hangover," after the Vietnam War. In that instance, the end of the war was accompanied by a strong anti-military reaction in the United States born of revulsion with the conflict's outcome—the United States lost—and the involuntary participation of many of the draftees. For the remainder of the decade, military and national security concerns were downgraded in public discussions because those topics reopened the sores of Vietnam. The ongoing concern with terrorism may dilute the hangover somewhat, but it will almost certainly be a factor in other potential American military involvements, notably the possibility of military action against Iran (*see* Chapter 7).

SELECTED BIBLIOGRAPHY

Friedman, Thomas L. "Neither Democrats Nor Republicans Offer Realistic Strategies for Leaving Iraq." *New York Times*, July 14, 2007.

Giuliani, Rudolph W. "Toward a Realistic Peace." *Foreign Affairs* 86, 5 (September/October 2007), 2–18.

Hilsman, Roger. *American Guerrilla: My War Behind Japanese Lines.* Washington, DC: Brassey's (U.S.), 1990.

Kattenburg, Paul M. *The Vietnam Trauma in American Foreign Policy, 1945–1973.* New Brunswick, NJ: Transaction Books, 1980.

McMaster, H. R. *Dereliction of Duty: Lyndon Johnson, Robert McNamara, The Joint Chiefs of Staff, and the Lies That Led to Vietnam.* New York: Harper Perennial, 1997.

Moore, Lt. Gen. Harold G., and Joseph L. Galloway. *We Were Soldiers Once . . . And Young.* New York: Harper Perennial, 1992.

Moyar, Mark. *Triumph Forsaken: The Vietnam War, 1945–1965.* New York: Cambridge University Press, 2007.

Pollack, Kenneth M. *The Threatening Storm: The Case for Invading Iraq.* New York: Random House (A Council on Foreign Relations Book), 2002.

Rozen, Laura. "Interview with Colonel H. R. McMaster, Advisor to General David Petraeus." *Mother Jones* (online), October 18, 2007.

Snow, Donald M. *Distant Thunder: Patterns of Conflict in the Developing World.* Second Edition. Armonk, NY: M. E. Sharpe, 1997.

————.*When America Fights: The Uses of U.S. Military Force.* Washington, DC: CQ Press, 2000.

————, and Dennis M. Drew. *From Lexington to Desert Storm and Beyond: War and Politics in the American Experience.* Armonk, NY: M. E. Shrape, 2000.

Sorley, Lewis. *A Better War: The Unexamined Victories and Final Tragedy of America's Last Years in Vietnam.* New York: Harvest Book, 2007.

Wiegley, Russell F. *The American Way of War.* New York: Macmillan, 1973.

Yingling, Lt. Col. Paul. "A Failure of Generalship." *Armed Forces Journal* (online edition), May 2007.

Chapter 3

On the Domestic Front

The Iraq War has created a very real division within the American political system. The American people have increasingly demanded an end to American involvement in Iraq. By the end of 2007, public opinion had stabilized with about two-thirds of the public demanding American withdrawal from the war and roughly one-third favoring continued support. Unlike Vietnam, opposition or support for the war has been divided along party lines, with a very high percentage of Republicans (and their presidential candidates) supporting a continuation of the conflict, an equally high percentage of Democrats (and their presidential candidates) in opposition, and Independents tending to side with the Democrats.

The voters voiced their unhappiness with the war in the 2006 election, but that outcome has not translated into a movement toward withdrawing or even reducing American force levels in Iraq. Indeed, as the polls were showing growing disaffection with the war, President Bush increased American troop levels from over 130,000 to over 160,000 during the 2007 troop surge. That increase has been widely condemned by opponents to the war, but strongly supported by those who favor the war's aims.

A clear picture has emerged—the majority of the American public wants disengagement from Iraq, and believes that the United States should withdraw much faster than the political system is moving in that direction. Among those who oppose the war, impatience with the failure of the political system to make meaningful—if any—progress toward meeting their demands is growing, as is their dismay and lack of comprehension over why their voices are apparently being ignored. They wonder what exactly is going on.

This chapter explores the American political reaction to the Iraq War. Using the analogy described in Fiorina et al.'s *Culture War?* as a starting point, it begins by examining and assessing the gap between the political leadership and the public regarding the direction of the war effort, and then explores the differences between the public and their leaders on the issues.

It then moves to other parts of the impact on the political system, including how Iraq has affected the general political debate, the economic impacts, and more underlying questions intermixed with the GWOT, including matters such as civil liberties, the use of so-called "enhanced interrogation methods" to support war aims, and how the Iraq commitment has an impact on other policy, including financial, priorities. Inevitably, the analogy with Vietnam enters the picture.

One of the undeniable comparisons between the wars in Vietnam and Iraq is that both became intensely unpopular within the United States. In some measure, the public reaction reflects the general aversion all political democracies have toward long-running wars, unless those wars are demonstrably wars of necessity, fought for a higher cause and with clear-cut endings on the horizon to justify national sacrifice. Modern Third World conflicts, however, are rarely depicted easily in these terms, the implication being that fighting such wars will always be problematical in achieving enduring public support.

The first clear evidence of the political unpopularity of Iraq occurred in the 2006 off-year national elections, when Republicans were swept out of control of both Houses of Congress. In that election, one of the strong motivating factors for voters was their opposition to the war in Iraq and their desire for an alternative leadership that would get the United States out of the war. Along with the economic downturn that became increasingly apparent in the latter months of 2007, the Iraq War is also a major factor in the 2008 election.

THE PUBLIC, THE ELITE, AND IRAQ

In some important ways, the presidential election of 2008 provides an analogy to the 1968 presidential election. In both cases, the contest pitted candidates who were not incumbents, although the Democratic candidate, Hubert H. Humphrey, was vice president and thus associated with the war policies—a position he tried to distance himself from as much as possible. In 1968, the Vietnam War had helped drive Lyndon Johnson from running for a second term, and constitutional provisions prevented George W. Bush from standing in 2008. In both elections, an unpopular war stood as a major campaign issue, forcing the candidates to adopt a position promising to bring the war to an end (although all were inexplicit about how long and under what conditions they would end American involvement). In 1968, there was ambiguity in the ways both candidates—Humphrey and Richard M. Nixon—claimed they would end the war, and public frustration only became a major consideration later, as President Nixon's "secret plan" for extrication dragged on for what turned out to be five years. Similarly, candidates on both sides in 2008 have hedged on the question of exactly how long withdrawal would take.

The war in Iraq has revealed a fissure between the voting public and the policy elite. Borrowing the distinctions made by Fiorina and his colleagues in *Culture War?*, the argument is basically that the real, deep divide in American politics does not reflect so much a fundamental division within the population, a culture war, as much as it reflects a deep fissure *within* the policy elite (those people who make or influence public policy) and *between* the policy elite and the general public. The Fiorina argument is that the public is in basic accord (or at least not deeply divided) on most policy issues, whereas the elite is very divided at the extremes of issues, and it overlays that depth of disagreement on the public—including producing candidates for public office who reflect the policy elite's strong differences much more than the comparatively small differences within the population.

The Iraq War has created a political fissure not unlike that described in *Culture War?*, but it has a twist. While Fiorina and his colleagues suggest a smaller fissure in the general than the elite public, this factor may be reversed in the case of Iraq. In polls, public opinion has fairly consistently registered opposition to the war and its continuation, although the percentages of opponents and supporters vary, depending on the specific question asked. When questions offer incremental answers, it is interesting that answers tend to congregate in the least extreme options (e.g., "somewhat agree," "somewhat disagree"), rather than the more strident option ("strongly agree" or "strongly disagree"), providing at least some indirect support for the Fiorina thesis that the public is not deeply divided on this—the most divisive current policy matter.

If public opinion was the major driver among political leaders in a presidential election year, it would be reasonable to find politicians following the Nixon-Humphrey model and advocating withdrawal, and to an extent they are. With the exception of John McCain and Mitt Romney, major candidates have explicitly suggested an open-ended commitment until victory is achieved, although all Republicans (except Ron Paul) have been circumspect about the terms and pace of withdrawal they accept. What is more interesting, and on the surface, surprising, is that major Democratic candidates with some realistic chance of gaining the nomination and thus potentially occupying the White House, have been guarded in their timing of withdrawal, and especially the rapid withdrawal that many of their supporters clearly want. Democratic candidates (as the currently most visible symbol of the policy elite) are more likely to voice opposition to the war (for instance, on whether the United States should have started the war in the first place) than their Republican counterparts (who are more likely to argue considerations about the beginning of the war distract from the "important issues" surrounding what to do now). Both mainstream Democratic and Republican political leaders, however, are significantly less forthright in advocating a rapid and total withdrawal from Iraq than the public at large. At this writing, it is only at the extremes among each party's contenders for the presidency (Dennis Kucinich and Mike Gravel among Democrats, and Ron Paul among Republicans) that one finds unconditional support for rapid withdrawal. Why?

Public Opinion. The public, of course, never has *an* opinion on anything, in the sense that everyone agrees with a particular position on any issue. Rather, what is referred to in shorthand terms as public opinion normally is a reflection of what a majority of the public feels about a particular issue at any point in time, or over a period of time. Moreover, public opinion on any issue is variable: people change their minds as time goes by and conditions surrounding the issue change. Public sentiment about the Iraq War is no exception.

As noted earlier, public support for the invasion of Iraq was quite high, and that support was reinforced and expanded by the relative ease of the invasion and conquest stage of the war, culminating in Bush's May 1, 2003 pronouncement of the liberation of Iraq and the end of major hostilities, standing proudly on the deck of the USS *Abraham Lincoln* with the "Mission Accomplished" banner waving behind him. By tying the conquest of Iraq to the general war on terror, the far less successful occupation stage was effectively shielded from adverse publicity for well over a year, and it was not until after the 2004 presidential election that public opinion began to turn against the war. As noted, that opinion began to move against the war, had reached a high enough level to influence the 2006 off-year elections, and continued into the 2008 election season at what became fairly stable levels of majority opposition.

Opinion polls taken in November 2007 offered a reasonable "snapshot" of public opinion on the war. Although the numbers varied marginally depending on the poll cited, a clear two-to-one margin opposed President Bush's handling of the war, which, given his insistence on continuing the war until achieving success, reflected what people thought about the war. The *NBC News/Wall Street Journal* Poll covering November 1–5, 2007, for instance, indicates 27 percent of respondents approved of the president's handling of the war, 68 percent disapproved, and five percent were unsure.

Throughout 2007, approval ratings of the war varied from 22 to 30 percent, opposition from 66 to 72 percent, with the variation largely attributable to reports of success or failure of the troop surge. Consistently, however, the public overwhelmingly endorsed a change in policies toward Iraq, and these results were consistent across polls (for a summary of polling results, *see* PollingReport.com, from which data reported here are taken). These figures narrow somewhat, however, when one asks more specific, detailed questions about what Americans think about the war, suggesting both a narrowing of the public gap on the issue, and, thus, differing messages being sent to the political elite.

Four examples illustrate more subtle opinions about the Iraq War. The prestigious Pew Research Center for the People and the Press asked people in October 2007 whether they thought the United States made the right decision or the wrong decision in using military force in Iraq. A majority, 54 percent, responded that it was a mistake, compared to the 40 percent who believed it was the right decision, a narrower margin against than the general opinion of "Bush's war."

A second set of questions focused on how people judged the war's progress. The Pew October 2007 poll also asked respondents, "How well is the U.S. military effort in Iraq going?" Then, results were negative but narrowly so: a bare majority (51 percent) believed the war was going "not too well" or "not well at all," compared to 44 percent who thought it was going "very well" or fairly well." In July 2007, the percentages had been 59 to 36 percent negative, suggesting the surge had some impact on the public's perceptions. This narrower judgment, however, was also reflected in opinion on getting the troops out of Iraq. An *ABC/Washington Post* poll of late September 2007 asked whether people thought the United States should maintain forces in Iraq until civil order is restored even if it meant additional American casualties. By a margin of 54 to 43 percent, respondents believed the forces should be withdrawn (the same poll revealed that 59 percent did not believe the benefits of the war outweighed the costs, while 38 percent disagreed). The *NBC/Wall Street Journal* Poll of November 1–5, 2007 reported that 55 percent believed the United States should "withdraw most troops by 2009," while 40 percent thought the United States should "remain until the country is stable."

The support issue also takes on some interesting dimensions when questions about the war are put in partisan political terms. The public is not enamored with either party's handling of the situation, but they are more critical of the Republicans than the Democrats. When a September 2007 *CBS News* poll asked 706 adults whether they approved of the way

Congressional Democrats were handling the "situation in Iraq," 31 percent approved and 57 percent disapproved. While this might initially appear to be encouraging for Republicans as the 2008 election campaign engages, it is not. An October 29–November 1, 2007 ABC/*Washington Post* poll asked 1,131 Americans, "Which party do you trust to do a better job handling the situation in Iraq?" The result was 50 percent for the Democrats and 34 percent for the Republicans, a finding reflected in a late September 2007 ABC/*Washington Post* poll that asked whether a Democratic or Republican president would do a better job resolving the situation in Iraq after the 2008 election. Fifty-one percent replied a Democratic president, while only 31 percent answered a Republican.

How much faith should one place in these kinds of poll results? It is easy to be mesmerized by the apparent precision of numbers, but poll results should be treated with some reserve. The results cited do, in fact, only represent a slice in time of opinion on the subject, and while the results have been fairly consistent since 2006, they could change. Moreover, surveying still contains elements of art as well as science: the answers one gets, for instance, depend on what questions are asked, how they are asked, to whom they are asked, and when they are asked. No individual results are unassailable, in other words. What the polls are helpful in doing, at a minimum, is tapping into the public's general attitudes.

What the polls do suggest, however, is that there is generalized opposition to the war effort, although the extent and content of that opposition varies, depending on what it is about the war one is questioning. If historical analogies are relevant, negative opinions are likely to increase the longer the war goes on, unless there is dramatic evidence that something that could be consensually agreed to as "victory" is imminent. The Vietnam example is the most obvious case in point. Moreover, if politicians are as driven by poll results as is often alleged, one would expect more of them to be seizing the banner of withdrawal as a, or even *the*, major objective of their quests for public office. But have they?

Policy Elites: The Presidential Candidates. The overall policy elite is divided on the war. Those directly outside the process—academic analysts, media spokespeople, for instance—offer a broad range of opinion based upon ideological positions that cover the gamut of opinion. As one gets closer to the actual centers of power, this range tends to narrow, at least partly because as one approaches the places in which policy decisions are made, there is a restriction of policies advocated, due to the sobering realization that a person might actually have to implement the policies he or she has advocated.

Nowhere is this restriction more pronounced than among the major candidates for the presidency, on whom this section focuses.

As the presidential primary campaign winnowed the field in both parties in 2008, party-based positions emerged: Republicans (notably McCain and Romney) supporting the war, and remaining Democrats Clinton and Obama in opposition. The reluctance to embrace an anti-war stance is more understandable among Republicans, who face political difficulties in abandoning and repudiating the policies of the Republican president. The reluctance of Democrats is more puzzling, because the Democrats have a lesser stake in the President's legacy, and would benefit by taking advantage of riding the crest of the anti-war wave of public opinion. In 1968, the Vietnam issue came down to which candidate could get the country out of the war first; the 2008 election would be more clearly drawn if the Iraq issue were either depicted in the same way as in 1968, or if one party clearly favored continuing the war and the other did not. The stances of the major 2008 candidates more closely resemble the latter scenario than the former.

The candidates and their parties do differ on the Iraq question, of course. In the latter half of 2007 and early 2008, each of the top-tier candidates was asked to write an article, outlining their foreign policy platforms for *Foreign Affairs*. These included assessments of Iraq that provide a database from which positions have evolved. One can gain some insight into their differing and similar positions by looking at three dimensions of what they had to say about Iraq: Should the United States have become involved in Iraq? Should the country stay or get out, and under what circumstances? And, how should withdrawal occur? While these statements were limited by space considerations and were not directed toward the specific questions posed here, they are representative of what the candidates wished to convey to the generally policy elite demographic that reads *Foreign Affairs*. The candidates surveyed were Democrats Hillary Clinton, John Edwards, Barack Obama, and Bill Richardson, and Republicans Rudolph Giuliani, Michael Huckabee, John McCain, and Mitt Romney.

On the question of whether the United States should have become involved in the war at all, the candidates differed by party. Democrats Edwards and Obama argued it was a mistake. Former candidate Edwards, for instance, described Iraq as "one of the greatest strategic failures in U.S. history" and publicly repudiated his 2003 vote in the Senate, which authorized Bush to pursue a war policy. Obama was equally explicit, adding a negative assessment of how the war had been conducted, arguing, "Incompetent prosecution of the war by America's civilian leadership compounded the strategic blunder of choosing to wage war in the first place." Of the three, Clinton was alone in stating no direct opinion on this subject in her *Foreign Affairs* article (she still maintains that she would not have supported the war if she had had complete information about it at the time). Richardson agreed that the war was a mistake.

The Republicans, by contrast, were more supportive of the decision to go to war. McCain, who has been the most consistent supporter of the war among contenders, stated the case most strongly as part of the anti-terrorist imperative in a post-9/11 environment: "Defeating radical Islamist extremists is the national security challenge of our time. Iraq is this war's central front." Before his withdrawal from the campaign, Giuliani offered an indirect endorsement, also based in the 9/11 connection that had been at the heart of his election campaign. He argued that the main foreign policy objective of the United States is "victory in the terrorists' war on the global order," of which Iraq is a primary theater. "Defeating the terrorists must be our principal priority in the near future," he added. Romney's endorsement in his article was less direct, tied instead to the need to continue the effort. Huckabee emphasized mismanagement of the war effort.

The positions coalesced more with regard to the question of how and when to get out of Iraq, with party differences more matters of degree than of kind. Edwards and Obama had been explicit in their advocacy of beginning the process of withdrawal, but not necessarily in how fast it would occur. Both Obama and Clinton, for instance, publicly said at the ABC-sponsored New Hampshire debate of January 5, 2008 that, in Clinton's words, she would get troops out "as quickly and responsibly" as she could. Richardson wanted complete withdrawal within six months of his inauguration. Obama promised troop withdrawal within a year of inauguration, arguing that withdrawal is necessary in order for the Iraqis to resolve their problems themselves. "The best way we have to leave Iraq a better place," he argues, "is to pressure these warring parties to find a lasting political solution. And the only effective way to apply this pressure is to begin a phased withdrawal of U.S. forces." He did not, however, set a firm guideline about when that withdrawal is to be completed. Edwards' call for a withdrawal was similarly hedged: "The United States must retain sufficient forces in the region to prevent a genocide, a regional spillover of the civil war, or the establishment of an al Qaeda haven." This residual force, Edwards maintained, would mostly be outside Iraq proper. Clinton's position was similar, suggesting, "we must withdraw from Iraq in a way that brings our troops home safely, begins to restore stability to the region, and replaces military force with a new diplomatic initiative."

Because they were mostly supportive of the decision to invade Iraq in the first place, the Republican candidates were somewhat reluctant to discuss withdrawal, short of some demonstrable success in the war, and thus argued the importance of remaining in Iraq. Romney, for instance, argued the negative consequences of withdrawal at the time, warning that "walking away now or dividing Iraq up into parts and walking away later would present grave risks to the United States and the world." Giuliani basically concurred, maintaining, "the consequences of abandoning Iraq would be averse," because "parts of Iraq would undoubtedly fall under the sway of our enemies, particularly Iran." More ominously, he argued, "some U.S. forces will need to remain for some time in order to deter external threats," an apparent reference to terrorism.

McCain, the only major candidate to be a forthright advocate of the war, was more explicit about why the United States must remain in Iraq. He lists four consequences of an American failure in Iraq: an extremist belief that the world "is going their way and that everything is possible"; a terrorist sanctuary emerging "in the heart of the Middle East"; "a decisive end to the prospect of a modern democracy in Iraq"; and "an invitation to Iran to dominate Iraq."

None of the Republican candidates was willing to project an end to the war, and thus methods for ending the war. Democratic candidates were equally substantively imprecise on this question. Clinton, for instance, referred to "a regional stabilization group composed of key allies, other global powers, and all the states bordering Iraq" as part of "a new diplomatic initiative" aimed at bringing peace to the region. Obama made a parallel appeal, calling for "a comprehensive regional and international diplomatic initiative to help broker an end to the civil war in Iraq, prevent its spread, and limit the suffering of the Iraqi people."

What emerges from these comparisons are views of Iraq on two different planes. Within the public at large, there is a strong majority that has consistently argued for well over a year against continuing the war, expressing their views most explicitly with regard to opposing the Bush policy on the war. The majority narrows when specifics about the war are asked, but it certainly can be argued that a mandate is available within public opinion to end the war. Democratic and Republican candidates are divided about continuing the war, but their disagreement is more over the length of time and conditions of withdrawal than about heeding the public mandate. The public, basically, wants out of Iraq, and is less concerned about the conditions or consequences of that withdrawal than are the candidates. Although the candidates differ on those conditions and their implications, they all agree that a precipitous withdrawal is not wise, because of the untoward consequences of such an action.

The only candidates who favor a rapid or immediate withdrawal have been the fringe candidates in both parties who have relatively little chance of gaining the nomination of their party and see opposition to continuing the war as a way to improve their chances, or simply feel unconstrained to express their true feelings. This latter distinction may help us understand why the major candidates seem out of step with the public on the question of the pace of withdrawal. It is generally true that, once elected, the options available to political candidates are fewer than the rhetorical positions they can advocate in campaigns—politicians can, and do, promise more than they can possibly deliver. What is sometimes called the "realm of policy possibility" constricts choices, and it may be that the leading candidates, especially Democrats, whose populist instincts must call for advocacy of rapid withdrawal, are indeed looking at the prospect they might actually be elected and held accountable for the positions they have advocated. At the same time, viewing themselves as potential incumbents may also lead them not to want to be encumbered with campaign promises that will prove embarrassing or impractical once they have taken the oath of office. In either case, the result is a gap between what the public clearly expresses as their desires and what those who would serve them promise to do.

IRAQ AND THE POLITICAL DEBATE

Frustration about the future of the Iraq War is a major issue in the 2008 political campaign, and, depending on how the American economy fares in the months leading up to November 2008, is likely to vie with the economy as the leading issue in deciding both the presidency and control of Congress. Iraq has, however, spawned other concerns that are a more-or-less direct spin-off from the war itself. One of these has been frustration with Congress' inability to rein in the war effort. The impact on the economy is also a major concern, particularly as the country flirts with what may be a new recession. Finally, Iraq, especially as it is portrayed as an extension of the war on terror, has raised a series of constitutional questions in areas like intrusion on civil liberties (e.g., warrantless wiretapping) and conformance to national and international legal obligations (e.g., torture, laws of war).

Controlling the War Effort

A Democratic majority was elected to both houses of Congress in 2006, and almost all observers attribute this victory to Democratic opposition to the war. Yet, since those Democratic majorities were sworn into office, there has been no measurable movement toward ending the conflict, and, due to the troop surge in mid-2007, American military involvement has actually increased physically, as already noted. The American public has become increasingly frustrated with the inability of Congress to put brakes on the prosecution of the war. In a late September 2007 *ABC/Washington Post* poll, for instance, 55 percent of respondents said the Democrats in Congress were not doing enough to end the war, and approval ratings for the Congress have fallen to record lows. To the extent Congress was elected to reverse the war, they have failed. Why?

The problem is both constitutional and political. Constitutionally, two principles apply. The first of these is the presidential authority as Commander-in-Chief of the Armed Forces to deploy and employ the armed forces. The U.S. Constitution limits that ability by declaring that only the Congress can declare war, but the last legally declared war the United States fought was World War II. Armed conflicts are no longer declared as wars because of international political and legal concerns: all signatories to the United Nations Charter forfeit the right to initiate wars, for instance, and the declaration of war engages international legal rights and obligations that parties to modern conflicts seek to avoid (e.g., laws of war regarding the treatment of prisoners). Maintaining the legal fiction that an armed conflict is not technically an act of war removes one source of complication for those at war.

This, of course, limits congressional authority, because the constitutional limit that only Congress can declare war does not apply to armed hostilities not declared as war. The only congressional action supporting the use of armed force against Iraq was the resolution of 2002 already mentioned, and that resolution was not legally necessary for the president to deploy armed forces to Iraq. The War Powers Resolution of 1973 was an attempt to recreate a mandatory congressional permission before the commander-in-chief invoked armed forces, but parts of it are of questionable constitutionality, thereby limiting its effectiveness (*see* Snow and Brown, 1997). Effectively, there is little formal limit on the ability of the president to use the armed forces within the limits of political, including public, acceptability. As the continuing Iraq War demonstrates, the president can act as if he is essentially unencumbered by limits on his authority in this area (a position the Bush administration has consistently argued throughout the war).

Congress' constitutional power is indirect in the form of "the power of the purse." The president cannot constitutionally expend any public funds not specifically authorized by Congress for the purposes that Congress has specified. All authorization bills, by constitutional provision, originate in the House of Representatives, making that chamber the focus of budgetary concern. If the Congress wants to limit the president's ability to act in particular ways, including using armed forces, the Congress' major tool is to deny him funds to act in areas of their disapproval.

Politically, of course, imposing such limits is easier said than done, particularly in areas where the funding decisions affect support for American forces deployed in harm's way. Proposing to use the power of the purse, as the Democratic leadership in the current Congress has indeed suggested, activates two quite contrary emotions in the American public, and opponents and supporters of the war have latched onto each emotion. Those who support the attempt to limit the conduct of the war, and even to force an end to American participation, have suggested cutting off funding for the war effort, thereby requiring the president either to withdraw American forces or to commit the impeachable offense of using funds appropriated for other purposes to conduct the war. Thus, the power of the purse is the power of war opponents, at least at one level.

The problem is that another emotion is in play; support for soldiers in the field. Those who support a continuation of the war argue that cutting off funding has the effect of denying soldiers the wherewithal to protect themselves against the enemy. Moreover, tying funding to withdrawal schedules (as the Democrats' November 2007 supplemental appropriations bill did) allegedly forces the military to engage in contingency planning that diverts them from their primary mission—the conduct of the war. Denying troops the funds for ammunition, body armor, or the like is clearly reprehensible and even unpatriotic and thus activates the scorn not only of those who actually favor the war, but also those who simply feel that troops should receive adequate support under any circumstances, but who may otherwise oppose the war. The effect is to broaden support for funding for the war and thus, indirectly, broaden support for the war on moral and patriotic grounds. A great number of Americans who oppose the war are unwilling to take the chance that anti-war action may endanger their fellow Americans in uniform.

The result is to add an emotional and frustrating dimension to the debate over continuing the war. The argument that withholding funding endangers troops is arguably false and disingenuous in any direct sense. When proponents argue for cutting off or limiting funds, they are generally talking about funding for *future*, not current, operations. At any given time, prior appropriations contain adequate provisions to continue robust support for troops in the field and to provide the needed funds for an orderly and well-protected withdrawal. Arguing that such restrictions endanger troops in the field is disingenuous, the war critics maintain, and, moreover, those who make such claims know this full well. Instead, the purpose of the accusation is to make those who oppose the war appear anti-military and unpatriotic in the sense of denying needed support for the armed forces. The counter claim—that the best way to protect the troops is to get them out of harm's way by ending the war—gets effectively drowned out in the acrimony of the debate.

The use of the power of the purse is frustrating for both sides, but especially to war opponents, who find themselves in a damned-if-you-do, damned-if-you-don't situation. If they attempt to use the one meaningful tool available to them to meet the public's demand for ending the war, they are accused of being unpatriotic and of unnecessarily hinder the military in its activities, including the protection of American soldiers in the field. If they honor the equally strong demand to adequately support troops in the field, they are accused of reneging on their promise to end the war. War proponents are frustrated because they have been unable to elicit adequate support for their position on the war with the majority of the population, but can find some solace in having placed war opponents in an absolutely untenable position. Among other things, reducing the issue to this level obscures a more open debate on the merits of continuing the war and also on the consequences, prominent among which is the economic impact of the war.

Economic Impact

When the war was first being proposed and its conduct projected, one of the major assertions arising from the administration and its supporters was that the economic impact would be minimal. This contention was based on what proved to be two false assumptions, both of which were arguably knowable at the time the arguments and decisions were being made. One argument was that the cost of the war itself would be minimal. The basis of this claim was that the war would be short and that American forces would be withdrawn quickly from Iraq, thereby avoiding the expense of a prolonged deployment. This argument in essence was based on the invasion and conquest phase of the war and ignored or denied the prospect of a lengthy occupation. The second argument was that rebuilding Iraq into a viable state would also not be expensive for the United States, because Iraqi oil revenues would be increased enough in a post-Saddam environment to pay for the cost of rebuilding the country. In fact, Iraqi oil output and revenues declined after the fighting and have only recently approached pre-invasion levels. There have been no Iraqi oil revenues to pay for the aftereffects of the war.

The Iraq War has become a very expensive economic albatross for the United States. Estimates of how much of a burden vary. It was, for instance, stated in a November 13, 2007 report by Democratic members of the House-

Senate Joint Economic Committee that the tab would reach $1.6 trillion by September 2009 under present spending levels. War proponents argue that this estimate is too high, but nonetheless, the actual figures are unquestionably very high. In turn, this ongoing economic burden creates a number of economic concerns, four of which will be mentioned here.

The first and most obvious economic concern is the cost of the war and how it is being financed. As noted directly above, the war has been vastly more expensive than was originally projected, and its open-ended pursuit will have further impact on federal spending in the future. How debilitating that future spending will be is, of course, a matter of speculation, and war supporters and proponents differ on how much the continuing amount and impact will be.

A major part of the concern over the mounting cost of the war is its contribution to governmental operating deficits (roughly the difference between the amount the government collects in revenue and the amount it spends in any given fiscal year) and government debt (the accumulation of deficits). During the Bush administration, annual deficits have ballooned and resulted in an accumulated debt estimated in 2007 as approaching $9 trillion. A major contributor to this accumulation has been the cost of the Iraq War, since it has involved the expenditure of a large amount of money for which there has been no offsetting increase in federal revenues in the form of increased taxes, decreased spending in other areas, or some other manner.

Part of the economic impact has been masked by the way in which the Iraq War has largely been funded, using the *supplemental appropriations process*, rather than the regular budget. Supplemental appropriations, as defined by the White House Office of Management and Budget Watch (OMB Watch), a non-profit watchdog group that studies and critiques governmental spending, is "spending legislation, generally but not exclusively requested by the President, intended to address a need not known or foreseen when the annual budget for a given fiscal year was drawn up." The use of supplemental funding is not new, dating back to the first Congress in 1790, but historically, the rationale for this form of legislation has been to deal with emergency situations. Post-Katrina funding for the immediate reaction to suffering in New Orleans is an example of the principle in action.

The problem is that the use of supplemental appropriations has expanded well beyond its original intent and has arguably been distorted, especially during the Bush administration. The expansion has been the result of increased use of the process to cover a broadening list of funding priorities, to the point that over six percent of government proposed spending for fiscal year (FY) 2007 was done through supplemental appropriations requests. The distortion has been that the original intent of the process—providing relief in the face of unforeseen disasters—has been essentially eliminated. The primary area where this has occurred is in funding for the wars in Afghanistan and Iraq. As the OMB Watch study asserts, "The use of supplemental appropriations has mushroomed during the Bush administration, and the emergency requirement has faded. The Iraq and Afghanistan wars have been almost entirely financed by emergency supplemental."

The amount of funds involved is not inconsequential. For FY 2006, for instance, Congress passed a supplemental appropriation of $91 billion on March 8, 2006. Of that amount, about $68 billion was earmarked for Afghanistan, Iraq, and the GWOT, which hardly met the criterion of unanticipated emergencies, about $19.5 billion was allocated to Hurricane Katrina relief, and another $4 billion was earmarked for international catastrophes like Darfur and a devastating earthquake in Pakistan. The FY 2007 request was $99.7 billion, and requests for FY 2008 have been even larger.

Why is this distinction important in understanding the Iraq War? For one thing, it helps clarify the actual costs of the war and their budgetary impact. A primary advantage of using supplemental appropriations is that they are "off-budget." What this means is that they do not appear in any way in the regular federal budget for any fiscal year. When the administration calculates what it spent for a given year, it uses figures from the regular federal budget that excludes these additional expenditures, which *include almost all the real spending on Iraq*. Since supplemental appropriations are not accompanied by compensating revenue proposals, they are essentially entirely deficit spending that, if included in the federal budget, would inflate deficit figures. Thus, hiding Iraq funding within supplemental appropriations obscures the contribution of that spending to federal deficits that are already a sore point for the administration: If Iraq funding had to be accounted within the regular budgetary process, deficit figures would look much worse than they already are.

If one wants to minimize public reaction to Iraq War spending, the supplemental appropriations process has other advantages as well. By declaring that a request represents a response to an emergency (as the administration routinely does with Iraq funding), the request also avoids the regular budget process and is immune from spending limits imposed by the annual budget resolution passed early in the year to set the parameters on permissible federal spending (the resolution sets broad guidelines for developing the detailed federal budget). In addition, since emergencies can occur at any time, supplemental appropriations can be requested at any time—and at multiple times—as the need arises.

The overall impact, of course, is to create the illusion that spending on Iraq, because it is not reflected in regular budget assessments, is much less consequential both in terms of the amounts expended and their impact on federal deficits. In the process, the original intent of the process has clearly been prostituted—some small aspects of funding for the war for any year may be the result of unforeseeable emergencies, but most of it is not. The Congress has cooperated with this effective budgetary "sleight of hand" for most of the Iraq War. Between 2003 and January 2007, the Republicans controlled both Houses of Congress, but Democrats have not objected vociferously since gaining control of the Congress. When Democrats raise questions about Iraq War spending now, it is in reaction to new supplemental requests (although that fact is not loudly acknowledged). Their acquiescence to administration demands, despite occasional restricting riders like withdrawal timetables, results largely from fears of being labeled as unsupportive of the troops, as noted earlier.

The contribution of Iraq spending to government deficits and debt raises the second and third economic concerns. The second economic concern deals with how the deficits caused by the Iraq War are being financed. Since the government has not proposed so-called "offsets" (proposals to decrease spending in other areas to compensate for supplemental appropriations) or created other sources of revenue to pay for these monies, the answer is through borrowing. More specifically, most of the borrowing has been from foreign sources, and notably from China. Exact amounts are not readily available on the extent to which the Chinese Government has financed the American involvement in Iraq, but a good deal of that financing has come in the form of borrowing back American dollars held by China as the result of trade surpluses with the United States.

The consequences of the fact that China has in effect been putting up the money to fight in Iraq are debatable, but they are not a matter the U.S. Government is anxious to publicize broadly. Historically, Americans have held most of the federal debt, in the forms of government bonds and securities, savings bonds, and the like, but increasingly foreign governments and foreign investors have become prominent holders of American debt. As long as the United States continues to run both a spending deficit and a negative trade balance, American dollars will flow out of the country to pay for the things Americans buy in excess of what they sell, and some of that cash will return to the United States as loans to the government held by overseas investors. How much this potentially compromises the United States in the future is uncharted ground and thus subject to disagreement. No one, however, endorses the accumulation of additional foreign debt in principle, and particularly when that debt is the result of questionable, arguably unwise, spending. It cannot be confidently predicted that foreign borrowing to fight in Iraq will compromise this or a future generation of Americans; the possibility that it will have negative effects cannot be discounted.

A third possibility with arguable antecedents in the Vietnam War flows from these dynamics: the possibility that spending on Iraq will contribute to an inflationary spiral and even a recession after the war is over. In some ways, the situations are parallel. In Vietnam, the government financed the war with deficit spending (although mostly through domestic borrowing), mainly because Lyndon Johnson chose to finance both the Vietnam conflict and his "Great Society" social programs without raising taxes. The dynamics are slightly different now, but with similar results. The Bush administration has not increased non-Iraq spending as systematically as under the Great Society entitlement package (the Medicare prescription plan is a notable exception), but it has continued or marginally increased other spending while decreasing taxes. The result in both cases is burgeoning current accounts deficits.

Will the economic consequences be the same as they were in the wake of Vietnam? Deficit spending on Vietnam was blamed for an inflationary spiral in the early 1970s—so-called "double digit" inflation rates (a rate of ten percent or more) that in turn caused an economic downturn and one of the last admitted recessions in the country. As 2008 began, the signs of economic weakening were occurring in the United States. Among the most serious signs were the weakening of the American dollar against other global currencies, making it more expensive for Americans to interact with other countries (for travel, or to buy merchandise, for instance) and raising the possibility that Americans would be able to buy less in the future, possibly with recessionary implications. Wars always distort economies to some degree, and the longer the war in Iraq continues, the greater distortion it will likely bring. While the predictions of such effects are often exaggerated, and Americans are willing to endure some hardships if they feel the effort is worth it, the economic impact may be increasingly controversial with the Iraq War.

A fourth economic effect surrounds the sacrifices in other areas that have been the result of spending on the Iraq War. Obviously, funds expended on the Iraq War cannot be applied to other priorities, and when economic issues are reduced to funding Iraq *or* other priorities that some Americans hold dear, it creates a real sense of sacrifice that supporters of the war have, by and large, sought to avoid. The question of whether the United States should spend scarce and precious resources on Iraq, or on other priorities, will certainly be part of the election-year political agenda.

Two health-related examples emerged in 2007 as notable examples. One involved American veterans of the Iraq War and the Veterans Affairs effort of the government. The lightning rod of this concern was the revelation of squalid conditions for recovering veterans in the crown jewel of the armed forces medical facilities, Walter Reed Hospital in Washington, D.C. Whether it was scenes of unsanitary living facilities or nonexistent rehabilitation programs and facilities, the Walter Reed case opened a Pandora's box of deficiencies in the system and revealed, among other things, that programs to deal with the physical and mental problems incurred by American veterans in Iraq had been badly underestimated by the Bush administration. As a result, it became increasingly evident that an administration that had regularly chided the Democratic opposition for opposing adequate support for American service members was itself beggaring those same soldiers, sailors, airmen, and marines when it came to medical care. In late 2007, President Bush vetoed a bill passed by the Democratic Congress to expand the State Children's Health Insurance Plan (SCHIP), on the grounds that at $35 billion it was too expensive and expanded the protection to middle-class children who did not need it. The Democrats replied that funds being diverted to fund the war would easily cover the cost of the expanded SCHIP and be more responsible in the process. In an election year, it is a virtual certainty that the SCHIP controversy will be the prototype of several other aspects of campaign debate.

There is a traditional bit of conventional wisdom that asserts that wars are good economically, because a war effort stimulates economic activity and is thus "good for business." World War II, for instance, is credited with ending the Great Depression in the United States, and conspiracy theorists are fond of blaming what Dwight Eisenhower called the "military-industrial complex" for promoting war (this is one of the standard arguments made by opponents of the Vietnam War, for instance). In the present context, no one argues that the economic impact of Iraq adds to its appeal or support. Rather, the impacts are generally viewed as uniformly negative, and as a result, proponents of the war have downplayed them as much as possible. Opponents have only recently begun to try to exploit these perceived negative consequences. At the same time, the war has spun off other political debates, especially in areas where Iraq and the GWOT have been intertwined.

Broader Policy Implications

The Iraq War has also become a political battleground in other areas of American politics. Part of this extension has been the result of the conscious equation of Iraq and the GWOT, which has the effect of entangling controversies about politics surrounding the GWOT with those relating directly to Iraq. This equation is clearest with regard to two issues: 1) The infringement of civil rights and liberties caused by, and attributed to, dictates of national security caused by both "wars." 2) The specific issue of torture and other alleged internationally illegal actions as practiced both in the names of the GWOT and the war in Iraq. Both are complex issues that cannot be explored fully in the limited space available here. They can, however, be introduced.

Iraq, the GWOT, and Civil Liberties. The idea that the conduct of war and lesser states of national emergency occasionally come into conflict with individual rights and liberties is certainly not a novel phenomenon in the current context. During the earliest years of U.S. history, the Alien and Sedition Act defined sedition as criticism of the president (John Adams at the time) and called for deporting resident aliens considered threatening to the country. President Lincoln suspended *habeas corpus* (designed to protect citizens from unlawful arrest and detention) during the Civil War, and both world wars produced legal actions against citizens suspected of actions against the war effort. In Vietnam, the FBI Counterintelligence (COINTEL) Program subjected anti-Vietnam activists to surveillance and occasional harassment.

The history of government infringement on civil rights during wartime has been based in the dictates of national security and, by and large, courts have upheld that argument by government across time. During times of peace, the issue is rarely raised, and although it is not universally the case, most of the time the infringements imposed during any particular war have been repudiated after the war is over: No one, for instance, defends the internment of American citizens of Japanese ethnicity during World War II, nor does anyone argue that Lincoln's suspension of *habeas corpus* is a useful precedent (except possibly against non-American citizens). Nonetheless, the idea that the government would deem it necessary to take actions that place limits on the exercise of some individual liberties in order to assist in the conduct of war has a long, if not necessarily distinguished, history. Actions by the Bush administration are thus not unusual responses to a condition of hostility, at least in general terms. Nor is opposition to those actions particularly unusual.

The precipitating event for the current round of restrictions and objections to them was, of course, the terrorist attacks of September 11, 2001. On September 12, 2001, President Bush stood defiantly on the rubble of the World Trade Towers in New York with a bullhorn. He promised retribution and, in effect, declared the "war on terror," now more often described as a war on Islamic extremism or radicalism. In the wake of this event and response, the Congress authorized the president to take whatever actions he deemed necessary to prosecute this new war, and, almost immediately, passed a controversial piece of legislation, the interpretation of which has formed the basis both of administration actions and critical responses. The piece of legislation was the Uniting and Strengthening America by Providing Appropriate Tools Required to Intercept and Obstruct Terrorists ("U.S.A. PATRIOT Act" is the symbolic acronym for a title contorted to fit the acronym) major provisions of which were renewed in 2006. The PATRIOT Act was passed in October 2001 and thus is not formally connected to the Iraq War, in that its inception predated the war by a year and a half. The continuing application of the Act, however, is at least partially justified by the needs of the war.

There are two particularly controversial outgrowths of the legislation (for more detailed accounts, *see* Dory, or Doyle) arising directly or indirectly from the PATRIOT Act: surveillance of American citizens through surreptitious wiretapping of telephone conversations, and the ongoing controversy over the detention of suspected terrorists at the Guantanamo Bay military facility in Cuba. There is controversy about the extent to which the actions taken in either area are the direct result of applications of the PATRIOT Act or whether controversial actions are interpretations that go beyond its provisions. In either case, the actions have provoked controversy that has carried over into the 2008 election campaign. Predictably, supporters of the continuing campaign in Iraq tend to support restrictions on civil liberties and the continued commission of Guantanamo, whereas opponents of the war oppose both of these sets of actions (indeed, this support or opposition may be the clearest link between these GWOT-inspired actions and Iraq).

The heart of the surveillance issue has been the practice of surveillance of electronic communications without first gaining warrants from the Foreign Intelligence Surveillance Act (FISA) court, as provided by law. The administration argues that such permission is unnecessary in the limited instances in which it permits such intrusions: the interception and monitoring of phone calls between suspected terrorists or sympathizers and known overseas terrorists. Their justification is both legal and practical—its legal basis is in the dictates or national security during wartime, and its practical basis is that the program would not be possible if such permission had to be obtained in specific instances (warrants could not be obtained fast enough). Opponents argue on principle that the whole idea of warrantless surveillance runs directly against codes of American jurisprudence (violating fundamental rights of privacy guaranteed in the Constitution) and that if current procedures are inadequate to permit a justifiable activity, then the proper course is to revise FISA, not to ignore the law.

The Guantanamo issue arises because those detained at the facility are denied almost all the legal rights of anyone else on American soil. The administration position is that these individuals, who are all suspected terrorists (by the government's definition), are beyond the categories of those protected either by the U.S. Constitution's provisions of individual rights (*habeas corpus*, most prominently) or even international standards as prisoners of war (they are defined, somewhat ambiguously, as detainees rather than as prisoners of war). To opponents of the Iraq War, the continuation of the Guantanamo facility is yet another instance of lawlessness by the Bush administration, hiding behind the protective veil of national security (the GWOT and Iraq). They believe that the facility represents an ongoing national embarrassment to the United States and should be shut down.

Torture. The second issue that has arisen as a part of the national security debate in the 2008 election is the question of torture, or what the administration prefers to call "enhanced interrogation" techniques. The context is, once again, the issue of national security versus civil rights. Those who defend the use of techniques that are arguably torture defend the practice on two grounds. The first is to deny that the practices actually used by Americans constitute torture, and President Bush has consistently argued that the United States never engages in acts of torture. The other justification is the nature of the competition with Islamic extremists who do not honor legal codes and who engage in acts of terror against American citizens, which justifies enhanced efforts to gain information about their plans. Opponents counter these arguments by maintaining that the actions that have been undertaken in the name of enhanced interrogation in fact do constitute torture (the case of "waterboarding," a technique that simulates drowning the person being interrogated, has received particular publicity in this regard), and that, under any circumstance, it is ludicrous, even anti-American, to think that the United States Government would engage in actions that could be argued as torture. The issue is not entirely clear-cut, and revolves on a conundrum of sorts. The nub of the disagreement, which reflects the classic wartime infringements debate, is the extent to which agents of the United States should go—or be allowed to go—to protect American citizens from attacks that would kill innocent American citizens. Is, in other words, national security or individual freedom the first order and responsibility of the American Government? In normal times, the two concepts are not usually at odds with one another, but particularly in this age of unconventional, asymmetrical warfare against enemies who do not accept or honor what Americans view as "civilized" rules of conducting conflict, is the use of unconventional means justified, or dictated by the situation?

In a specifically Iraq War context, this issue came up most dramatically in 2005 over revelations of American actions at the Abu Ghraib prison in Iraq. Leaked pictures of actions being taken by American military personnel against Iraqis who were suspected of being part of the Iraqi resistance that was killing American occupation forces indicated actions broadly describable as acts of torture, and the revelations inflamed the American debate. Critics (*see* Hersh, for instance) argued that the excesses of Abu Ghraib were in essence an extension of the hysteria of reactions to 9/11 transferred to the Iraq War, while those who supported the war tended to view at least some of the actions as necessary ways to gain information that could save the lives of American soldiers and marines. Were there not a condition (if not legal state) of war either against Islamic extremists (the GWOT) or in Iraq, these subjects would not arise as concerns in the 2008 election campaign. If the Iraq War alone were removed, the issues might be somewhat muted in their impact, but they would still remain. As long as there is both a GWOT and a military action in Iraq, however, they will remain matters of public debate and disagreement.

SELECTED BIBLIOGRAPHY

Clinton, Hillary. "Security and Opportunity for the Twenty-first Century." *Foreign Affairs* 86, 6 (November/December 2007), 2–18.

Dory, Amanda J. "American Civil Security: The U.S. Public and Homeland Security." *Washington Quarterly* 27, 1 (Winter 2003–04), 37–51.

Doyle, Charles. *The USA PATRIOT Act Sunset: Provisions That Expire on December 31, 2005.* Washington, DC: Congressional Research Service, June 29, 2005.

Edwards, John. "Reengaging with the World." *Foreign Affairs* 86, 5 (September/October 2007), 19–36.

Fiorina, Morris P., with Samuel J. Abrams and Jeremy C. Pope. *Culture War? The Myth of a Polarized America* (Second Edition). New York: Pearson Longman, 2006.

Fogarty, Gerald P. "Is Guantanamo Bay Undermining the Global War on Terror?" *Parameters* XXXV, 3 (Autumn 2005), 54–70.

Giuliani, Rudolph W. "Toward a Realistic Peace." *Foreign Affairs* 86, 5 (September/October 2007), 2–18.

Hersh, Seymour M. *Chain of Command: The Road from 9/11 to Abu Ghraib.* New York: HarperCollins, 2004.

Huckabee, Michael D. "America's Priorities in the War on Terror." *Foreign Affairs* 87, 1 (January/February 2008), 155–168.

Irwin, Paul M., and Larry Nowels. *FY 2006 Supplemental Appropriations: Iraq and Other International Activities, Additional Hurricane Katrina Relief.* Washington, DC: Congressional Research Service, March 10,2006.

McCain, John. "An Enduring Peace Built on Freedom." *Foreign Affairs* 86, 6 (November/December 2007), 19–34.

Obama, Barack. "Renewing American Leadership." *Foreign Affairs* 86, 4 (July/August 2007), 2–16.

OMB Watch. *Background Brief: Supplemental Appropriations.* Washington, DC: OMB Watch, March 2007 (http://www.ombwatch.org/budget/supplemental backgrounder.pdf)

PollingReport.com, November 13, 2007 (http://pollingreport.com/iraq.htm)

Richardson, Bill. "A New Realism." *Foreign Affairs* 87, 1 (January/February 2008), 142–154.

Romney, Mitt. "Rising to a New Generation of Global Consequences." *Foreign Affairs* 86, 4 (July/August 2007), 17–32.

Snow, Donald M. and Eugene Brown. *Beyond the Water's Edge: An Introduction to U.S. Foreign Policy.* New York: St. Martin's Press, 1997.

Watts, William L. "War Costs Could Top $1.6 Trillion, Panel Says." *Marketwatch* (online). November 13, 2007.

Chapter 4

Iraqification

A critical part of the debate over leaving Iraq is the questionable condition of that country once the United States withdraws. Those who defend a continuing U. S. presence argue that complete withdrawal would likely be disastrous—a spiral into a maelstrom of violence and increased insecurity that could seep across the borders and infect neighboring countries in the region. This chaos might invite intervention by Iraq's neighbors, out of feigned or real appall at the human devastation. Since the United States fomented the situation by overthrowing the previous order in Iraq, it bears responsibility for fixing what has been broken (remember Powell's Pottery Barn rule analogy in Chapter 1), and thus, has a moral obligation to stay long enough to repair the damage and to leave Iraq capable of taking care of its own affairs. Critics counter that the American presence is part of the problem, and that, in the long run, continued American presence simply impedes the establishment of Iraqi self-determination, while pointlessly sacrificing more American blood and resources in the futile effort.

Both of these arguments rest on two premises not in evidence, since they project into an uncertain future that cannot be known. One premise is a "description" of Iraq after the American withdrawal that is dire and unappealing. Those who support the war predict an apocalyptical future for Iraq if the United States withdraws precipitously, and see a more positive outcome if the United States "stays the course." Those who oppose staying the course generally concur that Iraq will undergo bloody turmoil after the United States leaves (but not, they say, as bloody as it would be if the United States remained), but maintain that American presence just prolongs the agony. As retired General Anthony Zinni puts it (*see* Schulman), "The short-term security benefits that we create are not long lasting, because you can't be there forever."

The other premise is based on the impact of continuing American presence in Iraq. Foreseeing the affect of maintaining American forces in Iraq is even more confused and confusing than what Iraq will look like (although the two are clearly related). The benefits of maintaining a U.S. presence tend to be associated with the military condition on the ground, and, since the summer of 2007, are associated with the surge of American forces. The successes that are proudly displayed describe military conditions in the country—lowered levels of Iraqi and American casualties, signs of increased security in different regions—that can be attributed to the increased presence of American forces and their suppression of Iraqi resistance activities. Accepting the salutary effects of this activity has become a patriotic mantra of support for the troops. As McMaster (*see* Rozen) summarizes the surge: "I believe that certainly it does have a strong chance of succeeding if we have the will to see it through. And that's the fundamental question, you know." The message is clear: The surge is succeeding, and it should be allowed to complete its work, which will produce a good outcome.

The problem is what kind of success continued American presence creates. It is undeniable that the surge and reduced hostile activity against Americans and Iraqis has coincided, but does that mean the ultimate outcome in Iraq is moving in a positive direction toward peace and stability? The alternative interpretation is that the effects of the surge are transitory and will last only as long as American troops are present to physically suppress the violence. The idea parallels a hypothesis about Vietnam put forward by Gelb and Betts in a 1979 book *The Irony of Vietnam: The System Worked*. Their thesis was that as long as the United States remained in Vietnam, the American political objective of a free and independent South Vietnam was indeed maintained, but after the United States left the situation reversed and the objective was lost. Could the same be true in Iraq?

The two positions are ironic. Those who believe in the need to stay in Iraq are particularly chary of historical analogies that suggest a negative outcome; using Vietnam as an example might highlight the futility of involvement, if they try to bolster their case by suggesting that if the United States had persevered in Vietnam, the outcome would have been different. This involves the double negative of asserting what would not have happened if what *was* done had *not* been done. Critics counter with the argument that the Vietnam analogy demonstrates the futility of involvement and even, by extension, that the worst-case outcome is not proven to be an unfavorable outcome (Vietnam is not, after all, currently an enemy of the United States). The irony is that both arguments are counter-factual, built on premises the truth or falsity of which cannot be demonstrated by facts and which cannot be proven until a decision is implemented.

The net effect of the debate over leaving Iraq is uncertainty, since critical elements about the outcome cannot be known. Instead, the arguments are necessarily extrapolations from a present situation with an unknowable future, making a straight-line projection questionable. Will, for instance, the military successes of the surge translate into improvements in the internal political situation in Iraq, which will then lead to its future political success? Or, are military and political success unrelated, or perhaps related in more complex ways? Whether staying makes sense depends critically on answering that question, but it cannot be answered with certainty.

The result is an environment of ambiguity surrounding the issue of withdrawal from Iraq. The discussion here will begin by looking at the three possibilities: success, failure, or something in between. Based on this assumption, the analysis suggests that neither extreme outcome is likely and that, by default if for no other reason, an intermediary outcome ("Iraqification") is most likely. After examining the possible shapes such an outcome could take, the chapter concludes by looking at some of the consequences of a policy of Iraqification.

THREE POSSIBLE OUTCOMES

There are three possible outcomes of the Iraq War: the United States can succeed in accomplishing all of its objectives (victory); the United States can be vanquished and forced to leave the country without achieving any of its objectives (defeat), or the result could be somewhere in between. These possibilities, and especially the extremes of victory or defeat, are thrown about in public debates without a great deal of precision in terms of what they mean or what is entailed in reaching them. Both their meaning and implications are critical to determining how the United States could and will leave Iraq. Confusion about exactly what the terms mean has had the effect of clouding the debate over preferred ways of ending the conflict.

What do "victory" and "defeat" mean? Is the essence of victory the military outcome of hostilities, as President Bush implicitly suggested when he declared a successful end to hostilities in May 2003? Or does victory mean—or require—achievement of the underlying political purposes that provided the reason for going to war in the first place? Can one, as the old military saw goes, "win the war yet lose the peace"? In other words, win the military confrontation yet fail to achieve the political goals that caused the war in the first place?

The answer to the latter question is "yes." The military conduct of war, in conventional terms, is the precondition for imposing the victor's conditions on the defeated enemy to bring about its political objectives. Thus, in World War II, the destruction of fascism required first defeating the military forces of Germany and Japan, which in turn allowed the overthrow of their fascist governments and thus the attainment of the political goal of the war. In modern asymmetrical war, however, the sequence is not so simple. As the joint U.S. Army-Marine doctrinal statement on asymmetrical wars (*FM 3–24, Counterinsurgency*) signed by and acknowledging the authorship of General Patraeus agrees, the process of defeating counterinsurgents is mostly political, with the military outcome not the only, and sometimes not even the most important, contributor to success. Military success *may* lead to achieving the political goal, but it also may *not*.

Discussions of progress in Iraq gain meaning in terms of this distinction. When supporters cite progress (especially since the surge began), they are generally talking about success on the military level, as already noted. Implicit in the assertion is that military success will lead to political success, but that connection is not absolute: Military success might be necessary, but solely, it is not necessarily sufficient to guarantee success. Opponents argue that, at the political level, despite the military successes, Iraq is not moving toward the political accords and reconciliations that would allow realization of the underlying political objectives of the war (i.e. a democratic Iraq). The recognition that the meaning of victory is a matter where the opposing sides in the debate essentially talk past one another is critical to assessing the possible outcomes.

Victory. In modern, largely internal Third World conflicts, victory means different things to different participants. In Iraq, the multi-ethnic and multi-confessional nature of the country means there is a power struggle among the various major factions (Sunnis, Shiites, and Kurds) that, in simplest terms, is a zero-sum game where one side triumphs at the expense of the others. Thus, many Shiite politicians favor something like a one-man-one-vote democracy (since they represent about 60 percent of the population). This would allow them to elect a Shiite majority that can enact legislation to effectively suppress the Sunnis and reduce Kurdish autonomy, an outcome that comes at the expense of Kurds and Sunnis. The same calculus can be applied to both the Sunnis and the Kurds, and the results are the same: The gains of one are the losses of the other. The only way Iraq benefits is if some arrangement can be found by which all factions can agree on a set of political outcomes, and by which each faction believes it benefits to an acceptable level to support that outcome. Such an outcome has proven elusive to this point, and since all of the factions distrust one another, forging an agreement that all can accept— and trust the others to honor—is the main, possibly insuperable, obstacle to future success.

As long as the Iraqis themselves think in terms of subnational rather than Iraqi terms, then the idea of an "Iraqi" victory will remain elusive. The point of the American effort to encourage Iraqi political reconciliation aims at creating the conditions to break the logjam of parochial solutions in order to allow the Iraqis to find an Iraqi solution. While the surge has suppressed the activities of military and paramilitary groups who represent one group or another, it has been totally unable to move the political process, which remains as unsuccessful since the surge began as it was before. In that circumstance, each side will retain its military forces in the form of armies or militias loyal to its particular group, and will be ready to use those forces against any that might try to suppress them. If the American goal, as stated, is to leave behind a stable Iraq that can stand on its own, then a definition of victory in both military and political terms must emerge within the Iraqi population. The question, explored later in the chapter, is whether that process of reconciliation is better served by a continuing American presence or by the removal of the United States from the equation.

From an American vantage point, the question of victory is somewhat different from either a military or political perspective. The initial goal of the United States was to overthrow the government of Saddam Hussein, for which the military objective was to defeat the Armed Forces of Iraq that protected the Iraqi dictator. That objective was accomplished, but it led to attacks on the Bush administration's reasons for overthrowing Saddam. When the first of these objectives (WMD and ties to terrorism) proved ethereal, the political objective became more explicitly the neoconservative aim of creating a model democracy in the region that could serve as the catalyst for reforming the region. A model democracy that would also grant oil leases to American and British firms would be the ideal solution.

Militarily, the objective changed as well. Once the Iraqi army had been defeated and disbanded, they no longer posed any barrier to achieving the political goals. As the occupation phase continued (accompanied by very little visible reconstruction), however, the various forms of Iraqi resistance emerged to oppose the occupiers, as well as to attack other segments within Iraq. These groups pose a different military and political problem than did the Iraqi Army. The army presented a conventional, symmetrical challenge that the United States is extremely efficient in combating. The resistance groups, however, pose an unconventional, asymmetrical threat that may be possible to repress and reduce, but is very difficult to eradicate altogether.

How does the United States define and claim victory in these circumstances? As defined in the run up to the war and in supporting arguments documented in Chapter 1, the apparent goal is an Iraq that is stable, self-sufficient and contributes to reinforcing and leading the peace in the region. In order to be such a force, the Bush administration (and its neoconservative allies) defined a democratic Iraq as the kind of country that would produce such a result.

The question is whether such an Iraq is possible. It is entirely possible to imagine either a stable *or* a democratic Iraq. Under Saddam Hussein, for instance, Iraq was stable enough, if one discounted the WMD program's supposed contribution to destabilization, and the emergence of a new Iraqi despot might well provide stability within Iraq. In the present situation, however, a new Iraqi strongman would likely be Shiite and probably would rule a theocratic state that might resemble Iran—hardly the outcome the United States wishes to achieve.

At the same time, it is at least possible to define some sort of democratic Iraq. The problem, of course, is what kind of democratic Iraq is desirable, and the answer depends on the group of Iraqis to whom one is addressing the question. In this case, the problem is that the form of democracy will largely determine which group(s) win or lose the zero-sum game of Iraqi politics. As noted, a one-man-one-vote democracy guarantees Shiite domination, almost certainly at the expense of the formerly ruling Sunnis and probably at the expense of the Kurds. Larry Diamond, a Stanford political scientist (and former colleague of Secretary of State Condoleezza Rice), who was sent to Iraq to advise on democratization, explains the problem this creates: "So many Iraqis, particularly the long-suppressed Shiite majority, view democracy as mainly consisting of rule by the majority. In a deeply divided country like Iraq, with well armed minority groups, such a one-dimensional concept of democracy cannot be viable."

A federal state favors the Sunnis if they are guaranteed part of the country's oil revenues (there is no oil in the traditional Sunni regions of the country) but provides a lesser victory for the Shiites (who have to share some of their oil revenues), and does not grant the Kurds as much autonomy as they desire. A confederal Iraq—one with minimal power for the central government—suits the Kurds best, because it maximizes their autonomy (a major Kurdish goal, in effect creating Kurdistan for them) but is not particularly acceptable to the other two contenders. Diamond is also skeptical of schemes built on power sharing: "Such systems have not fared well in the developing world, but rather, as in Lebanon, have further polarized ethnic groups in a way that intensifies political stability and even violent conflict." Trying to find a compromise acceptable to all sides has been a major part of U.S. efforts to find an acceptable solution to the Iraqi future and is the basis for proposals supporting each of these options.

In the end, the only political solution possible in Iraq is a choice between stability and democracy. A democratic Iraqi state is almost certain to be unstable, and a stable Iraqi state is almost certain to be undemocratic. The United States wants both; by insisting on that, and by defining a stable, democratic Iraq as its definition of victory, it could easily end up with neither (Iraq breaking into two or three countries, for instance).

No one should be surprised that these devil's choices are what confronts the United States and the Iraqis. There are at least three very good reasons that the kind of stable democracy the United States (and at least some Iraqis) want will not emerge from the occupation. First, such a state would be a new democracy arising from a condition of autocracy to which multi-ethnic and multi-communal concerns are added, and this is a recipe for instability in the short run. As this author argued in *Cases in International Relations*, "In part, this is a matter of the length and duration of their democratic experience. When people are suddenly given their freedom, for instance, their first reaction may be to express pent-up frustrations and anger" at those who have suppressed them in the past. Pietrrzyk argues that the moderation necessary to sustain stable democracy needs to be related to economic development, which the ongoing war has precluded. In these circumstances, a country that is moving toward democracy can be expected to have a long period of transition to democracy, and the interim period while this is occurring may well be more unstable than the autocratic period that preceded it. The academic literature on democratic transitions refers to these kinds of democracies as "immature" and "illiberal." Palestine and Lebanon may be models of what a democratic Iraq would look like, assuming some kind of democratic consensus can be achieved.

Second, Iraq is less than an ideal kind of country in which to implant political democracy. Indeed, one of the major prewar criticisms of getting involved in Iraq was precisely that there were few countries in the world more unlikely to make the peaceful transition to democracy than Iraq. The reasons, of course, include the multi-ethnic and multi-communal bases of the society (that guarantee a lack of common nationhood and deep divisions among groups) and the fact that Iraq itself is an entirely artificial state created in 1919 as a part of the treaty process ending World War I. Its closest semblance to a predecessor is the Kingdom of Uruk (from which the name Iraq is derived), which existed nearly 3,500 years ago. The lack of national identity reinforces societal divisions and means there is little common foundation of identity and loyalty from which Iraqis can surmount more parochial identities.

Third, the initial American occupation not only did not make reconciliation more likely, but made the prospects of a peaceful transition worse. In the process, the "model" of Iraq for the rest of the region was significantly tarnished. Diamond summarizes the effect based on his own experience. "But from the moment the war ended, Iraq fell into a deepening quagmire of chaos, criminality, insurgency, and terrorism." Elections in 2005 did not improve this situation, and as a result, "Iraq became a black hole of instability and a justification for neighboring regimes that insisted their societies were not culturally ready for a democracy."

What these three factors suggest is that the United States put itself in an extremely difficult position by attempting to implant political democracy in Iraq. Under the best of circumstances—which clearly did not exist in Iraq—the process would have been longer than the administration suggested, and the conditions in Iraq made that success problematical anyway. Bungling the occupation (discussed more fully in Chapter 5) only added to this difficulty. Hawk, based on her case studies of Bosnia, Kosovo, and Somalia, offers a very guarded optimistic note which may be as positive as any assessment can be: "External actors are able to create an opening for peace that local actors generally cannot bring about themselves. In this sense, external actions may not provide sufficient conditions for peace, but they are often necessary ones." In Iraq, democracy was impossible without getting rid of Saddam Hussein, but doing so has certainly not meant democracy will triumph.

What about the prospects of military victory? To understand the situation in military terms, one must divide the war into two phases: invasion and conquest, and occupation. The first phase, invasion and conquest, was a conventional military operation that began in March and was officially ended with the president's pronouncement of the cessation of major military operations in May 2003. Although the troops encountered some initial resistance from regular Iraqi army units at the beginning of the invasion (*see* Franks) and some attacks by irregular Iraqis that might have served as a harbinger of the resistance to come (*see* Gordon and Trainor), the conventional phase of the war was highly successful. The American forces swept through the countryside, entered and subdued Baghdad with minimal opposition, and caused and accepted the surrender of the Iraqi Army, which it quickly disbanded (one of the most controversial acts of the war, as described in Chapter 5). Military planning had concentrated on this phase of the war, virtually excluding consideration of so-called Phase IV operations (the occupation and rebuilding of the country), and the execution of the invasion and conquest were virtually flawless. It can be said (and often is) that the United States won this part of the war. Unfortunately, this part of the war was not the whole military problem.

The military conduct of the Iraq War must be extended to include the occupation and the resistance it has spawned, and which its continuation sustains. Whether one refers to the ongoing military atmosphere as a resistance, an insurgency, or a civil war, the situation on the ground in Iraq remains a state of violent opposition to the American occupation and an internal contest between various factions within the country jockeying for political power in the postwar Iraq. The conventional phase of the Iraq War may have ended in May 2003, but the Iraq War continues to the present.

The Iraq War has moved from being a symmetrical to being an asymmetrical war. The characteristics of the current conflict are complex and beyond the need to describe it in detail here (for a summary, *see* Snow, *National Security for a New Era,* third edition, chapter 11). This phase of the war involves the actions of multiple, loosely organized armed factions (militias loyal to different groups, for instance) and terrorist elements (Al Qaeda in Iraq, for example) resisting either the continuing American presence or the ascendancy of one group over the other (Shiites in traditional Sunni areas, for example). Their tactics include both terrorist acts (roadside bombings using improvised explosive devices or IEDs) and more standard guerrilla warfare methods, including ambushes and fading into the population when faced with superior opposition forces.

The problem of dealing with the various faces of the Iraqi resistance is an exercise in counterinsurgency, which is one of the reasons that General Petraeus, the author of *FM 3–24* on the subject, was brought in to command the forces as the surge mounted. The problem of counterinsurgency is extremely difficult. It involves opposing an enemy whose major purpose is not to defeat its opponents in direct conflict but to wear down the will of the opponent. Guerrillas, by whatever name, cannot confront and defeat conventional armed forces; they know this, and do not try. Rather, they seek to survive, inflict suffering on their opponent when possible, and wait for the opponent to tire of the contest and retire from the field. Tactically, the admonitions for insurgents go back to the teachings of the Chinese military strategist, Sun Tzu and forward through practitioners like Mao Tse-tung and Vietnam's General Giap (for a summary, *see* Snow, *Distant Thunder,* or Lowther). All have the common theme of defeating a militarily superior foe by applying patience and superior understanding of the situation and problem at hand.

Part of the Vietnam analogy holds up on this point. The North Vietnamese knew that they could not defeat the United States in conventional, European-style clashes of armies and so, after the 1965 Ia Drang battle, they ceased trying. Instead, they reverted to an insurgency style of warfare that preserved their own existence and coherence and gradually sapped the American will to continue the contest. The Vietnamese had successfully employed the same approach in repelling Kublai Khan in the thirteenth century, and it worked again. Eventually the same approach prevailed against the Americans, as public opinion turned against the war and forced withdrawal without victory.

The same dynamics can be applied to the occupation stage of the Iraq War, specifically to the likelihood that the surge will result in an American military victory. At a considerably lower level of violence than in Vietnam, the various Iraqi resistance elements have been following an asymmetrical campaign against the Americans, the purpose of which has been to turn American public opinion against the war and to force the Americans to withdraw. Like the North Vietnamese, it is the only way these groups can succeed in their goal of ridding the country of unwanted foreigners, either for the intrinsic value of ending a foreign occupation or to allow them to engage in whatever processes will settle the nature of the postwar order in Iraq. Tactically, this means they must avoid direct contact with the firepower-intensive Americans, so that they are not destroyed.

This dynamic affects how one evaluates the surge that has been going on since summer 2007. The surge has apparently succeeded in pacifying more areas than had previously been made violence-free. This reflects the fact that there are now more American forces in the field than there were previously, and thus they are present in more places. Where the Americans are physically present in substantial numbers, the insurgents are not likely to contest their presence (beyond occasional individual terrorist attacks), because they cannot match American firepower and would be destroyed if they tried. In such circumstances, they simply retreat tactically from the field. Doing so does not, in their view, constitute anything like defeat, because their tactical goal is simply to wait for the Americans to leave, which they inevitably will, and then to return. The situation is analogous to the Gelb and Betts analysis: The United States succeeds in suppressing the insurgency as long as American forces are in the field where the insurgency is active (the system works), but once they leave, the system ceases to work.

Is there any way to change this dynamic in such a way that the peace and stability created by the surge translates into a permanent stabilization that could be argued to constitute victory? Proponents of staying the course believe that it can succeed through the successful application of counterinsurgency techniques—hence the leadership of General David Petraeus as author of the counterinsurgency manual. To succeed, one or both, of two things must happen. One is the physical destruction of the insurgency so that it no longer has the physical ability to continue its resistance. The other is a transfer of political loyalties away from the insurgents and their causes toward the side of peace and stability. The two dynamics are related; if support is withdrawn from the insurgency, it will be easier to defeat the insurgents decisively. As counterinsurgency theory argues (including that contained in FM 3–24), this task is largely political in nature; insurgencies cannot thrive without some popular backing, and the continuing existence of a resistance implies at least some level of political support. Thus, in the current situation, the proclamation of military victory falls back on the need for political victory. If political victory is elusive, any meaningful sense of military victory is likely to be as well. These realizations are important to understand as the discussion moves to more likely resolutions of the conflict.

Defeat. If comprehensive, total victory in Iraq is improbable, what about the opposite, total defeat? To assess this possibility, it is first necessary to specify what defeat would mean in both political and military terms. This distinction is clarified by looking back at the Vietnam experience.

It is often alleged that Vietnam was the first war the United States ever lost. But what does that mean? The meaning cannot be military: The United States Armed Forces were not broken and defeated, and did not leave the field in disgrace or abject failure. Indeed, at the tactical level, Vietnam was largely a military success in the sense that American forces were generally always successful in individual engagements. At the same time, the United States did not *win* the war in Vietnam militarily, since it did not crush the hostile ability of its opponents' armed forces and cause them to quit the field (for instance, to surrender). Militarily, Vietnam was neither a victory nor a defeat for the United States.

Vietnam was, however, a defeat for the United States in political terms. If the purpose of war ultimately is the achievement of the political objectives for which one enters war in the first place, then Vietnam was a defeat. The American political objective in Vietnam was to stop communist aggression and to insure the continuing viability of South Vietnam as an independent, anti-communist redoubt. Presciently, that objective was modified to creating a *reasonable chance* of South Vietnamese independence as part of the strategy of Vietnamization. By either count, the American political objectives were not realized; in that sense, the United States lost the Vietnam War.

Is the United States likely to lose the Iraq War? Once again, the analogy of Vietnam and the meaning of the term "lose" define the prospects. In early 2008, there was a kind of euphoria in official governmental circles about the progress being made in the surge, and hence the prospect that American forces might indeed prevail and allow the declaration of victory in the occupation phase of the war. In some ways, the situation was similar to Vietnam after the 1968 Tet Offensive by the North Vietnamese and Viet Cong and the American-led counteroffensive against them. The net effect of those actions was to shatter the armed forces of the Democratic Republic of Vietnam (DRV), sending them reeling back across the border into the north, and it took them three years to regroup and rebuild their forces to adequate strength to mount major new actions. It is often argued by revisionist apologists for Vietnam that the United States had, at that point, won the war, but either did not realize it, or simply didn't take advantage of that victory. Could the United States be reaching a similar point in Iraq?

Possibly, but it depends on what the lesson really was in Vietnam, and how, or whether, it extends to Iraq. The evidence indicates that, at a strictly military level, the United States did break the North Vietnamese Army (NVA) in 1968, effectively overcoming the NVA's hostile ability (its capacity to compete in the field). It did not, however, overcome North Vietnamese hostile will, defined as its willingness to accept the American political objective of creating two Vietnamese states. While the North Vietnamese were regrouping and rebuilding militarily, after all, its representatives at the Paris peace talks refused to negotiate a two-state solution, instead conducting a diplomatic holding action while hostile ability was being reinvigorated. The United States might have used its military advantage to try to exact favorable terms in the peace talks by threatening military action against North Vietnam, but the North Vietnamese knew there were limits on what could be meaningfully threatened; strong action like a military invasion ran the risk of widening the war into a direct confrontation with the Soviets or the Chinese, an unacceptable prospect in Washington.

This analogy is potentially instructive because it frames both military outcomes and the meaning of victory and defeat. As already noted, the United States was certainly not defeated militarily in Vietnam, and it arguably won the war militarily. Yet, in the long run the United States lost the war because it could never force the Vietnamese to accept two Vietnams instead of one. Military victory (or the absence of defeat) could not be translated into winning the war. Iraq may be similar. One can argue that the surge has accomplished essentially what the Tet counteroffensive did, of either breaking or cowing the opposition into quitting the field—overcoming insurgent hostile ability. But is that outcome sufficient to bring about accomplishing the goal of political democratization of Iraq?

The North Vietnamese "defeated" the United States not by beating the Americans militarily, but by waiting them out. The reunification of Vietnam was, in the end, more important to the North Vietnamese than a free South Vietnam was to the Americans. Thus, the North Vietnamese simply waited until the American public turned against a long and indeterminate war, and forced a withdrawal, allowing the North Vietnamese to complete the job they started before the Americans intervened and interrupted their progress. And it worked.

Will the same thing be true in Iraq? As in Vietnam, there is no danger whatsoever of an American military defeat, and the surge has created at least the appearance of something akin to victory. But is that an illusion? Could it be that the insurgents have simply licked their wounds and gone underground, waiting for the surge to end, and with it the end of America's ability to interfere with their activities? The antidote for North Vietnamese success would have been a strong South Vietnamese nationalism, willing to resist unification at all costs, but that never clearly emerged (of course, some argue that the will was there once, but that the United States had emasculated the South Vietnamese ability to resist). The antidote to the Iraqi insurgency is the emergence of a strong sense of Iraqi nationalism that abjures more parochial identifications, and thus rejects the appeals of insurgents fighting for the ascendancy of one or another of the internal groups. The surge is designed to create Hawk's "necessary condition" for such a transformation to occur, but can it be a "sufficient condition" to create such change? Continuing advocacy or opposition to American presence in essence boils down to how one answers that question.

In any conventional sense, the United States will not be defeated in Iraq. This is most obviously true in a military sense, but it reflects a limited vision of victory and defeat. The continuing status of the American presence in Iraq is, from the vantage point of the Iraqis themselves, as an occupying power, and that fact alone will likely insure a continued resistance as long as occupation lasts. A more enlightened American policy (more rapid rebuilding of Iraq, for instance) could mollify the Iraqis somewhat, but many Iraqis will not be truly content until the last American has left. Moreover, it is not clear that the American presence helps create the consensus in Iraq that would lead to a democratic state. If the American political objective is to create a model democracy in Iraq, it could well fail and, if one thinks in those terms, constitute defeat.

Intermediate Outcomes. Notions of victory and defeat have an absolute aura about them that suggests finality and closure. In the era of "total war" (discussed in Snow and Drew), beginning with the American Civil War and going through World War II, wars were indeed fought for total purposes (the overthrow of enemy regimes, for instance) that required a commitment of total military resources for total purposes (the defeat and destruction of the opponent's military forces, as in World War II). The advent of nuclear weapons made such total wars impractical, since they would include the use of nuclear weapons which, if possessed by both combatants, would likely result in a catastrophe with no victors, only losers. Since the nuclear age, only countries that lack such weapons can fight total wars.

The result is a return to an era of limited war, where states fight for purposes less than the total overthrow of combatant societies, in which means are restrained. In Korea, for instance, the United States fought not to overthrow the government of the Democratic Republic of Korea (DPRK), although that was briefly its intent. Rather, it fought to remove the North Koreans from the south, a goal that did not require a total military victory or the toppling of the Pyongyang regime. In Vietnam, the objective of maintaining South Vietnamese independence was a limited goal that did not require overthrow of the DRV government (conversely, the North Vietnamese had the total goal of reunification, which *did* require overthrowing the South Vietnamese government).

The situation in Iraq defies these descriptions. The original goals of disarming WMD and severing connections to terrorism were limited in scope and, as such, probably did not require overthrowing the Hussein government. This goal was attainable but, as it turned out, unnecessary. When the objective became democratization, the objective was inflated to a total one, the overthrow of the Hussein government and its replacement with a democratic alternative. The first part of achieving this objective—getting rid of the Baghdad regime—was attainable and attained. The second goal remains elusive and may well prove to be unattainable, at least within the time frame of American interest and willingness to pursue it. (Democratic theory suggests that after a long—generational—period of adjustment, which is far longer than the United States can or will stay in Iraq, the goal might be achieved.)

Staying in Iraq for a long time in the hope that doing so may produce a victorious outcome is an increasingly difficult position to sustain, although it is the only position possible for those who support a continuation of the war. The evidence for such a position is the progress of the surge—military progress—but that may or may not translate into a successful political solution. Whether or when it will succeed (or fail) is speculative, as is the counterargument that it makes little difference how long the

United States fails in terms of the impact on the final outcome. Thus, those who argue either the extreme outcomes or the impact of U.S. vigilance are arguing counterfactually.

The argument here has been that neither victory nor defeat is the likely outcome of the war. Both represent absolute positions at the extremes of possibility, and arguing that one or the other must prevail commits the logical fallacy of the excluded middle (that there are possibilities between the extremes). If neither extreme—complete victory or complete defeat—is possible or acceptable, then the only possible outcomes are somewhere in between the two, a hybrid that redefines the situation's acceptable outcomes.

Consider for a moment why the absolutes will not occur. Based on the American public's angst over the perceived loss of the Vietnam War, an outcome that unambiguously signifies defeat is simply unacceptable to the United States. Further, anyone who either propounds or, even worse, presides, over an outcome that is viewed as defeat would be politically castigated and probably punished at the polls. This dynamic infested Vietnam war planning, as the seven presidents who presided over American participation in that war worried about being the president who lost South Vietnam to communism. The desire to avoid such an accusation may help explain why George W. Bush wants to be sure the war has not ended ignominiously by January 2009, and why contenders in the 2008 presidential race have hedged on the terms under which they would withdraw.

The ideal outcome would be one in which the United States could declare victory and everyone would accept that proclamation, but that is improbable, and practically impossible. After the president's "Mission Accomplished!" proclamation fiasco of May 2003, the public is rightly skeptical of such pronouncements, and the improbability of a stable political democracy emerging in Baghdad means that the stated political objective that would define victory is elusive.

The practical impossibility of victory and the equally absolute unacceptability of defeat lead to one of two possible outcomes. One is simply to let the war continue and to hope for the best. While it might seem cynical to state in this way, it is not politically unattractive, since it avoids making a definitive decision on a controversial issue that will, regardless of content, be unpopular with some. Moreover, avoiding such a definitive decision also avoids making the *wrong* decision. The problem with this option is that it is politically unsustainable, because it means an open-ended continuing commitment to an endeavor the public already opposes, and is likely to oppose even more strongly the longer it drags on (unless the evidence of progress is overwhelming).

The other alternative is to look for a more restrained acceptable outcome that is both attainable and acceptable to the greatest number of people. Once again, the Vietnam experience provides a guidepost. As noted, the 1968 presidential election featured two candidates who, because public opinion demanded an end to the war, were both publicly committed to ending American involvement in Southeast Asia. The prospects of total and unambiguous victory was practically unattainable (or at least perceived as such), and abject defeat was unacceptable—the United States could not, as Senator Claude Aiken of Vermont had suggested, simply pack its bags, declare victory, and let others figure what that meant. Instead, the expectations had to be changed in such a way as to leave the semblance of a continuing commitment to victory, but within the context of something that was attainable and politically defensible. The answer, formulated and executed by the Nixon administration, was the policy of Vietnamization. It was the third way between the extremes in Vietnam, and its equivalent is the only possible way out of the ongoing war in Iraq.

IRAQIFICATION

The term "Iraqification" was raised early in the debate about the Iraq War, but was fiercely opposed by supporters of the war, to the point that it is now rarely mentioned among public options. The opposition comes from supporters of the war because the term implicitly links Iraq and Vietnam, which Iraq supporters believe is inappropriate, and also because the policy of Vietnamization "failed" and led to the fall of South Vietnam to the Communists. And yet, *Iraqification without the name is precisely the policy the Bush administration is following, for the simple reason that it is the only policy it can follow.* The debate about Iraq is really about the pace of Iraqification, not about its desirability.

What is the policy of Vietnamization/Iraqification? Its essence is a means to turn over responsibility for the war and its aftermath to the Iraqis (or the Vietnamese) in such a way that allows the United States to exit that country. Its roots are in the assumption that the United States will not be able to remain in Iraq long enough to turn over a totally pacified Iraq to local authorities, or to assure the Iraqis and the American public that the result of a turnover will meet all U.S. objectives. This assumption can be based either in the observation that the United States (or its elected representatives) lack the political will to stay the course to ensure such an outcome, or from the premise that such an outcome is unattainable regardless of how long the United States stays. In either case, it assumes that the United States *will not* remain in Iraq until all its objectives are met. In other words, attaining victo-ry, as described earlier, will take longer than American patience will bear, if victory can be attained at all.

At the same time, a policy of Iraqification recognizes that it is politically unacceptable for the United States to abjectly fail in Iraq. With five years of resources invested in the war, the United States cannot simply throw its hands in the air in despair and declare the whole enterprise a fool's errand, even if many Americans believe it to have been so. Politically, such a stance would amount to declaring that the personal sacrifices of all those who have fought or died in Iraq were in vain, and that the United States wasted its energies and resources in the process. Embracing and implementing such a policy would likely be political suicide for any administration that enacted it.

A policy of Iraqification recognizes that the current political climate holds two contradictory goals: withdrawal from Iraq and success in that country. Neither position can be ignored completely, but must be given at least lip service. The purpose of the policy is to find a middle ground that gives recognition to both positions while allowing adherents of both posi-tions to feel that their desires have been considered. It seeks, in other words, a solution in the realm of the possible somewhere between the two poles of victory and defeat.

Iraqification, unlike the extremes, represents a series of graded choices, not a single option. To clarify: Think of Iraqification as resting along a con-tinuum, the extremities of which are victory and defeat. Defeat, or the fail-ure to achieve the objective, is represented by immediate withdrawal, not necessarily because defeat would be the result (although it could be, in the sense of the kind of Iraq that would emerge politically after the withdraw-al), but because that would certainly be the charge among war supporters. Victory, of course, would be to leave Iraq with a fully functioning, stable democracy that the Iraqis themselves would have the ability to maintain. Proposals to stay the course move the policy advocacy toward the victory end of the continuum and imply a longer stay. Proposals for withdrawal move toward the defeat end; the more rapid the pace of withdrawal advo-cated, the more it moves toward that end of the spectrum in the propenent's eyes. It should be noted that those who maintain that it makes little differ-ence how long the United States stays in Iraq will be included at the "defeat" end of the scale, even though they do not necessarily agree that defeat is made more likely by withdrawing rapidly.

Vietnam and the policy of Vietnamization provide an instructive exam-ple of how such a policy might work. That policy was born in the 1968 elec-tion campaign—arguably the equivalent of 2008 in Iraq. In 1968, the popular perception of the Vietnam War was largely honed from public horror over the Tet Offensive at the beginning of the year, but unleavened by recognition of the startling devastation of the NVA in the counteroffensive. In the public mind, the war had become unwinnable, and the only politically acceptable outcome was withdrawal—ending the war with minimal concern for the consequences of that withdrawal. At the same time, proponents of the war argued that the purpose of the war, stopping communist expansion in Southeast Asia, remained vital to the interests of the United States, and also cited the enormous investment the United States had made.

Vietnam in 1968 thus posed two contrary alternatives with public support, getting out or staying the course. They could not be pursued with the same policies, but neither could be ignored. What was needed was a compromise somewhere between the extremes. The answer was Vietnamization. The basis of this policy was that victory was not attainable within a time frame the American public would accept, but total abandonment of the South Vietnamese was also unacceptable.

Politically, the problem was that the United States had stated its objective as the maintenance of an independent South Vietnam, and the only way to insure that seemed to be an open-ended American presence that had become politically unsustainable. What could be done to resolve this dilemma? The answer was subtly to change the political objective in such a way as to engage a policy that would lead to disengagement. The political objective of "guaranteeing" the independence of South Vietnam was changed to providing the South Vietnamese with a "reasonable chance" of maintaining their independence from North Vietnamese rule.

The policy of Vietnamization flowed from this change of objectives. It consisted of both military and political dimensions. The military aspects were the most vital, because their purpose was to create an atmosphere in which the South Vietnamese could take over the war and, hopefully, withstand the North Vietnamese successfully. To this end, the military phase consisted of two parts. The first was attempting to beef up South Vietnamese military capability with an accelerated transfer of arms and supplies to the RVN, and additional training of the South Vietnamese in preparation for assaults by the North Vietnamese. Whether this aspect of Vietnamization could have worked is controversial, because Congress cut off military assistance to the RVN after the withdrawal of American combat forces in 1973, thereby leaving the South Vietnamese critically deficient in military supplies when the DRV began its final assault in 1975 (the army, for instance, ran out of fuel to power its mechanized military assets). The second aspect of the plan was to seal off South Vietnam from infiltration by the DRV from

Cambodia into the southern parts of RVN, and from Laos down the Ho Chi Minh Trail into northern and central parts of the country. A side effect of these efforts was to stimulate communist insurgencies in Laos and Cambodia that led to communist rule.

The political aspect of Vietnamization centered on attempting to create better governance in South Vietnam that would make citizens of the South more supportive of their government, a process that had been ongoing with limited success since the beginning of American direct involvement in the early 1960s. The success of political efforts became moot when the DRV swept into South Vietnam and routed the Army of the Republic of Vietnam (ARVN) in 1975.

The current policy of the United States, which the administration obdurately refuses to compare to Vietnam, nevertheless bears eerie resemblances to the policy that evolved thirty-five years ago. At the level of the political objective, the United States no longer trumpets a democratic model government as the objective. Rather, it has scaled the objective back to simply creating the conditions where, through self-determination, the Iraqis can freely choose a government. This modification is similar to the revised "reasonable chance" of success in Vietnam, in that it hopes to provide the Iraqis a reasonable chance of becoming democratic, but implicitly admits the possibility that the outcome will not be democratic in a way most Americans would recognize. It is an admission, never phrased as such, that the victory end of the outcome continuum is unattainable.

The policy for implementing this objective also follows the general contours of Vietnamization, especially the military dimension. The heart of the ongoing American effort is to do two things simultaneously. First, it seeks to reduce the insurgency to a much lower level of capability by establishing increased domestic security in the country—essentially a parallel goal to sealing South Vietnam from outside intruders (diplomatic efforts to reduce outside infiltration through Syria and Saudi Arabia have also been part of the plan). At the same time, the United States is accelerating the training and equipping of both Iraqi armed forces and the police so that they can gradually assume responsibilities currently being shouldered by American/coalition forces. The idea, of course, is to allow the gradual reduction of American forces as the Iraqis "stand up" and take over the job. Along with attempts to induce political reconciliation, the purpose clearly is to facilitate a withdrawal of American forces from the country with the reasonable prospect that it will be stable and peaceful after the withdrawal.

Thus, the current U.S. policy *is* Iraqification, whether the government chooses to use that term or not. The major question that remains about the implementation of the policy is the pace of withdrawal and the consequences of leaving at any given point in time. Here, the Vietnam analogy becomes troublesome to the discussion. Vietnamization took nearly five years from its announcement to the pullout of the final American combat troops, a wrenching process that many considered too long and which resulted in the deaths of many more American troops. Hardly anyone would like to reprise that aspect of Vietnamization. At the same time, the net result was a defeat of the American-backed South Vietnamese, the fall of the country to the DRV, and the abject failure of the United States to achieve any of its goals. The "reasonable chance" failed. Hardly anyone would want to reprise that aspect of Vietnamization either.

From a policy vantage point, the beauty of a policy of Iraqification is that it represents a series of possible outcomes rather than a set of objectives. In Vietnam, there was never a precise, measurable milestone at which point it could be said that America's allies could now defend themselves, and thereby allow American withdrawal with a reasonable chance that the South Vietnamese would succeed. Instead, the point of transition from American to South Vietnamese dominance was a subjective matter that could be affected by the situation on the ground in the RVN, estimates of the RVN's capability to maintain that situation, and the level of American patience with the continuation of the war. All of these matters, and especially estimates of RVN capacity, were speculative and controversial; speculative because they were future events, and controversial because they depended on U.S. actions, including the continuation or withdrawal of assistance to the erstwhile U.S. allies.

The process of implementation of Iraqification contains similar but subtly different dynamics. The critical questions remain the same: How much more involvement will American public opinion tolerate? And, what level of assurance of Iraqi success (at meeting U.S. objectives) must be achieved to allow withdrawal. Where the situations are apparently different is in the interplay between military and political aspects of "success" leading up to a decision to disengage, and whether the Iraqis share the American criteria for success. The former difference affects the decision to stay or withdraw at any point in time; the latter affects the withdrawal decision, but has a particular impact on what happens after the withdrawal. Neither question can be completely resolved before the fact. Both questions are crucial to how Americans will ultimately evaluate the Iraq experience.

The military-political progress question has gained particular prominence because of the apparent success of the surge. It has indeed reduced violence by the various resistance movements against both Americans and other

Iraqis, and it seems likely that the military situation will get no worse, and might improve, as long as surge levels of American and other coalition troops remain (the coalition contribution is, of course, not great). The result is a level of peace and tranquility on the streets of Baghdad and elsewhere unseen in recent years.

Two nagging questions surround this military success. One is whether it is being accompanied by political progress toward establishing a peaceful, stable post-occupation Iraq. The surge is designed basically to create a shield behind which political progress can occur. The shield is in place. But what happens after the shield is removed, which will happen eventually? Will peace hold, or are those who have disrupted the society simply waiting for the Americans to leave before they resume activities suspended by the surge? This problem is discussed more fully in Chapter 5.

The other question is about what is going on behind the shield while it is in place. Is political progress accompanying the military success on the ground? Critics point to the absence of visible progress by Iraqi politicians in creating the framework for a stable, peaceful political order. The solutions that form the basis for evaluating the conditions for future Iraqi tranquility sound remarkably American (a federal form of government, for instance) and may thus be irrelevant to the Iraqi situation. Even if the surge reduces violence in Iraq virtually to nothing, will the political framework be enough to ensure a peaceful post-surge environment?

The other major dynamic is what kind of post-occupation Iraq the *Iraqis* envisage. As already noted, it may be that there is no unifying vision that all Iraqis can share, and that any semblance of cooperation is merely a marriage of convenience to facilitate the American withdrawal. Polls taken in Iraq have, after all, overwhelmingly demonstrated that the Iraqis want the Americans to leave. Can they sustain a vision of their country that Americans can embrace as reward for the sacrifices Americans have made? What if the Iraqis' vision for Iraq (assuming they can agree) is different—and especially radically different—than the Iraq Americans foresee. If, after the United States leaves, the country slides or plunges into a form that repudiates American projections, how will the United States respond? What if a radical Shiite theocracy comes to power after American troop withdrawal, barring American oil companies from harvesting the Iraqi petroleum treasures, and demanding that the United States get out lock, stock, and barrel (including abandoning the permanent American bases currently under construction in Iraq)?

There is another variable that will, or at least arguably should, influence the pace of Iraqification: the cost of the Iraq War in monetary terms (the same basic argument can be made about the human costs). The impact cuts both ways. On one hand, the money already spent represents a "sunk cost," and some degree of success is necessary to justify this investment—an argument for continuing the effort until some positive "return" can be realized on the "investment." On the other hand, if the Iraq War is viewed as an unwinnable quagmire, the money already spent has essentially been wasted, and continuation means wasting more money ("throwing good money after bad"), magnifying the negative economic impact that spending on the war has created.

Many of the questions surrounding Iraqification are unanswerable in detail, and can only be viewed as possibilities along a continuum of "most acceptable" to "least acceptable" outcomes for the United States. What is certain is that some form of the middle option—Iraqification—will be the outcome, even though details are not currently knowable. Although one can argue about them, it is inevitable that the United States will withdraw from Iraq, and that it will do so with unanswered questions—primarily political—about what happens in Iraq afterward and how the American people will respond to those outcomes.

THE CONSEQUENCES OF IRAQIFICATION

Regardless of where on the continuum between victory and defeat the final implementation of Iraqification falls, there will be consequences—some foreseen and foreseeable, some not. In human terms, these consequences will be borne primarily by the Iraqis themselves, particularly as those consequences involve inevitable human suffering. The consequences for Americans (discussed further in Chapter 5) will primarily be political in terms of lessons learned and vindication of supporters, or recrimination of opponents, depending on the perceived outcomes. The shape and depth of the American reaction will, of course, depend to some degree on the impact of the withdrawal on Iraq's people.

The physical process of fully implementing Iraqification will be the transition in Iraq from physical occupation to fully restored Iraqi independence and sovereignty (although Iraq has "enjoyed" returned sovereignty in name, if not in fact, since 2004). American apologists for the war will describe this outcome as the final liberation of Iraq from Saddam Hussein's tyranny. Iraqis themselves will be divided on whether their liberation is from Saddam Hussein or from the Americans.

The major result of the American withdrawal from Iraq will be a power struggle in that country. By the end of 2007, it was clear that the prospects of the Iraqis reaching a viable political accord during the pre-withdrawal period had all but vanished, despite reduced physical violence as a result of the surge. Indeed, Thomas L. Friedman, who has generally supported the reasons for, if not the conduct of, the war, reported in a late November 2007 column in the *New York Times* that a growing consensus among military and political analysts close to the situation was that only informal arrangements were possible among the Iraqi groups—"accommodation not reconciliation"—would produce reasonable autonomy for the major groups and some tentative sharing of oil revenues. As Friedman puts it, "each of the Iraqi factions basically agrees to live and let live with the new lines drawn by the last two years of civil war and the Baghdad government serves as an ATM machine—supporting the army and local security groups and dispensing oil revenues to the provincial governors and tribal chiefs from each community." If this is the best that is possible, it does not sound very durable. Friedman quotes James Glanz, the *New York Times* Baghdad bureau chief, about the underlying malaise: "We don't know what is lurking back there (in the background), but we suspect, and the evidence suggests, that it is the same set of problems that were always there."

It is inevitable that some level of instability, including violence, will accompany the American withdrawal. Any violence that occurs is likely to be of two sorts. Some of it will be intercommunal: Sunnis and Shiites clashing over mixed territories, the settling of old scores, the redress of grievances, and the establishment of "turf" in the new Iraq. Inequities in the distribution of oil revenues—most likely Shiites trying to short-change Sunnis (at least in the Sunnis' view) could spark additional clashes. At the same time, clashes between Sunni and Shiite Arabs and Kurds are possible if an attempt is made to infringe upon and reduce Kurdish autonomy in the northern part of Iraq (Kurdistan). The other predictable source of violence is retribution against those Iraqis who have collaborated with the United States during the occupation—the fate of quislings after any occupation.

How severe will these acts of violence be? It is an important question for humanitarian and moral reasons, since a widespread bloodbath (as some have predicted, especially in the event of a "premature" American withdrawal) would be a humanitarian disaster for which the United States would bear some responsibility under any circumstances. Avoiding such a bloody outcome is, of course, the ultimate entreaty of Powell's Pottery Barn analogy: repairing the breakage includes leaving a repaired Iraq where such violence will not occur. A consensually democratic Iraq would be the best setting to avoid violence, but since that is almost certainly unattainable, the next best thing is to leave behind an Iraq where that violence is minimized. A catastrophic bloodletting is certainly a possibility when the Americans leave, given regional history, but it is neither inevitable nor is its extent predetermined. Anyone who claims to know what will happen one way or the other is extrapolating beyond the evidence.

Making some determination about the likelihood of various levels of violence is critical in planning withdrawal. Since the exact nature of how much violence will accompany withdrawal at any point in time cannot be determined, the best approach is to "stack the odds" against the worst possible scenario; a massive bloodletting for which the United States might believe it bears responsibility. There are three variables that can be manipulated as approaches to influence the outcome: 1) the level and extent of training given to Iraqi security forces, 2) the involvement of neighboring states in facilitating the peace, and 3) modulating the length of continuing American presence. Each deserves some discussion in trying to assess the consequences of American withdrawal.

The first approach is to ensure optimal levels of training and professionalism among Iraqi security forces, both the constabulary and the new Iraqi Army. Preparing the Iraqis to take over responsibility for their country is, of course, directly parallel to efforts made as part of Vietnamization, and those efforts, for whatever reasons, ultimately failed. The specific tasks are different. In South Vietnam, the problem was preparing and equipping the ARVN to a level where they could successfully repel a North Vietnamese invasion. Whether the preparations were inadequate or Congress' termination of funds to the ARVN was to blame, the effort ultimately came up short.

In Iraq, the task is preparing both the police and army to deal with elements of the various parts of the resistance. The army's task is presumably to deal with both foreign and internal insurgent groups, including sealing and enforcing the sanctity of borders. The role of the police is to ensure domestic tranquility where dissident groups threaten it, or where individuals seek to disrupt peace and stability. The trick in Iraq is creating *Iraqi* police and soldiers (officers whose loyalties are to Iraq and not the confessional groups or national groups from which they are recruited) who are willing to enforce the peace against any potential violators, including members of their own groups. In the past, many of the army and police units were recruited from the confessional groups—army units have often been sectarian or Kurdish *pesh merga* units donning Iraqi uniforms, but arguably still loyal to their sectarian groups. The elimination of this problem probably requires internal political progress among Iraqi factions to the point that confessional military or paramilitary groups can be persuaded or ordered to transfer their loyalty to the Iraqi government, rather than maintaining ties to the sectarian or tribal groups from which they sprang.

An important second approach, aimed at neutralizing negative outside influences on the unfolding Iraqi peace process, must be directed at regional involvement in creating and reinforcing whatever arrangements are arrived at internally. Once again, such efforts have a parallel in American efforts to neutralize Laos and Cambodia, and thus to cut off the flow of hostile arms and forces into South Vietnam. In Iraq, this "internationalization" of the process involves two basic parts. One is making sure that outside assistance to the various resistance movements is ended. The trick to this is getting those governments or organizations that are supplying such aid clandestinely to abandon policies they deny they are carrying out. The governments most affected will be Syria, Iran, and Saudi Arabia. The fact that the United States has almost no relations with Syria and none at all with Iran makes American leadership in brokering such agreements more difficult than it might otherwise be. The second part of internationalization is gaining foreign support to help in the rebuilding of Iraq, an effort that will still require large amounts of capital, particularly if developing Iraq's oil industry is included. Once again, America's ability to provide leadership is compromised by the unilateral nature of previous actions in Iraq. Some countries that might otherwise be donors have been alienated by America's decision to deny rebuilding contracts to countries that did not participate in the coalition occupation (including some of the same countries alienated by American unilateralism), and by American claims to primary, if not exclusive, access to development of the petroleum industry. International efforts could clearly contribute to "lubricating" the process of Iraqi transition; prior American actions may make providing leadership in this effort problematical.

The third approach surrounds the pace and timing of American withdrawal and how the prospects for Iraq will be affected based on those factors. As already suggested, there are two basic positions on this question that directly affect the consequences of Iraqification. One position is, of course, that the United States needs to stay in Iraq until conditions have stabilized sufficiently to allow a phased withdrawal that leaves behind a peaceful Iraq and at least the reasonable prospect that it will remain so. The success of the surge is used as evidence that this approach is effective. The contrary position is that continued American participation cannot materially affect the final, political outcome, and that the ongoing American presence simply delays an inevitable political process (with some violent aspects) that can only be concluded by the Iraqis themselves, most likely not until the United States has withdrawn. An enduring presence in which a residual American force remains garrisoned in and around Iraq may be a compromise solution.

The debate on this point is crucial, and it also displays the highly partisan political debate in the United States in its absolutely worst light. If there could be definitive knowledge that the American withdrawal would, or would not, create chaos in Iraq, it would certainly tilt the debate, although not necessarily its final outcome. If, for instance, it could be concluded that a precipitous U.S. withdrawal would produce otherwise avoidable widespread bloodletting in Iraq, the argument for staying would be buttressed as a means of stopping or forestalling that violence. But it is critical whether the effect would in fact be to stop and preclude the violence from ever occurring, or if it would simply delay the inevitable. If violence would not be the result of withdrawal, clearly the argument for staying is undermined. If putting off the violence (and even affecting its extent at the margins) is the effect of staying or leaving, the impact is more ambiguous.

Which of these things will happen? No one knows, and the highly partisan political debate in the United States adds heat but not light to the subject. The debate emphasizes the extremes; widespread communal slaughter if the United States leaves or continuing the needless expenditure of American human and financial resources in a lost cause if the war continues. The worst might happen, of course, but it also might not happen. Thus, the most one can responsibly do is to suggest what, based on past experience, would seem the likely consequences of American diligence of withdrawal.

The fundamental realization about predicting the future of Iraq is that it is an internal Iraqi problem that only the Iraqis themselves can ultimately decide. Unlike more conventional internal conflicts, the United States bears more responsibility than it would otherwise, since the American overthrow of the Saddam Hussein government ripped the artificial restraint off Iraqi society. Iraq was a country where there were great communal and ethnic differences, but the lid was kept on that situation by a tyrannical regime, which undoubtedly worsened the underling situation by favoring one group (the Sunnis) at the expense of the others (Shiites and Kurds). The Hussein regime kept the lid on the festering wounds that divided the country, and the American invasion removed that lid. The question is how the wounds will now be dressed. The American presence may provide ointment to soothe those wounds, but the ultimate cure has to be Iraqi.

The question is whether the continuing American presence aids in this healing process. At the military level, the U.S. occupation troops certainly suppress overt violence in places where they are physically present and presumably can continue to do so as long as they remain in place. Counterinsurgency theory, however, is fairly clear on the idea that this continuing military presence will not solve the broader problem. As Sir Robert

Thompson, the British commander, writing of his experience in suppressing the Malay insurgency in the 1940s, puts it, "Reliance on a military solution will always fail, particularly when sought by foreign troops." In a 2005 Heritage Foundation lecture on T. E. Lawrence, John Hulsman reaches the same conclusion in a specifically Arab context, warning particularly of avoiding the "imperial trap" by knowing "when to let the local elites take the reins in the state-building process." He describes this as the "litmus test as to whether a state-building effort has been successful—when the Western powers depart, the new political entity is capable of self-government." Following Lawrence of Arabia, he suggests that the indigenous population must take the lead in this area.

There is also reason to question whether continuing foreign presence—in this case American—contributes to greater progress in achieving the political end. Past experience (summarized in *Distant Thunder*) suggests three negative possibilities.

The first surrounds the question of leverage—the ability of the United States to induce the government of Iraq to take the steps necessary to produce stability. Although it may seem counterintuitive at first, it may be—and certainly was in Vietnam—that physical presence and leverage are inversely related; the greater the American presence, the less leverage it has over those it seeks to influence. Part of the reason is that continuing American involvement not only provides a shield against outside attacks, it also provides a veil that allows the Iraqis to avoid taking the necessary steps to create change, because the Americans are there to protect them from their own inaction. This dynamic has led Democrats Clinton and Obama, among others, to suggest that the United States can only jumpstart the political reform process in Iraq by establishing a firm withdrawal date that provides an incentive for action on their part. At the same time, this author argued in *Distant Thunder* over a decade ago, that a continuing occupation makes the Iraqi regime appear dependent on the American occupiers, and the more dependent it seems, "the more resentment is likely to be created in the population. The insurgents' propaganda will be fueled by that dependence." There is, in other words, a negative side to the continuing presence of American forces.

The second problem surrounds the issue of conversion of Iraqis to support for the regime, an obviously necessary part of the transformation in the country. This is the familiar battle for the hearts and minds of the Iraqi people, and it is not a process that can be induced by outsiders. While the occupying Americans can attempt to influence the process of building the Iraqi state by reestablishing security and aiding in infrastructure development, ultimately the process of transferring loyalty from subnational, communal or ethnic groups, to Iraq is a process that can only be achieved by the Iraqis themselves. Just as American occupiers could not win the hearts and minds battle in South Vietnam, it cannot win that battle in Iraq. Ironically, the only contribution may be negative: Opposition to continued American presence might serve as a projection object that creates some sense of common feeling among Iraqis. Since the Americans will eventually leave, that is not enough commonality to underwrite a stable peace.

The third problem is what Greentree called "the democratic contradiction" almost two decades ago. The heart of this dilemma is that for a regime to feel good enough about another regime to support it, that regime must be moving in the direction of producing civic virtue, roughly defined as adopting political and social reforms compatible with (in this case) American values and practices. These values, however, may be alien, even incompatible with the values and conditions of the target country, thereby resulting in the kinds of resistance to American prescriptions that seem to be current in Iraq. Yet virtue and support continue to be tied to conformance to these American yardsticks, and support wavers to the extent these are not met. The apparent fact that the Iraqis are not meeting the eighteen conditions set out for them by the Americans is thus criticized, and forms the basis for calls to withdraw. The point may be that only withdrawal will stimulate Iraqi solutions to Iraqi problems. Whether those solutions entail some recourse to violence may be beyond the American control under any circumstances.

What Iraq will look like when the United States withdraws is clearly a complex and indeterminate question that can, for better or worse, only truly be known when it occurs. Past experiences—Vietnam or otherwise—are only imperfect approximations, since no two events are identical. Iraq clearly stands alone in the American experience in that it is the only Third World conflict that the United States wholly created. Without the American invasion in 2003, there would be no war or insurgency in Iraq; there would probably still be a Sunni dictatorship, but there would not be a war.

What can be said about Iraq after the withdrawal? At the risk of going beyond the available evidence into the realm of speculation, two conclusions seem reasonable: One has been discussed, and the other has not been explored, but is an extrapolation from the Vietnam experience.

The first conclusion is that the United States will leave Iraq before all the issues surrounding the future of Iraq are determined. Putting aside the question of whether an indefinite occupation would move the situation closer to some closure the United States would view as successful, the United States will not stay that long. The process of Iraqification has in fact, if not in name, already begun, and its momentum is inexorable. The pace of Iraqification will depend upon the apparent progress of specifics like the surge and signs of political progress in Iraq. The situation in Iraq is too complex and the solutions too difficult to expect them to be worked out within the time frame the American public will permit for continued occupation. As has been argued, it is not clear how far toward a desirable outcome an ongoing American occupation would cause the situation to move on the continuum, and its presence may in fact impede as much as facilitate that outcome. It is possible that events will shift dramatically and that the light at the end of the tunnel will truly be visible in Iraq (as it never was in Vietnam), but that is unlikely. What is likely is that the United States will leave with the situation unsettled, and will have to sit on the sidelines as the final outcomes unfold. That process will almost certainly be disorderly, and those who have supported the war will be unhappy with at least parts of what unfolds.

The second conclusion is more controversial. Based on parallels between Vietnam and Iraq, the likelihood is that the American public will quickly turn its attention away from Iraq after the withdrawal occurs. Anticipating this, there are already plans and entreaties afoot to try to insure that American supporters in Iraq do not suffer the same abandonment as American South Vietnamese supporters suffered in 1975, when American forces quit the country and abandoned those who had supported them. In Iraq, there will be a residual American presence in the bases being built around that country, potentially leaving American garrisons there, and likely an "over the horizon" presence in places like Kuwait and Dubai. These remnants will leave the United States somewhat less helpless to moderate any disaster that withdrawal might entail, but the public will almost certainly not stand for a large reinsertion of American forces in the event that Iraq destabilizes and degenerates into a maelstrom of violence after its withdrawal. Americans, by and large, will wash their hands of Iraq as thoroughly and quickly as they did Vietnam. The only possible exception will be if American oil companies are denied access to post-occupation Iraq in the same way that Saddam Hussein denied them access during his rule.

SELECTED BIBLIOGRAPHY

Diamond, Larry. *Squandered Victory: The American Occupation and the Bungled Effort to Bring Democracy to Iraq.* New York: Times Books (Henry Holt and Company), 2005.

Field Manual 3–24: Counterinsurgency. Washington, DC: United States Army and United States Marine Corps, 2007.

Friedman, Thomas L. "Is Rice Avoiding Iraq or Does She Know Something That We Don't?" *Island Packet*, November 25, 2007, AA4 (reprinted from *New York Times*, November 24, 2007).

Franks, Tommy, with Malcolm McConnell. *American Soldier*. New York: Regan Books, 2004.

Gelb, Leslie H., and Richard K. Betts. *The Irony of Vietnam: The System Worked*. Washington, DC: Brookings Institution Press, 1979.

Gordon, Michael R. and General Bernard E. Trainor. *Cobra II: The Inside Story of the Invasion and Occupation of Iraq*. New York: Pantheon Books, 2006.

Greentree, Todd R. *The United States and the Politics of Conflict in the Developing World*. Washington, DC: U.S. State Department Center for the Study of Foreign Affairs, August 1990 (also released by the Center for Low-Intensity Conflict, Langley AFB, Va).

Hawk, Kathleen Hill. *Constructing the Stable State: Goals of Intervention and Peacebuilding*. Westport, CT: Praeger, 2002.

Hulsman, John. "Lawrence of Arabia and the Perils of State Building." Washington, DC: Heritage Foundation Lecture, October 2005.

Lowther, Adam B. *Americans and Asymmetrical Warfare: Lebanon, Somalia, and Afghanistan*. Westport, CT: Praeger Security International, 2007.

Pietrzyk, Mark E. *International Order and Individual Liberty: Effects of War and Peace on the Development of Governments*. Lanham, MD: University Press of America, 2002.

Rozen, Laura. "Interview with Colonel H. R. McMaster, adviser to General David Petraeus." *Mother Jones* (online), October 18, 2007. (http://www.motherjones.com/interview/2007/11/Iraq-war-hr-mcmaster.html)

Schulman, Dan. "Interview with General Anthony Zinni." *Mother Jones* (online), October 18, 2007.

Snow, Donald M. *Cases in International Relations: Portraits of the Future* (Third Edition). New York: Pearson Longman, 2008.

———. *Distant Thunder: Third World Conflict and the New International Order*. New York: St. Martin's Press, 1994.

———. *National Security for a New Era: Globalization and Geopolitics* (Second Edition). New York: Pearson Longman, 2007 (Third Edition, 2009).

Sun Tzu. *The Art of War*. (Translated by Samuel B. Griffith). Oxford, UK: Oxford University Press, 1963.

Thompson, Sir Robert. *Make for the Hills: Memories of Far Eastern Wars*. London: Lee Cooper, 1989.

THE CONSEQUENCES

Chapter 5

No More Iraqs

What can be learned from the American odyssey in Iraq? Part of the answer depends, of course, on how the war finally comes out, and that cannot be answered definitively until the war is over and there is time to develop some perspective on the outcome. There are, however, clearly parts of the experience that have occurred, or are occurring, on which it is possible to make judgments that both explain why certain actions were taken, and how it should help future decisions. Principally, these are, first, the events, processes, and reasons leading to the war, and second, the conduct of the war up to this point. Both—particularly the early conduct of the war—have been the subject of considerable analysis that will be noted but not replicated here. The full meaning of the legacy for the future remains somewhat more speculative, but parallel experiences (especially the Vietnam War) allow one to reach some reasonable, if tentative, conclusions.

The chief legacy of the Iraq War will be to avoid its repetition. The catch phrase, parallel to "No More Vietnams" a generation ago, will be "No More Iraqs." Even supporters of the war would, by and large, support this conclusion. In particular, even those who believe the United States must complete the mission it has begun (Arizona Senator John McCain is particularly clear on this point) agree that the mission should probably not have been undertaken and that if those who authorized it knew then what they know now, they would not have supported the decision to go to war (New York Senator Hillary Clinton dramatically represents this). The original reasons for the war lie in tatters. The long-time neoconservative fixation with the removal of Saddam Hussein has never been widely publicized or been used as public justification for the war, and alternative explanations for going in, like the capture of Iraqi oil, have never been publicly articulated by the Bush administration. From the vantage point of 2008, general references to the virtue of removing the shackles of Saddam's suppression from the Iraqis, and loose references to Iraq as a theater of the GWOT are about as far as anyone will go in defending the decision. This support largely melts away if one asks whether accomplishing even these goals was worth the long, expensive, and divisive proposition that the war has become. One way to think about that decision, which will be explored in the pages that follow, is that it was reached on the presumption of a short, decisive, and inexpensive campaign and that those who advocated and supported the war would not have done so if they had known what they were getting the country into when they made those decisions.

The same kind of criticism can be levied against how the war has been conducted since the initial invasion and conquest of Iraq. In particular, no one defends the absence of planning for so-called Phase IV operations, from the failure to respond to the initial lawlessness in Baghdad immediately after the Americans arrived, through the incredibly botched occupation, including the unfathomable decisions made (e.g., disbanding the Iraqi army and police) and the enormous ineptitude of those who were sent to carry it out (e.g., the Coalition Provisional Authority—CPA—"losing" several billions of dollars scheduled to pay for reconstruction efforts). The overall impression of this part of the war is that its conduct was insufficiently considered before the war because no one thought such a phase would exist (further evidence of the presumption the war would be quick and painless, a "walk over"). A question that must be addressed in assessing the longer-term impact is whether such bungling was so egregious that even the most valiant ongoing efforts cannot correct the situation.

The legacy of Iraq will almost certainly include a bitter heritage. It may not be as traumatic as the poisonous effects of the Vietnam experience, but it is likely to prejudice, even poison, the national security landscape for some years to come. Exactly how long and to what extent there will be an "Iraq hangover" has yet to be fully determined, but it is clear that there will indeed be negative consequences: The Iraq War has roiled the waters, but how?

To explore the legacies of Iraq for the future, the remainder of the chapter will focus on two aspects of that inheritance. It will begin, following standard military practice, by looking at "lessons learned" from the conflict. The discussion will be organized in two ways. One will be to divide the lessons into the three categories established in the subtitle: The process leading to the decision to invade Iraq ("getting in"); the evolution of the conflict leading to the effective process of Iraqification ("getting out"); and the general and specific effects of the outcome of the war ("the consequences"). Emphasis will be placed on the early stage, since different decisions at the outset would have rendered subsequent decisions moot. Second, each of these distinctions will be analyzed in both political and military terms.

These lessons learned are cumulative and worth previewing. The decision to invade Iraq will almost certainly appear anomalous to future historians. Iraq was indeed a troublesome, annoying country from an American perspective. The Saddam Hussein regime effectively defied American world leadership (e.g., dragging its feet on WMD inspections, and evicting American oil companies from competing for concessions), and acted outrageously internally (e.g., using chemical weapons against its Kurdish minority in 1987) and internationally (e.g., invading Kuwait in 1990), a litany of misbehavior that earned it the status of a rogue state. There are, however, abundant rogue states in the world, and what raised Iraq to the special status of prime candidacy for "regime change" remains controversial. Despite its record, the policy of "dual containment" of Iran and Iraq during the 1990s had arguably succeeded in maintaining at least an uneasy peace in the region, and it was hard to imagine any state in the world that was a less likely candidate for embracing an American-style democratization process than the highly fragmented, enormously artificial state of Iraq. Despite abundant objection, the decision was made anyway, and the question is why? Obviously, a different decision would have made the rest of the inquiry unnecessary. Having said that, an apparently reluctant, or at least unenthused, military leadership set aside what it had learned in Vietnam and marched to war as if the whole enterprise was going to be easy. They should have known better, and many did. Some spoke out (e.g., General Shinseki, the Army Chief of Staff who argued for a much larger invasion/occupying force), and they were dispatched in ways eerily reminiscent of Vietnam. McMaster's observations about the military in Vietnam seem to apply to Iraq as well.

The conduct of the war after the invasion and conquest stage is equally inexplicable. The presumption that the war would be swift and decisive was utterly fanciful from the beginning, yet few made the case debunking the presumption strongly enough to reverse it. That presumption was critical, because the war never could have been sold to the American public if what it could become had been known at the time. One can argue that war is always uncertain, and that the first victims of hostilities are prewar plans. But while that is true, it was the underlying assumptions of the plans that were tragically flawed, resulting, for instance, in too small a force being put into (and sustained) in Iraq, which initiated the process of administering an occupation the planners apparently believed would be unnecessary. How did this occur?

The lessons also extend to the ultimate legacies that the United States must continue to deal with, the second concern of this chapter. The essence of that legacy will almost certainly be revulsion with the war effort and a resolve that it not be repeated. The legacy of Iraq, in other words, is "No More Iraqs" in much the same way that the legacy of Vietnam was "No More Vietnams." Unfortunately, the ultimate legacy of Vietnam was apparently forgotten a generation later, resulting in involvement in another quixotic quest, this time in Iraq. Will American leaders learn something more permanently this time?

THE LESSONS OF IRAQ

The overwhelming judgment of the American public is that the Iraq War has been an unfortunate episode. As a result, a major emphasis of the lessons to be learned is what went wrong, allowing the United States to get into a war it should have avoided. History may judge the Iraq War in more or less negative terms than the public currently does. Historians may moderate some of the criticisms, or they may be even harsher than present judgments. It is impossible to say which with assurance.

Nonetheless, the virtual certainty of a negative reaction—the Iraq hangover, or Mueller's Iraq Syndrome—leads to an examination that emphasizes the pathologies associated with American involvement, while noting the successes, where possible. The purpose of a "lessons learned" exercise is to determine what positive things accompanied a particular action that should be repeated in the future, as opposed to what went wrong that should be modified or abandoned in the future.

Getting In: The Decision to Invade Iraq

Why did the United States Government decide to make war on Iraq? The decision was traumatic and dramatic, both because it involved an act of physical aggression by the United States—invading a sovereign state and fellow member of the United Nations—and because it was opposed by most of the rest of the world on legal and political grounds. The physical act of invasion violated the obligations to which the United States had agreed in signing the Charter of the United Nations, which includes renouncing the right to initiate war. The U.S. invasion of Iraq was only the second time since the Charter was ratified in 1945 that one member state invaded and conquered another. (The other, ironically, was Saddam Hussein's 1990 invasion of Kuwait, the repulse of which was led by the United States on the grounds that, among other things, it violated the UN Charter.) The Bush administration tried but failed to get UN sanction of the invasion through the Security Council, and tried to justify the invasion under the Bush doctrine of preemptive war, a principle not acknowledged in international law. Most countries condemned the proposed action and the actual invasion on a variety of political grounds, from Europe's concern over potential oil leases to concerns that reaction to the American invasion might have negative regional geopolitical impacts. In the end, the United States acted essentially on its own with the assistance of a "coalition of the willing" which, except in the case of Great Britain, was more symbolic than physical.

The Political Dimension. Was invading Iraq a good idea? The answer lies in examining the reasons—the political objectives—for attacking Iraq, overthrowing its leadership, and occupying it, and assessing whether these were adequate to justify the war. In turn, this involves the parallel questions of whether the United States should have done what it did, and if it can accomplish its goals.

The reasoning that led the Bush administration to invade Iraq was discussed in Chapter 1 and need not be reproduced here. Rather, what is useful is to group those reasons into units for analysis and judgment, keeping in mind that they have changed over time and were more or less explicitly stated when the decisions were made and support for them was solicited. Those judgments will be made largely on the basis of realist criteria based in the notion of vital interests. Those who made the decisions are not entirely comfortable with this framework, which their defenders maintain prejudices the analysis and conclusions drawn from that analysis.

The key element in whether to use force within the realist paradigm (*see* Snow, *National Security for a New Era*, Third Edition, for a description) is the criterion of vital interests. As already noted, the question of whether vital interests are involved and can be invoked in any relationship or situation is the intolerability of the worst possible outcome of the situation or relationship. Can the United States, or any other country, tolerate such an outcome? Or does that prospect justify the use of all measures available, including the use of force, to preclude it?

The political objectives articulated by the Bush administration can be divided into two categories using the vital interest designation. Two explanations for going to war, one explicit and implicit, can be described as being in America's vital interests: Iraqi possession and potential use of WMDs and their ties to terrorists, and the need to insure American access to, or control over, Iraqi oil reserves. Two other explanations can be thought of as expanded vital interest explanations: the desire to democratize Iraq as a regional beacon, and the positive effects of a transformed Iraq on Israeli, and by extension, American security. These extended vital interest rationales, of course, are associated with the neoconservative analysis. As Lewis and Reading-Smith point out, Bush and his closest advisors made almost 500 "false statements" alleging these reasons between September 11, 2001 and the start of the war.

The idea that Iraqi possession of WMD threatens the United States goes back to the Gulf War of 1990–1991, where Saddam Hussein was forced to accept disarming of his WMD capabilities as part of the settlement ending that war. The importance of Iraqi WMD was dramatized by Iraq's use of these weapons against Iranians in the Iran-Iraq War and against Iraqi Kurds, which established Saddam Hussein's presumed willingness to use these weapons in future conflicts. Since Hussein had evicted UN weapons inspectors from the country in 1998, there was suspicion that he was not honoring these obligations and had to be forced into compliance. Economic sanctions had not succeeded in bringing the regime into open compliance with WMD disarmament conditions, and the administration adopted the use of force as one means of gaining that compliance. The link of the Iraqi regime to terrorists, to whom they might provide some of their WMD for attacks on American soil following 9/11, established the worst case, and a claim to violation of American vital interests. Clearly, a WMD attack on the United States by terrorists using Iraqi weapons was totally intolerable and justified robust, including forceful, actions.

The problem with these justifications, of course, is that their truth has never been demonstrated. Before the invasion, Saddam Hussein did agree to open all facilities for WMD inspection, and none have been found to date. The link to terrorism, originally based in an alleged meeting between officials of Al Qaeda and the Iraqi regime in Eastern Europe, was never established. Moreover, the allegations of a connection between the Iraqis and terrorists flew in the face of reason; the generally secular Sunni regime in Baghdad and fundamentalist Islamist terrorists were rivals, even enemies, not natural allies. This link, had it been true, arguably could have made a realist justification for military action, but it was not established at the time and has largely been discredited since. The nagging question is whether those who argued for invasion, principally the Bush administration, and those who ratified that decision, principally the Congress, knew or should have known that these statements of political objective were spurious. Some observers, Pillar, Isikoff and Corn, for example, believe administration officials knew these arguments were, at best, shaky, and tried to manipulate intelligence to legitimize these bogus reasons. Isikoff and Corn state the case bluntly: "Bush and his aides were using intelligence not to guide their policy on Iraq but to market it."

Iraqi oil provides a second geopolitical explanation, although it is one that is categorically denied by administration officials and their supporters. As chronicled by Weissman, the list of denials is extensive, including President Bush's statement that the idea of American interest in Iraqi oil is a "wrong impression" of the war's motivations. The list also contains then-National Security Advisor Condoleezza Rice, then-Secretary of State Colin S. Powell, and then-Secretary of Defense Donald Rumsfeld, all of whom are quoted as saying, "it's not about oil." Also making the same claim include former CPA administrator L. Paul Bremer, Central Command military commander General John Abazaid, Secretary of Energy Spencer Abraham, and Richard Perle, among others. Vice President Cheney, on the other hand, told a Veterans of Foreign Wars convention on August 26, 2002, "Armed with an arsenal of these (WMD) weapons of terror, *and sitting atop ten percent of the world's oil reserves*, Saddam Hussein could then be expected to seek domination of the entire Middle East, *take control of a great portion of the world's energy supplies*, directly threaten America's friends throughout the region, and subject the United States or any other nation to nuclear blackmail," (emphasis added). This rationale certainly does not deny the salience of oil.

The oil explanation is very rarely made outside liberal circles that are generally hostile to the Bush administration. Other than Greenspan, quoted earlier, it is rarely mentioned except for summary denial. As Klare, a consistent critic, says, "When it came to the punditocracy just about the only discussion was restricted to dismissal of claims by the antiwar movement that oil was the (or a) significant factor in the invasion, a position supposedly too simpleminded to be taken seriously." Ferraro offers a more intriguing explanation: "Perhaps this objective is rarely mentioned because it's obvious, or maybe because no discussion was necessary among decision-makers well versed in petroleum politics."

The idea that Iraqi oil had nothing to do with the motivation to invade the country and overthrow its leadership is indeed difficult to sustain, for at least three reasons. The first is the prewar exclusion of the major American and British oil companies (U.S. companies Exxon Mobil and Chevron Texaco, British companies BP and Royal Dutch Shell) from the Iraqi oil fields. This exclusion goes back to 1972, when the Iraqi government nationalized the Iraq Petroleum Company (*see* either Paul article for a discussion). This nationalization slowed the development of Iraqi oil and left it in a shambles when the United States invaded, a fact noted by, among other sources, *The Iraq Study Group Report*, which is one of the reasons Iraqi oil is such an under-exploited bonanza. In the 1990s, the Iraqi regime of Saddam Hussein negotiated developmental contracts with French, Russian, and

Chinese companies, but continued to exclude American and British firms. Ferraro maintains that "Vice President Dick Cheney's energy task force was particularly concerned in March 2001 about non-American suitors for Iraqi oil, according to documents obtained by Judicial Watch." (Judicial Watch is a generally conservative Washington think tank.) In testimony before the Senate Armed Service Committee on April 13, 1999, General Anthony Zinni, then commander of Central Command, stated that as a matter of strategic vital interests, the United States "must have access to the region's (oil) resources" (quoted in Paul).

The second reason that the administration has difficulty in denying its intentions on Iraq's oil supply is the nature of the competition. It probably should not be surprising that the leading alternative suitors for Iraqi oil (France, Russia, and China) have also been leading opponents of the American effort in Iraq and were among the countries excluded early on from participating in the rebuilding of Iraq, especially its oil fields. The invasion has suspended implementation of the oil development contracts of those countries and has put the American and British firms in a much better position to gain control of these aspects of desired "upstream" development. Upstream refers to the actual pumping of oil from its sources, as opposed to less profitable "downstream" parts of the process like transportation and refining. Moreover, American and British control of the oil can also prevent other countries from overproducing from the Iraqi fields, leading to a surplus on the oil market and driving down prices and profits that are more easily managed if American and British firms control the oil fields.

The third reason is the special desirability of Iraqi oil. In addition to being extremely plentiful (proven reserves of 112.5 billion barrels—11 percent of known world reserves—and possible reserves the U.S. Department of Energy estimates at 400 billion barrels), Iraqi oil is more desirable than alternative sources for two reasons (both discussed in Paul). For one thing, it is of very high quality. As Paul puts it, "it has attractive chemical properties, notably high carbon content, lightness and low sulfur content, that make it especially attractive for refining into high-value products." In addition, extracting it is very easy, with low production costs and high profits for upstream producers because Iraqi oil is found at comparatively shallow depths, with one-third of the known reserves within 1,800 feet of the earth's surface. The result is oil that can be produced for $1–$1.50 per barrel. By comparison, it costs about $5 per barrel to produce at the next cheapest locations, like Malaysia and Oman. Mexico and Russia cost $6–8 per barrel, and North Sea oil is $12–16 per barrel. North American oil can cost as much as $20 a barrel to extract. Given the extent of Iraqi reserves and how inexpensive it is to extract, the total value of these yields will likely be in the trillions of dollars, and given the low production costs, profits could also be in the same range.

The problem, of course, is how to guarantee U.S. and British access to this cornucopia. The Saddam Hussein government consistently blocked that access, thereby providing a rationale for getting rid of it, and potentially voiding the contracts his government had made with French, Russian, and Chinese oil producers. In these circumstances, is it any wonder those countries have opposed the American-British-led invasion and occupation? Beyond removing the barriers to access, however, is the problem of assuring post-occupation access. This requires that the post-occupation government in Baghdad be amenable to granting primary—preferably exclusive—rights to the American-British conglomerate. One apparent hope was Ahmed Chalabi, the Iraqi exile leader of the Iraqi National Congress and charter neoconservative, who once declared that "American companies will have a big shot at Iraqi oil," presumably if there were a Chalabi regime. *The Iraq Study Group Report* endorses privatization of the Iraqi oil industry but does not commit to who should control it. Given the stakes involved, it is not surprising that the United States government has such a high level of interest in who governs postwar Iraq.

Gaining continuing access to, even control of, Iraq's vast oil reserves thus provides another, possibly even more geopolitically sound, political objective for military action. In addition to the arguments already made, this explanation is reinforced by the global energy situation briefly described in Chapter 1. Oil consumption is increasing at a time when oil production has or will soon peak, and it will soon begin to decline. As competition for oil resources intensifies, control or guaranteed access to exploitable reserves will provide an ever-greater advantage for those countries that have it. As the world's largest petroleum importer, the United States is particularly vulnerable in this competition, and the vast and generally underdeveloped Iraqi oil reserves represents an obviously tempting target. Control of that oil makes geopolitical sense to insure American oil independence over the next few decades, as the world makes the transition away from petroleum to other forms of energy. Achieving and protecting energy security certainly can be defended as vital to the United States.

No defender of the invasion has publicly made this justification. Maybe it is so obvious as not to require stating, or so naïve as to be easily dismissible. On the other hand, the oil is there, everyone knows it is there, and everyone understands that oil and power are closely related in the modern world. One can argue that gaining control is a side benefit of the invasion rather than the primary motivation, but ignoring that oil has something to do with the equation is simply unsustainable. One can ask if the United States would have had sufficient interest in Iraq to become involved if Iraq had no oil. When Condoleezza Rice was presented with that possibility, she replied curtly that "This cannot be further from the truth." It is not necessary to argue that oil is the only reason for invading Iraq, but one cannot honestly deny the benefits incurred by those who favored the invasion.

The control of oil is the one argument that makes traditional realist sense for the invasion of Iraq. Given the oil dependence of the United States, controlling such a large asset could help free the United States of the increasingly cut-throat global competition for oil and, by gaining leverage over the post-occupation Iraqi government, provide leverage for the United States, and presumably Great Britain, in that competition. This latter prospect puts British solidarity with the Americans on the topic of Iraq in a different light than it might otherwise be.

The other explanations for the war are extensions of vital interest arguments and are, as noted, based in neoconservative visions of the world (*see* Kagan and Kristol for a broad overview).The explanations are related. One is the argument for democratization. This argument maintains that Iraq was a singularly divisive and destabilizing force in the Middle East region, thanks to its dictatorial regime. The record of Saddam Hussein thus invited regime change to overthrow him. The Wilsonian side of neoconservatism argues that transforming Iraq into a "model" democracy would both reduce its destabilizing influence, since political democracies allegedly do not fight one another, and would serve as a beacon that would be emulated by other states in the region, thereby pacifying the oil-rich part of the Islamic world. A more peaceful, democratic Islamic Middle East would also pose less of a threat to Israel, because Israel and those countries would share democracy, and thus, be less warlike. The impact would increase Israeli security, which in turn would have a salutary effect on U.S. interests in the region (the neoconservatives tend to equate U.S. and Israeli interests in the region). From a strictly American vantage point, reconciling the historical tension between support for Israel and its continued existence and relations with the oil-producing Islamic states would ameliorate that policy inconsistency.

These arguments are also suspect. One issue is whether overthrowing non-democratic regimes and replacing them with democratic regimes is vital to the United States. There are, after all, plenty of authoritarian regimes in the world whose people would arguably be better off if their regimes were changed (Myanmar-Burma comes immediately to mind), but that does not mean the United States will invade and overthrow all those regimes. The spread of democracy is clearly an American preference, and its achievement is clearly in the interest of the United States. Whether the American interest in democratic outcomes is sufficient to justify the use of American force to achieve it, is a different story.

The more fundamental question is whether the use of American force is appropriate and effective for this kind of change. Clearly, American military forces can overthrow Third World regimes, as Iraq demonstrates. Whether democratization can be imposed by military force anywhere is a different matter. The post-World War II experience in Germany and Japan is often cited as evidence that an occupation can inculcate the occupied population with democratic values. But can the same methods work in the developing world? More to the point, was Iraq a good place to try such an experiment?

The answer is clearly negative. On any dimension one can imagine, Iraq was one of the most unlikely places in the world to try to induce political democracy. Iraq not only lacks any tradition of political democracy, it also lacks a tradition as a country. The history of the region now known as Iraq is long and complex, traceable back to the time when it was the heart of Mesopotamia, and it is a tumultuous history. What is important is that the political unit known as Iraq was largely a figment of the British imagination when Great Britain deposed the Ottoman Empire as the ruler of this territory (*see* Rayburn). Thus, the history of "Iraq" is less than eighty years old by even the most generous measure. It gained independence as a monarchy in 1932. In 1958 King Faisal was overthrown by the army, which established a leftist republic that aligned itself with the Soviet Union. In 1978, another military coup brought Iraq under the tyranny of Saddam Hussein, as leader of the Sunni Baathist movement. His regime lasted until he was overthrown by the United States in 2003. Throughout its brief history, it has been divided on communal (Sunni and Shiite), as well as ethnic grounds (Kurds versus Arabs as the most prominent example). Beneath these gross distinctions, the country is further divided along tribal and clan lines, with primary loyalty more often associated with local tribal areas than the country itself (Saddam Hussein's base in his native Tikrit is an example). Because of the harsh rule of the Sunni minority over the Shiite majority and Kurdish minority, there is enormous residual bitterness among and between groups, which manifests itself in cautiousness about associating or cooperating with other groups. The result is an explosive mix wherein the spirit and ability to engage in the levels of political give-and-take necessary to develop and sustain political democracy is all but entirely missing.

Iraq, in other words, is a classic *artificial state* (a country that lacks any historical or other basis for statehood) and, in many ways, a *failed state* (a political unit that has consistently shown an inability to govern itself other than through sheer dictatorial coercion). All of this was known when Americans were planning the invasion and conquest of the country by simply consulting the numerous books on the subject (for a variety of viewpoints, *see* Braude, Kristol and Kaplan, and Pitt and Ritter). Under these circumstances, it is extremely difficult to imagine how anyone could possibly have considered Iraq as candidate for transformation into the model democracy of the region. It was certainly possible to make the case that Saddam Hussein was a reprehensible leader who deserved to be overthrown, and it was indeed possible to accomplish that part of the overall goal of the United States. How the war planners could have concluded that the process of reconstituting Iraq after the overthrow could be a facile job simply defies credulity, unless they were painfully ignorant of country and its history. There was ample opinion in the expert and policy communities (notably intelligence and diplomatic) that Iraq was not the ideal place to engage in regime change; that advice was, however, systematically ignored, even denigrated, by those who made the various cases for the invasion. A chaotic Iraq after the overthrow of Saddam Hussein was absolutely predictable and was predicted.

To return to the question of whether invading Iraq was based on attainable political objectives, the answer is that it depends. If getting rid of Saddam's WMD or connections to terrorism is the standard, it was accomplished, although one can question whether it was worth the effort. If the reason was to control Iraqi oil, the jury is still out, since a post-occupation government does not exist, and thus, its willingness to cede primary access to the United States and Britain is not established. If the goal was to establish democracy, that was clearly an unattainable goal.

The Military Dimension. The military dimension of the war is somewhat more complicated. At one level, the war has been a success: The invasion and occupation phases went off without major hitches (*see* Gordon and Trainor, and Franks for alternative interpretations), and the surge has been a tactical success. At the same time, the various forms of asymmetrical resistance were either unanticipated or unacknowledged , and the United States has not been able to end the insurgency. Neither the military nor the political dimensions of the occupation were well thought-out or implemented, making the occupation more difficult than it needed to be. As part of any meaningful lessons learned from the Iraq War, both of these deficienciesas must be why these predictable problems arose.

The United States either did not anticipate, or refused to acknowledge, the insurgency that emerged in opposition to the occupation. Instead, the

American political leadership chose to view the invasion as a swift and painless liberation that would not require a long commitment, ending in a rapid turnover of power back to the Iraqis. Capturing this cavalier spirit, Gordon and Trainor quote Rumsfeld aide Larry Di Rita's response to the question of rebuilding Iraq: "We don't owe these people a thing. We gave them their freedom." This view existed at the highest levels. Gordon and Trainor report that President Bush convened a meeting at the White House on April 15, 2003 to consider plans for withdrawing American forces from the country. In 2000, Bush had campaigned against peacekeeping and nation (or state) building. Thus, as Gordon and Trainor report, "There would be no Balkans-like peacekeeping operation. The Iraq War would be like a thunderstorm: a short, violent episode that swept away the enemy but would not entail a burdensome, long-term troop commitment. The combat forces . . . should be prepared to pull out within 60 days. New units would arrive to help stabilize the country but most would stay no longer than 129 days. This calculation was made despite a January 2003 National Intelligence Council prediction that the 'Americans would be seen as occupiers' and their presence resisted, a fact also noted by Packer, who adds : 'the CIA had several secret prewar intelligence reports warning of the possibility of an insurgency.'" (Also, *see* Pillar.)

The rosy projections, of course, proved to be foolish, and their inaccuracy was known at the time. Even General Tommy Franks, who led the invasion and conquest phase, admits in his memoirs that he had different expectations: "It was understood that the final phase, Phase IV—post hostility ops—would last the longest: years, not months." Drawing an analogy with Afghanistan, he concluded "that Phase IV [in Afghanistan] could last as long as five years. . . . we can expect about the same in Iraq."

Why did the administration convince itself that there would not be a resistance, when it seemed obvious to many outside the inner circle of the White House? Certainly, part of the reason was wanton self-delusion; the administration wanted a quick and decisive war, and that is what they prepared for. This preference was undoubtedly reinforced by the success of the invasion and conquest phase. As Packer argues, "The guerrilla phase that followed the invasion of Iraq caught the U.S. military by surprise. It shouldn't have." A number of sources—including Franks—admit that the advancing U.S. forces confronted irregular resistance that served as a presage of the more organized resistance that would follow. Moreover, denying such resistance flew in the face of the administration's own assessment of the situation. As Gordon and Trainor explain, "The failure to read the early signs of the insurgency and to adapt accordingly was all the more surprising given the Bush administration's repeated assertions that Saddam's regime was allied with Osama bin Laden and terrorist organizations like Abu Musab al-Zarqawi's and given confirmed intelligence sources that jihadists had infiltrated from Syria. Had the administration taken its own counsel to heart, it would have been planning to wage a counterinsurgency." The idea that the Iraqis would simply submit to another foreign invader intruding on their soil, and accept that presence as a liberation, when the liberator failed to leave, strains credulity.

Should the military be blamed for this failure to anticipate the problems that arose? One of the powerful lessons of Vietnam had been the failure of the United States to prepare itself for the asymmetrical warfare it faced there. Part of what McMaster terms the "dereliction of duty" of the army leadership during the Vietnam period was that it did not inform the political leadership of the nature of that war and of the American forces' limitations in counteracting that style of fighting. An important lesson was that the United States should prepare itself for asymmetrical conflicts in the future, and much effort was expended within the professional military education (PME) system, general staff colleges, and military think tanks to that end, including when to engage and when to avoid them. General Petraeus' *Field Manual 3–24* is one of the fruits of that effort.

The problem was that asymmetrical warfare was so alien to military tradition that it was more accepted at the rhetorical level than within the core of the army. Lt. Colonel Yingling's critique of planning for the Iraq War is explicit: "The U.S. military gave very little thought to counterinsurgency during the 1990s. America's generals assumed without much reflection that the wars of the future would be much like the wars of the past." As a result, he maintains that in Iraq "America's generals have been checked by a form of war that they did not prepare for and do not understand. . . . Those few who saw clearly our vulnerability to insurgent tactics said and did little to prepare for those dangers." Gordon and Trainor put it more bluntly: "There has been much training, but for the wrong type of war." Former Central Command commander General Zinni, in a May 4, 2004 CBS interview, concurs: "The president is owed the finest strategic thinking. He is owed the finest operational planning. He is owed the finest tactical execution on the ground. He got the latter. He didn't get the first two."

Why not? The most obvious answer is that the "truth" was not what the White House wanted to hear. The Bush administration planned for a short and glorious war, and all they wanted to hear was evidence that supported their vision. When someone offered conflicting counsel, they were messengers to be executed. The clearest case involved Army Chief of Staff General Eric Shinseki, who advocated sending a force nearly twice the size of what was dispatched to Iraq. His reasoning was that this size force was what Central Command, had planned for, and that such a force (over 300,000) would be needed for the occupation. Nearly all military analysts, such as Zinni, agreed. As Zinni put it, "I think there was dereliction in insufficient forces being put on the ground and fully understanding the military dimensions of the plan." The administration disagreed, and Shinseki was forced into retirement (the administration and its supporters deny he was forced to retire). Secretary of Defense Rumsfeld, however, did not attend Shinseki's retirement ceremony, a serious breach of protocol that suggests Rumsfeld's disdain for the general's rejection of his invasion plan.

The United States military has no legitimate excuse for not warning policymakers what was to evolve in Iraq. Based on the lessons learned in Vietnam, they could anticipate what might well transpire in Iraq. Like the military leaders pilloried by McMaster in *Dereliction of Duty*, they did not object, at least publicly. The Shinseki example probably influenced some to remain silent, fearing repercussions, but their silence allowed the war to proceed without adequate consideration of the possible ramifications. Yingling states this burden most directly in his conclusions, and is worth quoting in its entirety: "America's generals have repeated the mistakes of Vietnam in Iraq. First, through the 1990s our generals failed to envision the conditions of future combat and prepare their forces accordingly. Second, America's generals failed to estimate correctly both the means and the ways necessary to achieve the aims of policy prior to beginning the war in Iraq. Finally, America's generals did not provide Congress and the public with an accurate assessment of the conflict in Iraq."

Here, Yingling criticizes the role of the military leadership more than has generally been true in assessments of the war. By and large, the military's role has been applauded, a stark contrast between Iraq and Vietnam. At the tactical level, the record warrants that support, but what about the advice that was factored into getting into Iraq in the first place? An enduring critique of the military in Vietnam was that it never said "can't do" to its political leaders and their political objectives. It was supposedly one of the lessons of Vietnam that the military would not allow itself to be cowed in the future, as McMaster maintains it was in Vietnam. So what happened in Iraq?

Answering that question is critical both in assessing the military's role in the war and in determining the lessons to be learned from Iraq.

Did, or should, the U.S. military—at the highest levels—know that the war would be less like the Bush administration predicted, and foresee it as it now is? Certainly, much lip service had been given to asymmetrical warfare preparations for a quarter century, but had none of it taken hold? Did the American military join the administration in predicting the war they wanted, rather than the war they should have known they would get?

If the answer to the latter question is positive, it is extremely devastating to the role the military has played in the Iraq War. When the decisions were made to authorize and conduct the war, they were based on short war scenarios: the liberation and rapid withdrawal from the country, and the rehabilitation—which would be lubricated by Iraqi oil profits. If, however, had the certainty, or even the possibility, that the war would devolve as it has, been made known, the public and its elected representatives almost certainly would not have approved or supported the war. Telling the truth about what might happen—the long, protracted, expensive, and unpopular war that Iraq has become—almost certainly would have resulted in different decisions about going to war. Had the prospect of a long occupation been anticipated in the first place, for instance, it is entirely possible that the decision to invade Iraq would not have been made, which would have been the most obvious way to avoid the consequences of the occupation.

Both the political rationale for making war on Iraq and the estimation of the military conduct of those hostilities are controversial and suspect. The political objectives have changed, some have been explicit and some implicit, and it is not clear whether a lucid and dispassionate analysis would have concluded that the United States should have invaded that country. Ironically, the one reason that might be considered adequate for the action—gaining permanent access or control of Iraqi oil—is never cited as an official reason. Similarly, the question of whether the various objectives were reasonably attainable was simply assumed, despite evidence that achieving the goals would be difficult, possibly unattainable. At the same time, the military implications of invading Iraq, including the prospect of the insurgency that eventuated, were known but ignored or underplayed. As House Majority Leader Richard Armey told Bush before the war began: "Mr. President, if you go in there, you're likely to be stuck in a quagmire," (quoted in Isikoff and Corn).

But the military did not offer contrary advice that carried the day. The United States has waged a war of choice for over five years, has achieved none of its political objectives, and despite military progress in the surge, this administration appears to have no plans to impose lasting military solutions to political problems of national reconciliation in Iraq. A lesson of Iraq must surely be that a more open, thorough, and unprejudiced prewar examination of whether the United States should go to war, and a more open and thorough assessment of the military possibilities might have been cautionary. Would the Iraq War have occurred if the consequences had been known? Or would it have occurred if the predictable consequences had not been ignored or suppressed?

Getting Out: Ending the Imbroglio

Had any of the planning scenarios for invading and liberating Iraq in 2003 proven true, there would not have been an imbroglio in that country that continues to churn in 2008 and displays no short-term probability of successful resolution and closure. If dealing with Iraqi WMD and connections to terror had been the honest and total political objective, there was no need for the war at all, and the only remaining question is whether those who decided to invade knew so at the time—or at least should have. If the neoconservative dream of a regionally stabilizing model democracy was the objective, it is not clear that *any* action would have worked. If it was as easy as its proponents portrayed, that process should be complete, and the United States's mission should be over and the troops home. Instead, Americans fight and die while Iraqi politicians use the Americans as a shield behind which to avoid hard decisions. If control of oil is also part of the objective, then finding an acceptable Iraqi government is complicated, because such a government must both be democratic, which, for reason previously mentioned, might be impossible, and also amenable to negotiating oil deals with American and British petroleum companies, denied by Hussein and Iraqi governments dating back to 1972. Since many Iraqis apparently believe oil is the real reason Americans are in their country, granting oil concessions would add to the inevitable difficulty a postoccupation Iraqi regime would have in establishing that it was not an American quisling regime—a designation that would greatly prejudice its ability to function.

As the Iraq War has continued, most of the debate over what the United States is seeking to accomplish in the war have faded from public discussions. Particularly within the administration and its shrinking cohort of supporters in the general public, there is great disdain for discussing why or whether the United States should have gone to war. Such discussions are viewed as defeatist distractions from the real task of prevailing in Iraq.

Instead, the objective is "victory" (generally, not well defined). And the reason victory is necessary is because the alternative, defeat or at least not victory, would have unacceptable consequences. Galbraith, for instance, quotes Bush from a July 2007 speech to the American Legion making this negative justification: "For all those who ask whether the fight in Iraq is worth it, imagine an Iraq where militia units backed by Iran control parts of the country." Among other political figures, Senator McCain has been the most articulate spokesman for this position. Summarized in Chapter 3, his reasoning emphasizes the abrogation of American position in the region; it would promote Iranian domination, a victory for terrorists and vindication of their actions, and a belief among Islamic extremists that the world "is going their way and anything is possible." The emphasis is not on the positive achievement of prewar political objectives; it is on avoiding negative consequences arising from the conduct of the war.

Examining the occupation for lessons to be learned muddies the distinction between political and military dimensions because the critique naturally gravitates to, and emphasizes, the role of so-called *Phase IV operations,* the Department of Defense's designation for tasks to be performed after the invasion and conquest phase of the war was completed. The process leading to Phase IV admixed political and military concerns, and it is difficult to separate the two dimensions except artificially. Because of this, discussion of the occupation phase will be divided into three parts: prewar planning that had an impact on Phase IV, the actual, physical content of the occupation plan, and execution of the phase. Each has contributed to the problems that dog the United States and militate toward a longer tenure in Iraq.

Prewar Planning for Phase IV

The process by which the administration moved toward war, including planning and executing the occupation, has been subjected to careful scrutiny in a number of books and articles to which little can be added here, and the interested reader is encouraged to sample the best of these (Chandrasekaran, Ricks, and Diamond are particularly readable). The overarching commonality that all the analyses share is that this stage was flawed, in at least two separate but overlapping ways.

The first source of criticism is the size of the force assembled to fight the war. There was basic disagreement between the military and the Rumsfeld Defense Department on this issue. Contingency planning for an invasion had been made and honed during the 1990s (in itself not very surprising, as the United States has contingency plans for invading a wide variety of places. The fact that plans exist does not necessarily entail intent to use them). This plan (OPLAN 1003) had been developed and updated in 1998 by the U.S. Central Command (CENTCOM), which has operational authority for military activity in the Middle East. It called for an invasion force of between 275–300,000 to conquer and pacify the country. General Shinseki's assessment was based on concurrence with this plan, most of which was developed and honed while General Zinni commanded CENT-COM during the 1990s, and is a force size Shinseki has subsequently continued to justify (*see* Clancy with Zinni and Gordon and Trainor).

The Pentagon, largely at the insistence of Secretary Rumsfeld, rejected this formulation. Rumsfeld believed that the mission could be accomplished with a much smaller force of no more than 150–160,000. Such a force conformed more closely to the streamlined force model he was attempting to develop for the future U.S. Army and Marines, and would not overly stress existing American force levels—presuming the force could be inserted, accomplish its job, and then be rapidly withdrawn. Although most military leaders sided with Shinseki and Zinni, at least privately, Rumsfeld found in Zinni's chief deputy, General Franks, an acolyte who believed the force Rumsfeld proposed would be adequate (Franks explains his reasoning in his memoir). Based on a variant of highly mobile *blitzkrieg* warfare, featuring massive American displays of firepower (so-called "shock and awe"), the smaller force indeed proved adequate for the initial invasion and conquest phase of the war.

The problem was that the very success of the invasion and conquest masked the basic criticism of the size of the U.S. invading force, which was its inability to pacify and occupy the country it conquered. The deficiencies of the force were visible even as it streaked across the Iraqi countryside. The force was too small, for instance, to leave contingents behind to guard weapons caches it uncovered as it moved toward Baghdad, and these unguarded arsenals were seized by Iraqi resisters (including the disbanded Iraqi military) and used later against the Americans. In the glow of the initial success leading to Bush's May 2003 declaration of the end of major combat operations, however, these deficiencies were generally ignored. Moreover, the Rumsfeld vision was vindicated, adding to his power in determining what would happen next. The naysayers, who argued the force might be adequate for conquering the country but not for the occupation, were silenced by this apparent success.

The second problem was the bureaucratic location of prewar planning for postwar Iraq. Part of the criticism is that planning for the occupation was limited because Rumsfeld and those around him did not think this would be much of a problem. If, indeed, almost all the troops would be gone within 129 days of the war as predicted, there was no need for elaborate plans after that short interim; instead, planning should be concentrated on the actual conduct of the war, not on its aftermath. At the base of this reasoning was what proved to be an egregious assumption most closely associated with Vice President Cheney. Cheney reasoned that the Americans would have little to do, since the Iraqis would view the Americans as liberators and would greet them accordingly, quickly moving to restore order to their own country. It is not clear whether anyone beyond the Vice President's office believed this assertion, but, once again, in the very early days after the invasion, there were sufficient Iraqi expressions of gratitude toward the Americans for ridding them of the Hussein regime to reinforce this view. However, the most overt expression of that enthusiasm, the international television coverage of an enormous statue of Saddam Hussein toppled in a city square, was actually done by American forces rather than the Iraqis to whom it was initially ascribed. Only after it became clear that the liberators were becoming occupiers did this perception fade.

The war planning process took place in the Defense Department and, thus, under the control of Rumsfeld, which added to the problems. Prior to the George W. Bush era, postwar recovery efforts had traditionally been handled through interagency cooperation, with the State Department designated as the lead agency in planning and execution. Rumsfeld objected to this designation, because the State Department had objected to the idea of an invasion in the first place (the majority of the government's experts on Iraq were in the State Department, and they had raised continuing objections to plans for the conquest. Indeed, a document had been developed in the State Department that included a prescient list of problems that would be faced after the invasion, and mirrored similar CIA assessments (*see* Pillar). These difficulties were at odds with prevailing sentiment among the neoconservatives who dominated the planning function in both the Pentagon and the Vice President's office. Similarly, the advice of United Nations experts on peacekeeping and nation-building (many of whom were retired American military officers) was ignored as "too liberal." Rumsfeld convinced the president to assign total operational authority and responsibility for postwar administration to the Defense Department. The President concurred. The planning function fell to the Office of Special Plans within the Pentagon, headed by a particularly abrasive neoconservative, Douglas Feith, of whom the normally compliant General Franks said, "Feith was a theorist whose ideas were often impractical; among some uniformed officers in the Building, he had a reputation for confusing abstract memoranda with results in the field." Feith's office was at the middle management level within the DOD, and placing the planning function there downgraded its prominence and effectively isolated it from the interagency process—thereby excluding almost all of the government's experience and expertise from that planning.

Content of Phase IV

The result of this planning process was a plan that was, to put it kindly, inadequate, and the deficiencies were manifested in the first days after the arrival of the Americans in Baghdad. A first principle in the conduct of an occupation is that the initial, indispensable role of an occupying force is to restore the order that its intrusion has broken. As Zinni put it in his CBS interview, "The first requirement is to freeze the situation, is to gain control of the security. To patrol the streets. To prevent the looting. To prevent the 'revenge' killings that might occur. To prevent bands or gangs or militias that might not have your best interests at heart from growing or developing." American forces entering Baghdad had no instructions to restore order, and when looting and lawlessness broke out, they lacked the training, equipment, or orders to intervene. As the city of Baghdad was systematically torn apart by looters, including the ransacking of the National Museum and loss or destruction of irreplaceable artifacts dating back to antiquity, coalition soldiers stood by, powerless without orders to intervene and restore order. Rumsfeld's cavalier response to a reporter's question about the chaos on Iraqi streets was that "freedom's untidy." The official expectation was that, despite the fact of physical conquest, the Iraqi police would report for duty and restore order as if nothing had happened.

The arrival of Ambassador L. Paul ("Jerry") Bremer III to head the Coalition Provisional Authority (CPA) compounded the situation. Bremer, a career diplomat, had absolutely no experience in, or detailed knowledge of, Iraq (some have argued that that was the reason he was chosen), and when he tried to bring in Islamists from the State Department with expertise on the Middle East, his efforts were blocked by Rumsfeld and his staff. In the confusion and chaos of the scene, however, Bremer made decisions that effectively created the unsatisfactory situation that persists to this day.

In his first days on the scene in Baghdad, Bremer disbanded the Iraqi army, the Baath Party (the ruling Sunni-based party under Saddam

Hussein), and the intelligence service. In addition, he mandated that all Baathists be removed from public office. His rationale was that the major peacekeeping institutions, the army and police, were permeated by and loyal to the overthrown regime and had to be purged before an acceptable set of structures could be assembled. These actions were part of the process of regime change, one of the stated objectives of the invasion, intended to serve as evidence of their liberation to the Iraqis.

The results have been almost universally condemned, because, as Galbraith summarizes it, "By taking these actions, the United States eliminated the institutions that had held Iraq together. It was hardly surprising that the country fell apart." While these institutions had undoubtedly been part of the repression that marked the Hussein regime, they were also the only sources of normal governance in the country. The effect was to create a vacuum—especially in the critical area of security—which the Americans were unprepared to fill, since doing so had not been part of the prewar planning process. In addition, and also unanticipated, the order threw literally hundreds of thousands of Sunnis—including trained soldiers—out of work with no alternative jobs available. Inevitably, they became disaffected and bitter, and in an Iraq where weapons were freely available (partly because the United States had not secured military depots during the invasion), some took up arms and became part of the resistance with which the United States is still dealing. A major result has been that the United States has struggled ever since to develop Iraqi police and armed forces, with mixed results. Basically, both forms of security forces have been drawn from sectarian militias and the like, to the point that, Galbraith maintains, "The security forces are *more* sectarian than the population," (emphasis in the original).

Execution of the Occupation

The occupation of Iraq now spans half a decade and could, depending on the next administration and its priorities, extend more or less indefinitely beyond that. With regard to the structure and execution of the occupation itself—what it has set out to do and how it has done it—it is hard to conclude anything other than that it was a poor plan, poorly executed. Whether the occupation is making progress depends on one's definition of success, and the means by which that progress is measured. The question of so-called "metrics" (measures) of progress is particularly vexing, as in the attempt to assess the arguments for continuing in, or exiting from, Iraq.

Criticism of the execution of the occupation has two bases. One, that the planning itself was deficient, has already been discussed. Those efforts, concentrated around Feith and his associates in the DOD, clearly underestimated the problem and thus made inadequate plans for dealing with difficulties that should have been, but were not, anticipated. As an example, one of the surest effects of a military invasion is the disruption of sources of electrical power, particularly in urban areas like Baghdad. Moreover, the climate in Baghdad is very hot, with temperatures not unlike those in Arizona cities, but with higher humidity. A primary dictate of restoring civil society in a place like Baghdad is to maintain electrical power, so that air conditioning and other amenities are provided for the citizenry to enjoy the benefits of their liberation. Yet, this simple dictate was either overlooked or assigned a very low priority, and to date, electric service is sporadic in the Iraqi capital. An exception, of course, is the "Green Zone"—the Baghdad enclave in which the United States maintains its headquarters—where electrical service is fully functional. This lack of anticipation and preparation has been symptomatic of the overall effort, and is especially egregious since the State Department and the CIA, among others had anticipated many of the problems. The administration, and particularly Rumsfeld and his associates, clearly underestimated the problems they would confront.

These deficiencies were compounded by the quality and qualifications of the administrators sent to implement the reconstruction and occupation. Chandrasekaran has most thoroughly detailed the incompetence, ineptitude, and inexperience of those recruited for duty in Baghdad. He notes, for instance, that in many cases the major criterion for appointment was not competence or expertise, but political loyalty to the Republican Party and, more specifically, to President Bush. A large percentage of the administrators were in their twenties, fresh out of college, and had left American soil for the first time, traveling to Baghdad. Moreover, their commitment was to the creation of an American-style political democracy and a capitalist-based, privatized economy. These goals, which comported with the stated objective of the American invasion, often came into conflict with political realities and traditions in Iraq itself. Most of the personnel brought in were unacquainted with Iraq, and didn't know about these conflicts. (Chandrasekaran relates stories of new personnel reading tourist guides on their flights to Iraq to learn about their new posts). At the same time, people with substantial expertise about Iraq were generally excluded, because their expertise made them unacceptably skeptical of the enterprise and the prospects of its success.

Assessing the success or failure of the occupation is further complicated by the problem of accurately measuring that success. During the period between the 2004 elections and the middle of 2007, there was growing consensus in the American public that progress was not being made, based primarily on indecisive military reports that contained sufficient American casualties to raise concerns about whether these losses were worth the gains. Partly to rectify the situation and partly to alter public perceptions, the administration's response was the surge.

The ongoing question, which is critical to whether the effort should be sustained, is whether the surge has worked. Supporters of the war say it has, and cite reduced casualty statistics in those areas where the surge is active (e.g., Baghdad, Anbar province) as evidence. They rarely include more than hopefulness about political progress toward reconciliation. Critics acknowledge the reductions in casualties, but argue that the statistics are are misleading. Part of their critique is that attacks do indeed decrease when the Americans are present, but that the lull is tactical and attacks would resume once the Americans leave (essentially the Gelb and Betts thesis about Vietnam described in the last chapter). Thus, progress is ephemeral. Moreover, the lull may reflect that ethnic cleansing—forcefully removing Sunnis from Shiite areas and vice versa—has essentially been completed in these areas. As Rosen argues, "To the extent that violence among Iraqis has gone down, it is largely because there are fewer people to kill." Moreover, the real measure of progress is whether Iraq is moving toward a political reconciliation, and there are few signs that it is. Rosen's December 2007 assessment of the political situation is that "Iraq will never again exist as a state. . . . America's latest strategy [the surge] will prolong the fighting instead of allowing there to be a winner in the civil war." The surge, in other words, is producing cosmetic evidence of improvements, but the underlying, fundamental situation remains bleak and is not—possibly cannot—be improved.

It is difficult to assess these competing explanations. Part of the reason is visibility; the effects of the surge are much more evident through reduced casualty figures than is the lack of political progress. Those who claim that the situation in Iraq is irretrievable and that withdrawal is the only sensible recourse do not have the same clear "metrics" of non-progress from which to argue as those who maintain that progress is being made. At the same time, champions of the military progress resulting from the surge admit that political problems have not been solved, and that progress on the political level remains critical to overall success of the enterprise.

LEGACIES FROM THE LESSONS

What do these lessons learned tell the reader about Iraq and similar experiences in the future? As a matter of perspective, some of the most obvious legacies are similar to the legacies of Vietnam, while a few are unique to Iraq.

The trail of legacies begins with the decision-making process leading to intervention in an ongoing war (Vietnam), or instigation of a war (Iraq). In both cases, the decisions were based on flawed assessments, attributable to a failure to examine all aspects of the situation, and unheeded expert advice that would have prevented ill-advised actions.

Part of the error involved the increasing stakes the United States had in both situations. In Vietnam, the stakes were clearly identified—the fall of South Vietnam to communism. But, although that threat proved prophetic, its implications were not: No vital interests of the United States were, in the long run, jeopardized by the truth of the domino theory. In Iraq, the initial assessment was false (WMD, terrorism), and the subsequent statement of the objective of a democratic Iraq was arguably not vital to the United States. In both cases, the attainability of the objectives was questionable, leading to the accusation they were fool's errands.

Ironically, the objective that might have met the dual criteria of importance and attainability was—and continues to be—control or guaranteed access to the vast oil reserves of Iraq: overall at least 115 billion barrels or Kurdistan (estimated by the Environmental News Service, or ENS, at upwards of 55 billion barrels of the overall total if Ninewah Province is included in Kurdistan). This argument has never been made publicly as the rationale for the war, probably because it seems cynical and difficult to sell domestically, and even more so internationally. Securing the oil, however, could be defended as an extension of the Carter Doctrine, establishing it as vital to the United States. Stating it as a goal independent of the other objectives would also make it more attainable, because it might be negotiable with a less-than democratic Iraqi government, or a Kurdish government grateful for its delivery from Iraq. As the Iraq War winds down, a movement toward the latter solution (a *de facto* or *de jure* Kurdistan, for instance) might indicate that oil really is the justification for the war. The fate of Ninewah Province in Northern Iraq, and the American position on that fate, may provide a good indicator of the likelihood of the Kurdistan "option." If Ninewah is excluded from Kurdistan, its oil reserves drop to around 25 billion barrels, a considerable, but lesser, prize. As Kumins points out in a 2005 Congressional Research Service (CRS) study, the Kurdish oil industry is also tied to the state of development of the Kirkuk-Ceyhan (Turkey) oil pipeline, which can deliver Kurdish oil to the West without going through the rest of Iraq and the Persian Gulf.

Had the real dynamics of the war been made public and openly discussed, would the United States have become involved? Such an examination would have revealed the prospect of a protracted conflict along the lines of what the war devolved into—a sharp contrast to the rosy and utterly false projections that were made (whether those making these projections were honest or deceitful is a separate question). A clear and thorough vetting, including the expert community discussing both the political situation and the military probabilities, would have yielded a different environment for making the fateful decisions. Instead, there was a rush to judgment resulting in the herd behavior of Congress. Those members of Congress who voted to authorize military action against Iraq and who have since recanted (especially those with presidential ambitions) would have much less excuse for their decisions and endorsements, had a full and open debate occurred. However, their decisions were made in the atmosphere of anguish and recriminations against dissenters. A thorough prewar discussion might also have had the salutary effect of revealing the real motives of those who counseled war (as discussed in Chapter 1), and of disentangling the Iraq War from the 9/11 attacks.

Had the hard questions been raised and held out for public scrutiny; the questions of how important the outcome was, and whether it was attainable; and had it been insisted upon that the public have sufficient time to be persuaded, the chances are there would not have been an Iraq War. The war proposal would have been identified as calling for a war of choice rather than a war of necessity, as it was depicted, one that would be both costly and divisive—wildly beyond the projections of those who beat the war drums. Accurate visions of Iraq's potential for chaos were available before the decisions were made, but competed unsuccessfully with optimistic estimates, and, ultimately, were overwhelmed by the patriotic aura skillfully attached to the rush to war by its proponents. The result was arguably the most unnecessary war in United States history, save possibly the War of 1812. The United States declared war in 1812 in order to cease the forced impressment of American sailors onto British ships, a policy the British had rescinded before war was declared. The parallel to Iraqi WMD and ties to terrorism is not entirely without merit.

Had there been no decision to attack Iraq, there would, of course, be no Iraq remorse, hangover, or syndrome. Regardless of the final decision, a thorough vetting of the situation might have at least resulted in a better American policy. The predictions about how the war would unfold have been demonstrated to be utterly fanciful. The war was supposed to be short and decisive; it is now five years old and counting. The war was not supposed to put a strain on American resources, because of the decisiveness of the campaign; the American military system has been strained nearly to the breaking point and will require years of concerted effort to repair. The war was also supposed to be cheap, with a lightning liberation campaign followed by an equally rapid withdrawal and the use of Iraqi oil revenues to restore the country; the war has cost the United States nearly a trillion dollars in money mostly borrowed from foreign lenders. The economic bleeding continues, masked behind the veil of special appropriations that obscure its dilatory effects on the U.S. economy.

The people who proposed and made these decisions, and those who acceded to and supported them have no excuse for their actions. The assertions that were made at the time were, at their very best, questionable, and they should have been questioned with much more vigor than they were. Once the war was underway, a cooler assessment of its reality might have made the occupation less damaging than it has been. For over two years after the emergence of the Iraqi resistance, those who defended the war engaged in rhetorical warfare denying that the resistance existed, or that it was anything more than the actions of a few disgruntled Iraqis and foreign provocateurs, especially terrorists. In fact, the issues and problems were much more complex. A clearer vision of the situation might have led to an earlier implementation of the counterinsurgency approach introduced with the appointment of General Petraeus. Alternately, it might have led to the conclusion that military closure was impossible and that a political solution was the only recourse. Either alternative might have shortened the agony and the suffering for Iraqis and Americans alike.

Two additional parts of the legacy should be added. One is that, at this point, there almost certainly is no "final" resolution to the Iraq War that will be satisfactory to the American people as a whole. Americans like decisive ends to their conflicts, and there is no decisive goal in the policy of Iraqification that forms the single, logical outcome to the war. Moreover, Americans (or at least their leaders) are too polarized for there to be a point where all opinions and positions can be vindicated. The other part of this legacy is that the war is going to leave a sour taste in the mouths of essentially all observers, and the ultimate legacy of the war, as it was phrased after the Vietnam conflict, is "No More Iraqs."

Some, possibly most, Americans will be unhappy with the outcome in Iraq, regardless of what it is. If one rules out a decisive military victory and a political outcome that features a stable political democracy embraced by all groups in Iraq, all the alternatives are less desirable and unacceptable to some. Movement toward a policy of Iraqification admits implicitly that ideal outcomes are unattainable, and that American sights must be lowered to some more achievable result. In the present political climate in Iraq, the most that can reasonably be expected is some sustained reduction of the internal violence, behind which an exchange of responsibility from the Americans to the Iraqis can be affected. Despite the rhetoric that will accompany such an exchange (e.g., the successful "standing up" of Iraqi security forces), no one will seriously believe this result will hold. The question is the extent to which the violence returns: Will it be the violent bloodbath that some have predicted, or some lesser form of intercommunal violence? A totally pacified Iraq would, of course, be the ideal, but that is undoubtedly unattainable.

How bad it gets in Iraq as the Americans and coalition forces are withdrawing, and after they are gone, will largely depend on the political agreements the Iraqis themselves can negotiate. There must be a reckoning between various groups in Iraq and, as Galbraith opines, "America's latest strategy will prolong the fighting instead of allowing there to be a winner in the civil war." How bloody that civil war turns out to be will depend on the kind of political agreement that can be forged. Iraq may simply fracture: There is already a de facto separation of Kurdistan from the rest of the country. Kurdish *pesh merga*, for instance, "treat the border between Kurdistan and the rest of Iraq with the same vigilance they would display toward an international border," according to Galbraith. Kurdish secession may or may not occur, and may or may not be encouraged by the United States. Whether the Kurds remain part of Iraq or try to escape is, however, one of the big and complicated questions that will have to be resolved in order to determine the face of postwar Iraq. Turkish opposition to an independent Kurdistan is a factor, especially given the pipeline for Kurdish oil that travels across Turkey.

The Iraq that existed before the invasion will likely never be reconstituted, an improvement for some Iraqis (mostly Shiite), but not for others (mostly Sunni). In the aftermath, Americans will come to realize that their country bears a strong responsibility for whatever suffering the Iraqi people and their state have endured, and Americans are likely to respond with revulsion. At least for a while, "No More Iraqs" will likely dampen any enthusiasm for other foreign adventures.

The aftermath of the war will leave the United States with some difficult decisions of its own. The most obvious will be how to repair the American military system, which has been badly stressed by the Iraq experience and will require major attention, just as it did after the Vietnam War. The core of much of that concern will be military manpower, which is the subject of Chapter 6. At the same time, revulsion with the Iraq experience is likely to result in a debate over the propriety of American activism—mainly, but not exclusively, military—in solving America's own remaining problems, some of which have been made arguably worse by the Iraq War. Assessing some of these problems is the subject of Chapter 7.

SELECTED BIBLIOGRAPHY

Baker, James A. III, and Lee H. Hamilton (co-chairs). *The Iraq Study Group Report: The Way Forward—A New Approach* (authorized edition). New York: Vintage Books, 2006.

Braude, Joseph. *The New Iraq: Rebuilding the Country for Its People. The Middle East, and the World.* New York: Basic Books, 2003.

Chandrasekaran, Rajiv. *Imperial Life in the Emerald City: Inside Iraq's Green Zone.* New York: Alfred A. Knopf, 2007.

Cheney, Richard. "Vice President Speaks at VFW 103rd National Convention." Washington, DC: The White House, August 26, 2002.

Clancy, Tom, with General Tony Zinni and Tony Koltz. *Battle Ready.* New York: G. P. Putnam's Sons, 2004.

Clarke, Richard. *Against All Enemies: Inside America's War on Terror.* New York: Free Press, 2004.

Diamond, Larry. *Squandering Victory: The American Occupation and the Bungled Effort to Bring Democracy to Iraq.* New York: Times Books (Henry Holt and Company), 2005.

Ferraro, Vincent. "Another Motive for Iraq War: Stabilizing Oil Market." *Hartford Currant* (online), August 12, 2003.

Galbraith, Peter W. "After Iraq: Picking Up the Pieces." *Current History* 106, 704 (December 2007), 403–408.

Franks, Tommy with Michael McConnell. *American Soldier.* New York: Regan Books, 2004.

Gordon, Michael R., and General Bernard E. Trainor. *Cobra II: The Inside Story of the Invasion and Occupation of Iraq.* New York: Pantheon Books, 2006.

Isikoff, Michael, and David Corn. *Hubris: The Inside Story of Spin, Scandal, and the Selling of the Iraq War.* New York: Three Rivers Press, 2007.

Kagan, Robert, and William Kristol (eds.). *Present Dangers: Crisis and Opportunity in American Foreign and Defense Policy.* San Francisco, CA: Encounter Books, 2000.

Klare, Michael T. "Michael Klare on Iraq's Missing Sea of Oil." (A Project of the Nation Institute). *TomDispath.com.* September 30, 2005

Kumins, Lawrence. "Iraqi Oil: Reserves, Production, and Potential Resources." *CRS Report for Congress.* Washington, DC: Congressional Research Service, April 13, 2005.

Lewis, Charles and Mark Reading-Smith. "False Pretenses: Iraq: The War Card." Washington DC: Center for Public Integrity, 2008.

McCain, John. "An Enduring Peace Built on Freedom." *Foreign Affairs* 86, 6 (November/December 2007), 2–18.

McMaster, H. R. *Dereliction of Duty: Lyndon Johnson, Robert McNamara, The Joint Chiefs of Staff, and the Lies That Led to Vietnam.* New York: Harper Perennials, 1997.

Morgan, Dan, and David B. Ottoway. "In Iraq War Scenario, Oil Is Key Issue." *Washington Post,* September 15, 2002. A01.

Mueller, John. "The Iraq Syndrome." *Foreign Affairs* 85, 6 (November/December 2006), 44–54.

"Oil and Corruption in Iraq Part III: Kurdistan's Gushing Crude Spawns Conflict." *Environmental News Service* (online), September 12, 2007. (http://www.ens-newswire.com/ens/Spe2007/2007-07-12-01.asp)

Packer, George. *The Assassin's Gate: America in Iraq.* New York: Farrar, Straus, and Giroux. 2005.

Paul, James A. "Oil in Iraq: The Heart of the Crisis." *Global Policy Forum, December 2002.*

Pillar, Paul. "Intelligence, Policy, and the War in Iraq." *Foreign Affairs* 85, 2 (March/April 2006), 15–28.

Pitt, William Rivers, and Scott Ritter. *War on Iraq: What Team Bush Doesn't Want You to Know.* New York: Context Books, 2003.

Rayburn, Joel. "The Last Exit from Iraq." *Foreign Affairs* 85, 2 (March/April 2006), 29–39.

Record, Jeffrey. *Dark Victory: America's Second War Against Iraq.* Annapolis, MD: Naval Institute Press, 2004.

Ricks, Thomas E. *Fiasco: The American Military Adventure in Iraq.* New York: Penguin Press, 2006.

Rosen, Nir. "The Death of Iraq." *Current History* 106, 704 (December 2007), 409–413.

Weissman, Robert. "Greenspan, Kissinger: Oil Drives U.S. in Iraq, Iran." *Common Dreams News Center*, September 17, 2007 (http://www.common dreams.org/archive/2007.09/17/3910)

Yingling, Lt. Colonel Paul. "A Failure in Generalship." *Armed Force Journal* (online), May 2007.

Zinni, General Tony. "They Screwed Up." *CBS Interview with General Anthony Zinni* (online). May 21, 2004. (http://www.cbsnews.com/stories/2004/05/21/60minutes/printable618896.shtml)

Chapter 6

Repairing American Military Power

One institution endangered by the Iraq war, ironically enough, has been the U.S. military. The irony is that the United States entered the war with what was generally considered the most capable, professional armed force in the world, comparable to the legions of Rome, and it continues to perform admirably, in the eyes of its own leadership and nearly all Americans. Yet, in the words of Admiral Michael G. Mullen, chairman of the Joint Chiefs of Staff in an October 25, 2007, interview (quoted in Baker), "It's not broken, but it's breaking."

The reason is the Iraq War. It has been exactly the kind of war for which the U.S. armed forces, based on the All-Volunteer Force (AVF) concept, is the least suited. For one thing, the AVF is organized around the idea of a compact, professional force. It is a highly compact and efficient force, but it is compact, and military occupations require large armies. It is also a force designed primarily to fight conventional, symmetrical warfare, not the asymmetrical opponent it has faced in Iraq. The numbers game has meant stressful repeat deployments; occupation in the face of irregular enemy warriors has added to the stress. Iraq was not what those who constructed the American armed forces had in mind. Whether they should have is a different point; Rome, after all, was eventually worn down by what is now called asymmetrical warfare on the peripheries of its empire.

As a result, when the Iraq War finally winds to an end, one of the most important and potentially traumatic residual problems facing the United States will be rebuilding the armed forces, and in no area will that need be greater than military manpower. It has become commonplace in recent years to observe that the U.S. military has been stretched to the limits by the demands of this war, and the clearest example of this truism is its application to military manpower. The forces of the United States have been used—and some would say abused—to the point of near dysfunction by the requisites of fighting a war where there was hardly any reservoir of fresh manpower to replace or replenish existing active duty or reserve component soldiers, sailors, marines, and airmen. As a result, tours have been extended, multiple deployments have been endured, and service members have been kept involuntarily in uniform or on duty beyond the terms for which they had originally enlisted.

The question the American military must face is what happens to that force after the war is over. Not all troops will come home, if projections about forces remaining either in garrison duty inside bases in Iraq, or over the horizon in neighboring countries, are accurate—which they almost certainly are (see Chapter 7). No one knows how many soldiers and marines will remain in the Middle East, but it will be a significant number. But what will happen to the rest of the force?

The problem is the danger, even likelihood, that large numbers of those who return and cannot be kept involuntarily under arms on the basis of national security (called "stop loss") requirements will elect to leave the service at the first opportunity. Indeed, some who have been extended against their will most likely request immediate separation from the service. Will there be ready replacements—new highly qualified recruits—to fill the ranks? In addition, one of the apparent military lessons of the occupation is that the United States needs a larger army and Marine Corps for the future. Where will these additional soldiers and marines come from?

The problem that lies ahead is largely unprecedented for the United States. Before the Cold War, the United States kept only small armed forces during peacetime, recruited voluntarily and involuntarily. At the threat of war, a built-up fighting force was trained, but then rapidly demobilized after the war was over. World War II was the last war in which the United States used this model.

The Cold War, and especially the Korean conflict, invalidated that model. In 1945, with the end of World War II, the United States had demobilized (going from an armed force of over 12 million to less than one million in less than a year). When North Korea attacked South Korea (the Republic of Korea, or ROK) on June 26, 1950, the standing, active duty American army was inadequate for a sustained defense of the ROK. Fortunately, there were enough World War II veterans still in the reserves who could be activated to provide a stopgap and to stabilize the situation. But would such an option be available in the future?

As planners looked at the Cold War after Korea, they operated from two new assumptions about future wars. One was that war could break out anytime, virtually without warning, and forces would have to be available to meet such contingencies. Moreover, the technology of major war had become so violent that it was further believed that wars would be fought very rapidly, as both Cold War enemies engaged in an orgy of enormous destruction that would leave both exhausted, and in which the winner might well be simply whichever side had anything left after the onslaught. Thus, *large* forces—called "forces-in-being"—were necessary for this military prospect. In these changing assessments was born the requirement for large standing armed forces in peacetime, a first in American military history. These forces combined volunteers and conscripts (draftees), but since the pre-Vietnam draftees (Elvis Presley may have been the most famous) never had to go to war, the draft was acceptable.

The Vietnam War broke the mold. The initial fighting in that war was by the professional U.S. Army and Marines—mostly volunteers or original draftees who found they enjoyed service and stayed in the service—but once they had served initial tours in Vietnam, their replacements were mostly draftees. As the fighting wore on and became increasingly unpopular, the draft became a political albatross that accentuated the unpopularity of the war. To quiet some of the opposition, the draft was suspended on January 1, 1973. The All-Volunteer Force (AVF), the underlying principles of which guide military manpower recruitment and retention to this day, replaced it.

The history of the AVF has somewhat mixed reviews. In the years immediately after Vietnam, it was not an enormous success. Part of the Vietnam hangover was a reluctance to join or have anything to do with the armed forces (a possible harbinger for the post-Iraq period, as examined in this chapter). In that circumstance, the only way the armed forces could meet manpower quotas was to relax standards for accession, a practice that has been reprised in Iraq. The unfortunate result was an armed force of lesser quality than most Americans would have preferred. The good news was that during the remainder of the 1970s and early 1980s that force was not put to any major tests that it might have failed. By the mid-1980s, public attitude toward the military had improved, better and more recruits were donning uniforms, and the issue of quality receded and nearly disappeared. By the beginning of the 1990s, a high-quality U.S. armed force that was a source of national pride had emerged.

There was a further legacy of Vietnam that affected the U.S. military, the so-called Abrams reforms, named after Army General Creighton Abrams. One of the lessons of Vietnam for the armed forces was that the American public had turned against the military, breaking the famous Clausewitzian trinity of support between the people, the army, and the government. In evaluating Vietnam, army leaders decided the reason for this rupture was the failure to gain a public commitment to the war at the beginning. Since wars were no longer declared (the act of which forced such a commitment), the army would have to look for a different way to get the public to voice its support, or opposition. Their solution was to incorporate the reserves into war planning; any future large-scale military action would necessitate activation of reserves, now cast in vital roles, without whom war could not be sustained. The result would be to force Americans to see their neighbors called to duty, and to voice their approval or disapproval. Reserves had not been called up since the Korean conflict, and were first activated for the Persian Gulf War of 1990–1991. That experience seemed to vindicate the concept, but the war was over so rapidly that it did not provide an adequate precedent for a long engagement, such as Iraq.

The end of the Cold War introduced another change. With the communist threat evaporated, the United States no longer had any major opponent that posed the same kind of threat the Cold War military faced. As a result, there was no compelling need for such large standing forces, and the result was a downsizing of the force (sometimes described oxymoronically as "negative growth"). This reduction in size was accompanied by budgetary constrictions initiated by President George H. W. Bush and continued by his successor, William J. Clinton that began, according to Kagan, the beginning of the current "crisis" (Kagan's term) in the AVF.

The AVF at the turn of the millennium would thus be a smaller force as well, and Secretary Rumsfeld's reforms (discussed below) reinforced this trend by adding the idea that future wars would be won by smaller, more mobile, and more lethal forces than had fought in the past. The invasion and conquest phase of the Iraq War was the first application of the Rumsfeld imprint and, because of its apparent initial success, seemed to vindicate this principle.

All of these influences came together in the Iraq War, and have produced the current dilemma for American force planners. None of the problems, it should be noted, would have been severe had the original conception of the war occurred: the brief, overwhelming victory followed by rapid disengagement. Had Rumsfeld's projection that most American forces would be repatriated within 129 days of the invasion been true, none of the negative effects would have been experienced—no long tours, no frequent, forced redeployments, and the like. In that case, the model of Operation Desert Shield/ Desert Storm (the Persian Gulf War) would have applied. That was, of course, not what happened, and the war instead came to resemble Vietnam, at least terms of in its length and the degree of frustration surrounding it. But the Vietnam analogy does not hold in the case of manpower, since up to 1972, conscription produced a steady stream of replacements for the armed forces in Vietnam. There has been no equivalent source of manpower in Iraq.

Three factors from the past have defined the Iraq War predicament and thus its postwar resolution. The end of the Cold War meant that the force available to fight American wars would be considerably smaller than it had been in the past. This smaller size decreased military flexibility, particularly during the long occupation, because it placed constraints on the ability of the armed forces to rotate service members in and out of the country on desirable schedules, keeping a rested force with high morale on the ground. There simply were not enough forces available. One solution was to form the coalition in the hopes of augmenting American forces, but the results have been sparse, with only Great Britain providing sizable forces to support the effort (and those began withdrawing after Tony Blair stepped down as Prime Minister in 2007). The result is the ongoing problem of deployments and the privations associated with them.

The Abrams reforms specified that the national guard and reserves would be part of the military force on extended duty, since a number of vital military tasks are entrusted in part or in whole to reserves. The result has been particularly perverse. The Abrams principle was that reserve activation would signal levels of support for war, and the initial response was gratifying, as reserves were activated virtually without complaint. The perversity is that the reformers had not anticipated lengthy reserve activations like Iraq, and the activation itself became the basis of dissatisfaction with the war. Reservists who have been called for multiple deployments did not, by and large, sign up for that kind of duty and have reacted angrily to it. The hemorrhaging of the military that will likely accompany the end of the war could be particularly acute among current reservists, who will be reluctant to reenlist for fear of a future reprise, and for future recruits, who will be wary about what might happen to them.

The end of the draft has exacerbated the problem, in two almost independent ways. One is that the absence of a draft, and the political recognition that a reinstatement of the draft is highly unlikely, has resulted in very little personalization of the war among the 18- to 24-year olds who are potential armed service members. In the past, the shadow of the draft meant potential draftees had a stake in the outcome of wars, which is simply lacking today; young Americans are no longer motivated to sign up out of patriotic zeal or a sense of service to a noble cause. At the same time, this lack of personal investment undoubtedly has created less opposition to the Iraq

War than would have been the case had Americans been looking down the barrel of a gun at involuntary military service, in a cause for which they had little enthusiasm. This lack of enthusiasm is particularly true of college students. The other problem arising from the end of the draft is that there is no mechanism by which the armed forces can rapidly expand, or even replenish personnel. Neither compulsion nor patriotic appeals will expand the manpower base and relieve the pressure for things like reduced tours or longer periods between deployments, because there is nobody available to take the places of the troops.

The result is the conundrum that the armed forces find themselves facing. In a peculiar sense, the Iraq War has revived the Cold War concept of force-in-being, but in a different context. The all-volunteer force is, like the Cold War force, what is available to fight conflicts like Iraq. During the Cold War, it was assumed that it would take too long to augment that force because of the likely brevity of the unleashed violence that would occur. In Europe, the presumption was a thirty-day war, hardly time to get reinforcements to the scene and clearly not enough time to recruit and train replacements. Thus, the United States would fight with the forces available at the beginning of the war. In Iraq, the force-in-being was the smaller force that had evolved since Vietnam. It was not constrained by the brevity of the conflict but by its length, and its constraint was the inability to expand or replenish it. The dynamics were different, but the effect was largely the same.

This background helps to frame the dilemma that will face the United States in manning the force for the future. The war has made that problem more severe than it might otherwise be. Both recruitment and retention are almost certain to suffer because of the war and its outcome. Potential service members can look at what happened to soldiers, sailors, marines, and airmen in Iraq, and some will conclude that they do not want to take the chance of getting ensnared in a similar spider web. Others will be disgusted at the outcome of the war, will be part of the Iraq hangover, and will avoid military considerations in the same way that their peers did a generation ago. The results were unfortunate after Vietnam. Will the same be true after Iraq?

IRAQ AND MILITARY MANPOWER

An irony of the post-Iraq period may well be that the environment in which the United States finds itself could be more dangerous than it was before the war. As a result, the United States may need the military option more than ever, in order to face a more dangerous world. Yet, the impact of the Iraq War threatens to result in a diminished military capability for the United States, as Americans reject military options as reprises of what they view as the errant involvement in Iraq. According to many, the Iraq War itself has contributed to this greater danger by roiling political conditions (and especially anti-Americanism) in the Middle East. What can be done in these circumstances?

Military Transformation and Iraq

The impact of the Iraq War on the American military and perceptions about the military have been stunning. American military strength distanced itself from the military power of other countries during the 1990s. Although the United States was reducing commitments to defense, other countries were cutting their forces even more. It was common to refer to the United States as the remaining superpower in military and political terms. Indeed, there were even guarded comparisons of American military with the power of Rome during the glory days of its empire. The perception was widespread within the United States and elsewhere that the American military machine was a juggernaut that could not be defeated, and which would be foolhardy to confront.

The myth of an omnipotent United States was first called into dramatic question by the terrorist attacks of 9/11, which punctured the idea of America's invulnerability. The subsequent experience in Iraq has only reinforced this perception, as a reasonably disorganized and small group of insurgents has effectively tied down the American military machine for almost five years. The United States not only has been unable to end the insurgency with its armed might, it is committed in Iraq to the point that it could only confront another major threat in the world by dismantling and relocating many of its forces out of Iraq . How did this happen?

The answer lies in the point of distinction between conventional (or symmetrical) warfare and unconventional (or asymmetrical) warfare, and the two phases of the military effort in Iraq—the invasion and conquest and the occupation phases. The United States military was built (and under Rumsfeld's reforms was honed) for one kind of warfare, but not for the other. Its unpreparedness for military occupation has resulted in the prolongation of the war and the crisis of military manpower in the United States.

The debate over what kind of military force the United States should feature goes back at least to the post-Vietnam period. It is not an either-or proposition. The question is not whether the United States should have a conventional armed force *or* an unconventional force, but the relative extent to which it should feature one or the other. The debate goes back to what kind of war Vietnam was. Was it a conventional, European-style war involving the clash of two conventionally organized and equipped armies (the NVA versus the U.S. Army and the ARVN), or an unconventional, guerrilla, or what is now called asymmetrical war? The army, and its chief apologists like Harry Summers, preferred to see it as a conventional war; others, notably the U.S. Marines, saw it more in unconventional terms. In the period between Vietnam and Iraq a debate raged within the American military establishment first about Vietnam, and then about the kind of army the United States would need in the future. Within the armed forces, the terms of the debate tilted toward the supporters of conventional war, reflecting a historic doctrinal belief in the efficacy and preference for that style of war. The successful outcome of the Persian Gulf War helped tilt the debate decisively toward the conventional warriors, although believers in unconventional war like David Petraeus did not give up the fight.

The force that the United States possessed at the turn of the millennium, and the force available when the decision was made to attack Iraq reflect this debate. Rumsfeld's famous statement that "one fights wars with the force one has rather than the force one wants," is somewhat disingenuous, because the Rumsfeld reform process had been in progress for nearly two years before the invasion began. It was, however, a force better suited for the invasion and conquest phase than for the subsequent occupation phase.

Rumsfeld argued the requisites for the twenty-first century U.S. military in terms of transformation in a 2002 *Foreign Affairs* article. In 2001, he had ordered the creation of an Office of Transformation in the Pentagon to oversee the process of changing the military to conform to his vision. At the heart of his formulation was the need for flexibility and adaptation of forces. In the *Foreign Affairs* article, he argues, "Preparing for the future will require new ways of thinking, and the development of forces and capabilities that can adapt quickly to new challenges and unexpected circumstances." In Rumsfeld's mind, this meant forces that were highly mobile and highly lethal—incorporating new and deadlier weapons technologies arising from the "revolution in military affairs" (RMA, the incorporation of advanced scientific principles into military applications), but smaller and lighter than traditional conventional or "heavy" forces (for a discussion, *see* Snow, *National Security for a New Era*). The penultimate illustration of this new armed force was the "shock and awe" campaign incorporated into the guiding principles of the invasion of Iraq: The United States would act with such overwhelming, rapidly moving force that the enemy would be so discombobulated it would be paralyzed into inaction and would capitulate in a confused, shell-shocked state.

The heart of the Rumsfeld approach was a modern form of *blitzkrieg* (German for "lightning war"), where the objective is not so much to confront and slug it out with an opposing force as it is to dazzle and confuse it into submission. Relying on rapid movement and overwhelming firepower, it was a less manpower-intensive approach to warfare than the traditional U.S. Army approach, which suggested defeating enemy armed forces in direct battle. As such, it also was less manpower-intensive than traditional approaches to conventional warfare, and Rumsfeld insisted that the war could be fought with much smaller forces than the generals, who were steeped in more traditional approaches (and anticipating a post-combat phase), preferred. In the planning stages for the war, there was a great deal of well-chronicled dissension over the size of the force needed for the war (*see* Gordon and Trainor, and Ricks for examples), but Rumsfeld prevailed, finding in General Franks a commander who would accept the force size of his preferences, and the United States invaded Iraq with a force of no more than 150,000 (after second and third echelon reinforcement troops entered the country), rather than the 250–300,000 troops the armed forces, notably the army and marines, preferred. It is interesting, and probably important, that the Chairman of the Joint Chiefs of Staff during this period was General Richard Meyers, an Air Force officer.

Forces and the Iraq Mission

The force that invaded and conquered Iraq was appropriate for that task. As Rumsfeld had correctly predicted, the conquest went quickly and smoothly, with, as mentioned earlier, only some early signs of unconventional resistance that would congeal later. A force of 150,000 did not, moreover, stress to the limits the capacities of the combined army and marines, which had a combined size of around 700,000 at the time of the invasion. As long as the involvement was over quickly, a reasonable rotation policy that did not overly strain the force could be implemented, and all the problems of multiple tours and the like could be avoided. If the end of active combat operations declared by Bush in May 2003 and the end of the war had coincided, there would have been no manpower stress, as the vast bulk of those forces would have come marching home after the magic 129 days of deployment.

Reality, in the form of the requisites of the occupation, mugged these assumptions. Occupying Iraq, a country roughly the size of Texas, with 150,000 troops, proved much more difficult than the rosy estimates would have it. Part of the problem was the actual combat size of the force. Modern armies are, after all, complex organizations, and it requires an elaborate, manpower-intensive effort to support an army in the field. Indeed, the "tooth to tail" ratio of modern armies often approaches seven or eight support personnel for every combat soldier, meaning the actual fighting force in Iraq—the soldiers and marines available to enforce the peace in the occupation—was more like 20,000 rather than 150,000. These forces, of course, were augmented by nearly 100,000 civilian contractors, including about 20,000 armed personnel who performed some of the functions soldiers and marines otherwise would have been forced to perform (e.g., serving as bodyguards for CPA personnel), but their use has been controversial, as discussed later in the chapter.

A conventional force of limited size may have been adequate for the invasion and conquest phase of the war, but it has proven patently inadequate for a prolonged occupation for which the top decision makers neither anticipated nor planned. A force of 20,000 combat soldiers, even augmented by private contractors, has proven too small to pacify Iraq. The occupation has been opposed by the various elements of the Iraqi resistance and is a complex task, since there are several independent elements of this asymmetrical threat, some of which are communal and are engaged in inter-communal or inter-ethnic warfare, and some of which oppose the American presence (most prominently the Al Qaeda in Iraq forces that the American presence helped create by its very presence). In this swirling instability, the task of pacification requires not only clearing hotbeds of resistance, but also remaining in place to assure the combatants do not return when the occupiers leave.

Even augmented by the 30,000 troops of the surge, most of whom are combat forces, the forces available to the United States are far short of this need, and this leaves three options, none of which solves the problem. 1) The United States can sweep through hotbeds of resistance, attack and disable the opposition, and then move on to other places; the problem is that once the Americans leave, the insurgents return (in accordance to their doctrine discussed in Chapter 4). 2) The United States can enter selected areas, liberate those areas, and then stay and pacify these regions; the problem is that doing so leaves too many vulnerable places elsewhere in the country. Or 3) the United States can do the liberating and turn the pacified areas over to Iraqi forces. The latter is, of course, the ultimate goal of Iraqification, but since local forces are often more loyal to their communal base than to Iraq, they are ineffective against their co-religionists and repressive of other groups—a kind of fox in the henhouse problem.

The Effects on Manpower

It is, however, the manpower aspects of the occupation that are of current concern. With regard to that problem, it does not really matter that the occupation was unanticipated, in the sense that those requirements would have been roughly the same whether planned for or not. What might have made a difference was feasibility planning for the entire operation. Manpower strains were not, based on the publicly available evidence, much of a concern in deciding whether to invade Iraq because, as noted, it was anticipated that the war would be over too fast for strains to appear: the model of the Persian Gulf War, not Vietnam. The possibility of a long and protracted deployment may have been anticipated and rejected as unlikely or politically explosive: Would the American public have supported a five-year effort had they been told in advance that was the likely consequence of invasion? Moreover, planners had to know they were constrained in that they could not readily expand the force if exigency suggested the need to do so. The options were to fight with what was available (and maintain that configuration for the duration) or to reject the idea of invasion because of its negative manpower consequences. The decision was to employ the available force. The consequences have been manifest.

The size of the American armed forces at the time of the invasion and since has proven more constraining than those who described the American military colossus ever envisaged. Between the end of the Cold War and the present, the armed forces of the United States have shrunk by about one-third. In 1987, the force still stood at about 2.15 million in active duty strength, with about another million in the guard and reserves, and about an equal number of civilians. This included an army of around 800,000 and a Marine Corps in the vicinity of 225,000 active duty personnel. According to Department of Defense figures, the equivalent sizes for October 31, 2007, were an army of 522,388 active duty and a Marine Corps of 186,209, a total of slightly over 700,000 compared to the Cold War force of over one million. The extra 300,000 or so soldiers and sailors would make an enormous difference in both filling out the occupation force so it could physically remain in many more places (thereby increasing pacification), and in maintaining a rotation policy that would reduce and shorten both the frequency and length of tours in the Iraqi theater. It might also leave additional residual forces in reserve in the event of a major crisis somewhere else in the world, a contingency for which the United States currently has essentially no manpower capability, without removing troops from Iraq.

No one, of course, advocates a return to either the structure or size of the Cold War force, which was designed for a quantitatively and qualitatively different environment than that which confronts the contemporary military. The problem is not even that the size of the military was cut back too far, because such an assertion begs the question, "Too far for what?" In the national security euphoria of the 1990s, rather, planners assumed that the end of the Cold War indeed reduced military problems and thus allowed for reductions that could realize a "peace dividend" that proved an illusion. Military manpower is, after all, a particularly important military expense (Kagan, for instance, suggests the cost of "maintaining one service member on active duty for one year" was $112,000 in 2006), making reductions in the size of the force a reasonable cost-cutting idea. This attraction is further enhanced if one assumes the fruits of the RMA will substitute technological innovation for "muddy boots on the ground" and that the United States will be unlikely to encounter major manpower-intensive military actions in the future that might tie down the force that exists.

The Iraq occupation has invalidated this reasoning. Occupations require manpower, for which there is no ready substitute. Military "action" campaigns—the invasion and conquest phase of the Iraq War—can take advantage of the RMA in terms of applying technological advances for tasks like identifying and destroying enemy troop concentrations and other military targets. These advances do not, however, apply equally to the difficult tasks of occupation. Kagan states the case: "Military occupation and crowd control will remain human endeavors and will be less amenable to technological enhancement than any other aspect of war." As an example, he argues that RMA technologies may be useful and efficient for identifying and calling in air strikes to destroy a crowd, but that it takes many soldiers to control rather than kill the members of that crowd.

The simple fact is that those who planned the modern American military and its manpower did not plan adequately, if at all, for a major military occupation as part of the missions for which the force would be employed in the future. As Kagan explains the dictates of occupation, "The size of the ground force needed to control conquered territory is determined by the size of that territory, the density of its population, and the nature and size of the resistance." Iraq is a tough nut to crack on all of those criteria: Its territory is certainly not inconsequential, its population, especially in the Baghdad area, is large, and the extremely diverse nature of the resistance makes it impossible to isolate its critical elements for elimination. There is no single center of gravity in Iraq to attack.

Moreover, the ultimate "success" of the occupier depends on the restoration of some kind of order with which both the occupier and the occupied population can live. The conditions must be acceptable to the occupier so that it can claim the occupation has achieved the political objectives of the military action. The conditions must satisfy the occupied population, because they will have to live with its consequences. The problem is reconciling these two images of acceptable conditions where they conflict (and if they did not conflict, there would be no need for the military action in the first place). That process may be impossible; the sets of acceptable conditions for the two sides may be irreconcilable. Or, compromise might be possible. The outcome of that process is, however, political, not military. The two (or more, in the case of Iraq) sides must agree on the outcome, it cannot be imposed by force if it is to endure.

The occupation can only contribute indirectly to this dynamic. At its best, that contribution consists of calming the physical violence to the point that negotiations can proceed in a less emotional, less confrontational environment than an open state of insurgency. Occupying forces can, in other words, provide the shield behind which political processes can occur. But that is essentially all that the occupation can accomplish, and to ask more of it, as has been the case with the surge in Iraq, is to ask military occupiers to perform tasks beyond their capacities. The idea that the surge is somehow "winning" the war represents an unobtainable expectation, asking soldiers to do what soldiers cannot be expected to do. The surge will be a "success" if it materially strengthens the shield behind which the politicians act. It cannot substitute for those actions.

The results are by now manifest, despite claims surrounding the surge. General Barry McCaffrey, quoted in Kagan, says it succinctly, "the wheels are coming off" the military as the occupation extends into the future. The symptoms are easy to identify: combat tours that have gone from six months to a year and even to 15 months recently, for instance. When Senator James Webb of Virginia proposed a rotation policy in 2007 that would require one day of non-combat duty for each day exposed to combat, the idea was dismissed as impractical. Reenlistment rates have remained fairly high, but first-time enlistments are down, especially in the guard and reserves. There is a particular hemorrhage at the level of lieutenants and captains in the army, and it is not clear how much more bleeding will occur once the stop-loss program is rescinded. Libertarian and anti-war Republican candidate Ron Paul could even claim in late 2007 he was receiving more campaign contributions from active duty military than any other candidate, due to his strong commitment to ending the war and bringing the troops home.

There is another aspect of the manpower crisis that is less often discussed. The United States armed forces have been thrust into a mission for which they were not designed, and the effect has been to reduce what was less than a decade ago referred to as a "military colossus" to a much more reduced status. It is a simple fact that with the bulk of American ground forces committed to occupation duty in Iraq, the United States lacks the ability to engage in a major ground action anywhere else in the world without stripping forces out of Iraq. Occupation duty in Iraq has become quicksand for the greatest military force since the Roman legions. If a crisis breaks out somewhere else in the world engaging American vital interests that cannot be solved by airpower (bombardment), the United States is hard put to respond.

There is another implication of the predicament. There is a lesson in Iraq for other possible enemies of the United States who might have previously felt impotent in the face of American power. One-on-one, the American soldier may remain someone to be feared, but the Iraqi resistance has shown that it is possible to stalemate the military advantage the United States possesses. The lesson is clear: It may not be possible to defeat the Americans, but it may be possible to neutralize them. Supporters of the war have already seized on this prospect. When Senator McCain argues that the failure to defeat the insurgents in Iraq will lead to the belief that the world "is going their way and that anything is possible," he is admitting that they have already largely succeeded. The next opponents with whom the United States faces off are likely to oppose the Americans with variants of what has worked in Iraq, and continuing the war simply reinforces the desirability of that strategy. Even if the United States could totally destroy all elements of the resistance tomorrow, would outsiders not conclude that the resistance had been a success, holding the mighty American military at bay for that long? Would they not conclude further that the United States would be very reluctant to start another enormously expensive military adventure that would last over five years? As long as the American military continues to look the way it does today, it is hard to argue that this will not be the conclusion any future opponents will have learned.

FIXING THE POST-IRAQ MILITARY

No one denies that the American armed forces will require considerable rebuilding after the Iraq War is over, or that the military manpower problem will be at or near the top of the list of items to be fixed. In January 2007, for instance, President Bush called for an increase of 92,000 members of the

American ground forces (27,000 new Marines, 65,000 new soldiers), and others have suggested the need for larger forces as well (Kagan, for instance, favors an increase of 100–200,000, including active duty and reserve components). In addition, the major candidates have weighed in on the subject of future manpower, although with different levels of specificity.

Unsurprisingly, all the major candidates favor increasing the strength of the post-Iraq military. The Democrats tend to be less specific. Hillary Clinton, for instance, simply wrote in her *Foreign Affairs* article, "I will work to expand and modernize the military." John Edwards was similarly vague, stating, "The force structure of our military should match its mission." Only Barack Obama offered specific numbers, adopting President Bush's goal of 65,000 soldiers and 27,000 Marines.

The Republican candidates are more specific when it comes to increased manpower as part of the post-Iraq equation. Rudolph Giuliani, while still a candidate, stated, "The U.S. Army needs a minimum of ten new combat brigades." The Army defines a brigade as 3–5,000 troops, with 3,500 as a kind of average figure. The others propound larger increases: McCain called for the largest growth, "from the currently planned level of 750,000 to 900,000 troops." Romney, on the other hand, advocated "adding at least 100,000 troops." Former Arkansas Governor Mike Huckabee did not list numerical increases on his web page. Rather, he stated that "our current armed forces aren't large enough," and that he proposed an increase in defense spending from the current 3.9 percent of gross domestic product (GDP) to 6 percent (the percentage of GDP spent on defense by President Reagan).

None of the candidates, or others, has suggested very specifically the source of these increases: Where are they going to come from? If recruitment levels are difficult to maintain today because of recruitment problems and these problems are likely to worsen when the end of stop-loss has an impact on retention, where are all these "extra" military personnel supposed to be found? Moreover, it is not clear from the candidates the purposes for which these additional forces are needed, and to which they will be assigned. Presumably, no one is going to propose that they be trained and prepared for occupation duty somewhere other than Iraq, and if not that, then for what will they be prepared? Will some stay in Iraq? Simply saying that more troops are needed does not answer all the relevant questions.

Unless the United States adopts the unlikely policy of reducing military manpower after the Iraq War ends, the problem of maintaining current or expanded levels of manpower will arise. Clearly, the problem is more difficult the larger the force is projected to be, and the difficulty is also affected by other variables. Two of the most prominent of these variables are the state of the American economy and the perceived level of threat to the country. The economy is a factor because the 18- to 24-year olds who are a staple of military manpower are generally at the bottom of the employment scale, and their ability to get desirable jobs, or any jobs at all, is affected by the robustness of the economy, and thus the extent that the job market (along with higher education) competes for the services of the target population. Generally speaking, the stronger the economy, the more recruitment difficulties the military experiences; conversely, a weak economy benefits military recruiters by narrowing the options for 18- to 24-year olds. An enhanced threat presumably contributes to more patriotic incentive to join the military than does a reduced perception of threat.

The military manpower problem facing the post-Iraq military will be exacerbated by Iraq hangover, and it will have an impact in two ways. One will be a reluctance to sign up, or reenlist, based on the likelihood of being placed in the same situation as Iraqi veterans. This is particularly true in the reserves. Active duty soldiers and marines knew they might be getting themselves into wars when they enlisted, but reservists are more likely not to have anticipated the demands that have been made of them. It will be difficult to convince potential reservists that they will not face the same surprises and privations that current reservists have faced. The other impact is likely to be a general reluctance to engage in military actions, for fear they will turn into a reprise of Iraq. There will, of course, be attempts to maintain the perception of a highly hostile environment through the war on terror, but the public will be more skeptical of those appeals due to the Iraq experience than they were previously.

The problem of military manpower is really two problems: recruitment and retention. Recruitment refers to the process by which current non-members of the military service are enticed into becoming members. Retention, on the other hand, refers to the process by which current members are convinced to reenlist for periods beyond their initial enlistment. The two processes are, of course, related. The goal of the manpower system is to produce a force the size of which is determined by Congress. The recruitment problem is the numerical difference between the authorized goal and the number of current members. The more members who are retained for service, the larger the current number is, and thus the fewer new members are needed. Conversely, the less who "re-up" (reenlist), the more new members must be recruited to take their places.

Maintaining or increasing the size of the armed forces will be difficult. The current economic downturn in the United States may help inflate the numbers of new recruits driven into the services by economic necessity, and some current members may be convinced that staying in avoids entrance into a hazardous economy. Nonetheless, there will be a problem. There are essentially three ways in which this problem can be addressed: Through continuation and enhancement of the current all-volunteer system; through a reinstatement of some form of conscription to compensate for shortfalls in voluntary enlistment; and through the use of private security forces to augment the regular military. Conscription, of course, has not been used in the United States since the Vietnam War, and the use of private firms has become controversial due to the alleged difficulties with the Blackwater security firm.

The attractiveness of the options varies greatly. The AVF is by far the preferred option. Continuing the AVF concept is both the preferred and least politically painful option, and it is the option most preferred by the military itself. Hardly anyone actively advocates a return to conscription, although it is the method that can most readily provide manpower at whatever levels are required. Privatization provides an avenue for recruiting additional personnel, but its use has been tainted by the Blackwater experience in Iraq. Although continuing—or enhancing—the AVF is clearly the preferred option, the Iraq experience raises the question of whether it will prove adequate for attracting and maintaining adequate manpower in a demanding future, or whether other, less desirable, options will have to be explored in the post-Iraq environment.

The All-Volunteer Option

Since its inception on January 1, 1973, the All-Volunteer Force (AVF) has been the overwhelmingly popular method for providing personnel for the armed forces. The concept took most of the 1970s to begin producing the kind and quality of force that the armed forces (principally the army, for which recruitment and retention is the biggest problem) desired, because the Vietnam hangover made military service seem unattractive to many young Americans. This, of course, may be a factor as the military faces the post-Iraq environment as well.

Both the Army and politicians prefer the AVF concept to the alternatives. The Army likes it. It provides an alternative to the draft, with which the armed forces became very disillusioned during the Vietnam War. Admiral Michael G. Mullen, the current chairman of the Joint Chiefs of Staff, in a "town hall" session with army officers (reported by Baker), said recently, "I watched the military break apart. . . . To the best of my ability, I'm never going to let that happen. I was there, so I know; I understand the quality that we had back then." The complaints about soldiers in a largely conscript Vietnam force as that the war evolved centered on discipline and the willingness to obey orders, particularly when they involved combat. By contrast, the AVF produces a superior force. As Mullen puts it, "The quality, the professional level of our armed forces right now, every single branch . . . is so exceptionally high, and it's that which I believe we have to preserve." Moreover, as cited earlier, advocates argue that the force has, despite the high cost of maintaining individual soldiers, been affordable in economic terms. Summarizing the case for the AVF, Mullen states, "This is the best military I think this nation has ever had. I'm old enough to remember when we were a draft force, and I am not anxious to return to that."

Politicians also like the AVF. First and foremost among its attractions is that it is not the draft. The army favored moving to an all-volunteer, professional force because it would improve the quality of service members that it attracted: People would wear the uniform because they wanted to, rather than as a result of compulsion that left them sullen and uncooperative. The main, underlying reason the draft was eliminated (and why it will almost certainly not return, as discussed below) is that the draft had become politically unpopular. Compulsory service in Vietnam, where thousands of American draftees were being killed in what many viewed a pointless war, sealed the fate of the draft.

To suggest reinstating the draft has become political suicide, and the AVF provides a politically painless alternative, because no constituent who might retaliate at the polls is personally conscripted, or has loved ones conscripted. While the AVF is more expensive than a draftee-based armed force, there are compensations. Draftees cost less to maintain (they do not have to be paid competitively), but they turn over more rapidly, raising training costs. Avoiding the political headaches of a conscription system, however, more than compensates for the added costs. Moreover, the AVF has performed adequately, even admirably, for over three decades and has performed well in Iraq.

Nonetheless, the system is "breaking," in Admiral Mullen's words, as quoted at the beginning of the chapter. At the outset, two factors were identified as the sources of current angst in the armed forces. One of these was fighting the kind of asymmetrical war the AVF was not designed to fight, but that has arguably been remedied by experience and the infusion of new leadership in the form of General Petraeus. The other problem, which is at the heart of the current crisis, is the adequacy of manpower. The armed forces needed to be bigger to have fought an Iraq-type war, and the solution many politicians put forward for the future is to increase the size of that force. But how?

The armed forces face problems both in the area of recruitment and retention due to the effects of the Iraq war. Even though retention among active duty service members in Iraq has actually been higher than Pentagon estimates, there is an expected hemorrhage after the war ends and stop-loss is suspended. At the same time, recruitment has become more difficult. This is the direct result of the Iraq War. Parents, for instance, are less likely than before Iraq to recommend military service to their children for fear they will be sent to another Iraq. At the same time, Mullen points out, "The propensity for service is going down. Decision makers, who are dominated by parents and family and coaches and teachers . . . are not as supportive of the military service as they were a few years ago." Moreover, lower birth rates in the 1980s and 1990s mean the cohort group of potential new recruits is contracting, meaning there will be increased competition between the military, the economy, and higher education for the decreased numbers of 18-year olds available.

If the AVF principle is to remain the basis of military manpower acquisition and retention, it must answer the question of how it can produce an adequate size and quality of force. Traditionally, proposals to increase the size of the AVF have come in two categories: incentives for greater recruitment and retention, and a broadening of the recruitment base. The hallmark of the AVF has been the quality of the force it develops, and that emphasis may conflict with measures to attract a larger force.

The incentives approach seeks to attract greater numbers of recruits, and it does so by trying to narrow the gap between military service and the civilian alternatives for the target population. To compete with the marketplace, incentives have included better pay and benefits, greater enlistment and reenlistment bonuses (incrementally better for the less attractive duties—combat soldiers get larger bonuses than computer technicians), shorter terms of enlistment, and better living conditions. While these all provide incentive, they also have limits. First, they are expensive, and add to the general high cost of the AVF. Second, although they can make military service more akin to civilian work, they cannot erase the distinction that military members could face ultimate danger and sacrifice, which most civilian employment does not entail. The services compete with higher education by offering educational benefits for veterans in the hope of enticing young people to defer college by going into the service first. These appeals are most effective among those who cannot afford post-secondary education, adding to the economic divide between service and non-service components of the population.

The other approach is to broaden recruitment. One way to do so is to reach out to specific target groups, such as minority groups and females. Minorities are already overrepresented compared to their proportions in the general population. Women are not: 20 percent of the Air Force is female, 14.9 percent of the Navy, 14 percent of the Army, and 6.2 percent of the Marines are female according to 2007 statistics. The problem is that women are prohibited from direct combat roles by legislation, and while the distinction between combatant and noncombatant roles is blurred in modern warfare, it still restricts the number and kind of jobs for which females can be recruited.

The most controversial forms of broader recruitment open the service to individuals with lower intellectual abilities and to people with criminal records through waivers of existing regulations. Both of these methods have been undertaken in Iraq, although surreptitiously, and both tax the distinction between quantitative and qualitative adequacy of the force. Recruits of lower intellectual capability, generally measured by means such as high school diplomas, reduce the competence of the force to carry out complex tasks. Allowing those with minor criminal records (generally juvenile, nonviolent crimes) could lead to discipline problems. The result may be, in Baker's reporting, "more discipline problems." In either case, the quality of the force might be compromised—however slightly—by attempts to rectify the quantitative problems.

Fixing the AVF is by far the preferred solution politically and militarily, but what if it cannot be accomplished? Three other possibilities exist: a return to some form of conscription; a movement toward greater reliance on privatized forces; or a reconciliation of reduced force size and reduced missions. By stressing the manpower system to the point of breakage, the Iraq experience has made consideration of each of these options necessary.

A Return to Conscription

The selective service system (the draft) has been a political and military pariah since it was suspended at the end of 1972. It had an enigmatic history in the United States. The United States has resorted to the involuntary induction of its residents into military service a total of only thirty-five years of its history. Most of these calls came during wartime: the first large call-up occurred on the Union side of the Civil War, and the largest draft occurred in World War II. The Cold War was the first time in which the draft was regularly used to procure service participation during peacetime, and the selective service system supplied an increasing proportion of service members for the Vietnam effort before it was suspended. Very few want to see it reinstated, and since reactivating the system would require congressional action with presidential concurrence, it is unlikely to occur.

A RAND Corporation study summarizes why the draft was suspended at the end of 1972, and the dynamics largely hold today. Demographically, the population was producing far more eligible young men (women were not included, but might be today) than the system could possibly find military uses for, meaning the system had become *selective* rather than *universal*, which created problems discussed below. The Army, as noted, had become frustrated by quality and disciplinary problems associated with a largely conscript army, and the draft had become a bellwether for opposition to the Vietnam War. In addition, an odd political coalition had come out in opposition to its continuation. Conservatives and libertarians argued the government had no right to impose involuntary service on its citizens, while liberals argued the draft was socially unfair, since members of the lower classes were far more likely to get caught in the draft net than were more affluent Americans.

Much of the criticism surrounded the operation of the selective service system of the time. The basic problem the system faced was excess potential manpower—far more young men turned eighteen (the age of initial eligibility) than the military could possibly absorb, despite unsuccessful calls for alternate forms of national service that could absorb more of the eligible population. The consequence was that the system was indeed selective: some were chosen for service, and others were not. This in turn created a dual problem. One was what can be called *equity of vulnerability:* what parts of the eligible population were put in the potential manpower pool. Since all males were required to register with the selective service board on their eighteenth birthdays, this aspect of the system was universal and thus, equitable.

The problem was that only some would have to serve, creating the problem of *equity of sacrifice.* Since the military only had use (even during Vietnam) for a portion of those eligible, some would be forced to serve and sacrifice, while others would not. The equity problem arose in how these selections were made. The most controversial method was deferment—otherwise eligible potential service members could have their service delayed, in some cases until beyond the age where they were eligible to be drafted, for a variety of reasons, including higher education, marital or parental status, and occupation. Some professions were declared vital to the national security and thus excluded. For a time, even college professors fell under this protection. The deferment system became notorious because it provided a shield for the middle and upper-middle classes who possessed financial and other resources to take advantage of its provisions. Proposals for a renewed conscription option generally call for rescinding any deferments as a way to deal with the inequities inherent in the old system, but they cannot remove the problem of equity of sacrifice entirely, since some would still have to serve while others will not. In fact, the selection process would be more difficult in one respect, since women would be included in a renewed system, thereby essentially doubling the pool while not increasing the combat manpower needed.

Advocates of a renewed draft argue at least three reasons for reinstatement. One is to rekindle a sense of duty among young Americans, especially among the middle and upper-middle classes who are hardly represented at all in the current armed forces. The idea is that vulnerability would make those not currently affected think more seriously about the prospects of service. Related to this is the idea that a draft would create a more socially representative force than the country has today, particularly if deferments were eliminated. This virtue of the draft has primarily been championed by Representative Charles Rangel, D-NY, who is probably the most outspoken public advocate of returning to conscription. Finally, the draft is defended as providing a cheap and ready supply of manpower, since new conscripts who are both plentiful and reasonably inexpensive, do not have to be paid competitive wages, and can replenish any shortfalls in force size. The result is that the country can have any sized armed force it feels it needs at any time, and many of the problems of troop rotation associated with Iraq could readily be addressed.

Despite these arguments, the draft is unlikely to be reinstated. In many ways, conscription is the reverse side of the AVF, and arguments against the draft and for the AVF tend to coincide. From a military vantage point, because of the Vietnam experience, the military institution overwhelmingly opposes a return to the draft. The Army, which is the service into which nearly all conscripts would be drafted, likes the quality of force the AVF has produced, and would bristle at the idea of dealing with conscripts who would create problems in Iraq reminiscent of the Vietnam draft army (disciplinary problems, for instance).

More fundamentally, however, the draft is political poison. One of the principal appeals of the AVF is that it eradicates the prospect of involuntary service from the families of the politically influential, who would put pressure on their elected officials if their sons and daughters suddenly became vulnerable to service, and who might retaliate against anyone who serious-ly suggested reinstituting the system. Moreover, the AVF system has indeed proven adequate to meet the manpower needs of the country for thirty-five years, making the prospect of involuntary service not only foreign to most upcoming eligible 18-year olds, but to their parents as well. Reviving the draft is akin politically to poking a hornet's nest with a stick.

Could a return to conscription become necessary, despite its unattrac-tiveness as an option? History suggests that the American people will accept conscription when a true national emergency, such as World War II, arises. Crawford H. Greenewalt, a member of the Gates Commission that recom-mended a movement toward the AVF in 1969 in a memorandum to com-mission chairman Thomas Gates (quoted in the RAND study), stated the case clearly: "While there is a reasonable possibility that a peacetime armed force could be entirely voluntary, I am certain that an armed force involved in a major conflict could *not* be voluntary," (emphasis in original). In terms of its manpower demands, the Iraq War stands on the edge of being the kind of major war that Greemewalt believed would necessitate something other than an AVF. Conscription is one way to raise a larger force; the private sec-tor may be another.

The Privatization Option

The privatization of part of the military effort is largely an artifact of Iraq, although certain more peripheral aspects of the military system had previ-ously been turned over to private contractors. During the period since the end of the Cold War, a number of routine, mundane functions—aspects of food service, for instance—have been turned over to private sources. Doing so relieves the military of having to assign its own scarce resources to such activities and thus makes the "tooth" in the "tooth to tail" ratio of combatants to noncombatants in the service larger. It has also set the precedent for expanding this Reagan-era practice to other parts of the mil-itary effort in Iraq.

The extent to which the military effort in Iraq has been privatized is not insignificant. One analyst (Avant), for instance, estimated in 2004 that there were 20,000 private security personnel in the country, making them "the second largest member of the 'coalition of the willing'" in that coun-try. Scahill has updated these numbers in a pair of 2007 articles in *The Nation*. He reports that "by the end of Rumsfeld's tenure in late 2006, there were an estimated 100,000 private contractors on the ground in Iraq." While many of these contractors were engaged in non-military tasks associated with reconstructing the country, nonetheless their presence is extensive. The most famous of these private security contractors (PSCs), Blackwater, has been awarded "more than $700 million in 'diplomatic security' contracts through the State Department alone."

The Blackwater firm, located in North Carolina, has brought the use of PSCs into the public spotlight. Prior to accusations of its personnel's physical excesses against Iraqi civilians, the existence, and especially prominence, of these organizations was hardly known outside the professional national security community. The actions of these organizations have come under increased public scrutiny, mostly because of Blackwater activities. Because they also provide an alternative, if limited, form of additional personnel parallel to the AVF system, they deserve some examination.

The first question to be asked is exactly who are these PSCs? The answer is that they are a diverse lot of organizations that provide a variety of functions, from security for private firms and individuals, like business executives to contracted services for governments. This latter use is what raises concerns. Because PSCs exist in the private sector, their most basic underlying value is profit. This has led to the characterization of those PSCs in the active security business as mercenaries, professional soldiers of fortune who will work for the highest bidder. American firms like Blackwater staunchly reject this label. They argue that they only make their services available to the United States Government, whereas mercenaries will work for anyone who will pay them. Thus, by definition, they are professional soldiers, but they are not mercenaries.

Avant lists some of the primary advantages of PSCs. Among their advantages are the flexibility they provide and their surge capacity, meaning they can be mobilized quickly and moved into necessary situations with dispatch. Because they are often recruited from retired military personnel (especially Special Forces), they possess special operating capability for use in special circumstances where general forces would be inappropriate or ineffective. Moreover, they can be recruited internationally, broadening the net for potential recruits, and they are politically less expensive than regular American forces by being the ultimate "voluntary" forces. They provide, in other words, a highly specialized, flexible adjunct to the AVF forces. As an example, they can, in some circumstances, replace regular American forces, thus freeing up those forces for military use. Many of the Blackwater forces in Iraq, for instance, are assigned to providing physical protection for U.S. civilian personnel in the country (especially State Department personnel), and this bodyguard duty would have to fall to military forces—traditionally Marines—in the absence of the service Blackwater provides.

However, there are disadvantages as well. The scandal surrounding Blackwater (Blackwater personnel allegedly fired into a crowd of Iraqi civilians, killing a number of them) has highlighted these limitations. There is the matter of accountability: before the Blackwater scandal, these forces were not part of the military chain of command, did not report to that command chain, and were thus outside the normal command structure of the overall military effort. The Blackwater imbroglio of 2007 has caused these personnel to become part of that chain. At that, their legal status remains ambiguous. Because they are not formally combatants, their status under the Geneva rules of war is not entirely clear. These ambiguities make them difficult, if not impossible, to integrate into regular forces. Also, they are very costly in monetary terms. Although reports are somewhat obscure, the normal PSC member earns in excess of $100,000 in salary alone, making the individual more expensive than even the AVF soldier.

Privatization of military forces creates an ambivalence that may best be expressed in an analogy between PSCs and the famous French Foreign Legion. Officially, the French Foreign Legion is composed of mercenaries, none of whom can legally be French citizens, although some are (by lying about their nationality), and they can be employed by the French government wherever the needs arises. They tend to be deployed in desperate situations, where there may be high casualty rates. The major virtue of these forces is that, since they are officially not French citizens, expending them does not entail spilling French blood. This provides a level of flexibility in using armed force that is not available in using regular forces, for whose safety the government is more directly accountable.

PSCs provide some of this same flexibility and advantage when dealing with controversial situations that might not receive public support. That advantage, however, is a double-edged sword, because it can remove the inhibitions that serve to govern actions the public would call into question. As a matter of using PSCs to augment regular forces in the event of short-falls, their utility is quite limited because of their expense, and the fact that they are not numerous enough to provide much relief in filling the ranks. Their advantage is that they add specialized capability outside the regular military structure, but that comes with a price in terms of accountability.

Does the United States want its own Foreign Legion? Or is the country more comfortable with a citizen force recruited from the general population? What if that population will not voluntarily provide the numbers of service members necessary to carry out the national purpose? One answer is to expand the force to meet the mission, but that may prove difficult. The other solution is to size the missions to match the available forces.

Smaller Forces, Smaller Missions

The conduct of national security affairs is an exercise in *risk management*. The number of threats, or risks, the country faces will always exceed its capacity to blunt or neutralize all of them, meaning some will be alleviated whereas others will remain problems, or potential problems. Managing that dynamic condition is what risk management is all about (for a more detailed discussion, *see* Snow, *National Security for a New Era*, Third Edition, Chapter 7).

Although it may oversimplify reality somewhat, risk can be thought of as the product of a simple formula: Risk=Threat (the total number and intensity of challenges to national security) minus Capability (the capacity to counter threats), *ergo*, Risk=Threat-Capability. It is the goal of national security policy to reduce risk to the barest minimum possible, and it seeks to accomplish this either by reducing the threats faced or by increasing its capability to reduce threats. One important element of capability in this formulation is military force, the manipulation of which is relevant in the discussion of military manpower.

Virtually all observers project an equally or more hostile post-Iraq environment, and this translates into as great or greater threat than in the current environment. Some, of course, argue that the extent of the threat will depend on how the Iraq War ends, with defenders on both sides. Thus, supporters of the president argue an unsuccessful outcome will embolden enemies and thereby increase threat, and opponents of the war argue that ending the war will remove an irritant to America's opponents and reduce threat. At any rate, essentially all the candidates in the 2008 presidential election call for a larger American armed force, which translates into a call for increasing capability. As the discussion directly above has sought to clarify, the ability to increase that capability within realistic political constraints is problematic. The size of American armed forces may not be expandable without taking actions for which there are varying degrees of opposition, e.g., from lowering accession standards into the service to increased privatization to conscription. Had the United States not undergone the military trauma of Iraq, this might not be a major national security concern, but it is.

If it proves impossible or politically improbable that the capability of the armed forces measured in manpower can be increased, how does the country deal with the consequent risk implications that flow from that realization? The political response has been to increase capability to reduce risk. If that is not possible, what may be the alternatives to redefine threats to fit the capabilities of the armed forces? One is to reduce missions to match the forces available.

The idea is not as outlandish as it may first appear. Before American involvement in Iraq, the United States armed forces were deemed adequate for the country's needs. The Rumsfeld reforms called for a modernization and fine-tuning of those forces, but there were few public demands for a much larger and more capable force. Part of the reason may have been on overestimation of what those forces were capable of, a concern the Iraq experience would seem to validate. There was not, however, a widely perceived gap between the threats facing the United States and its capability to deal with them.

The Iraq War has revealed that the current U.S. Armed Forces are too small for Iraq-sized operations, if one includes an open-ended occupation in those calculations. The upshot is that unless those armed forces are changed in the future, the United States would be ill advised to embark on a similar military adventure without substantially increasing the capabilities of the military. A major component in increasing capabilities is creating a larger armed force that could, among other things, carry out the occupation of another Iraq without creating the strains the ongoing occupation has entailed.

In the face of this realization, there are general calls for enlarging the United States Armed Forces, presumably to levels that would alleviate the current dilemmas. Enigmatically, some of these calls come from political figures opposed to the current war, but apparently wanting to create conditions so that the United States can more successfully wage a similar war in the future. Does this not represent a contradiction of thinking? The Iraq hangover dynamic suggests Americans will be unlikely to view a reprise of the Iraq dynamic anytime soon—No More Iraqs! If one takes Iraq-style actions off the table, after all, one has essentially redefined risks and thus potential missions in basically the same terms as they existed before the Iraq invasion. In that atmosphere, the Iraq threat was "downgraded" to an annoyance that could be controlled diplomatically (the "dual containment" policy toward Iraq and Iran). Since a major military action against Iraq was not part of the American military mission, American capabilities were quite adequate to maintain an acceptable level of risk. Only when the Iraqi threat was upgraded to a national security emergency did capability come into question.

What if the United States redefined the military mission to include only major military actions in wars of necessity rather than wars of choice? There would, of course, be disagreement on whether individual situations fell into one category or the other. One way to look at the public relations effort preceding the Iraq War is as an effort to convince the public and political figures that it was a war of necessity—which it turned out not to have been. The suggestion that the United States might have cause to attack Iran has raised this question, and the reaction of the American public has been overwhelmingly negative. An attack on Iran would be an undesirable war of choice. If the Iraq hangover inhibits the promiscuous application of American force in arguably frivolous locations (deployments of choice rather than necessity), is that entirely bad? Would redefining the debate over the use of American force into these terms be an undesirable reorientation?

The horror scenario that is often put forward is that a negative reaction to the Iraq experience will reduce American will and capability to deal with "real" national emergencies (wars of necessity) that might be foisted on the United States with little notice. The Persian Gulf War, which no one foresaw as little as a few months before Saddam Hussein moved into Kuwait, is often cited as an example, and the rapid and total destabilization of a nuclear arms-possessing Pakistan (especially following the assassination of Benazir Bhutto) is often raised as a prospect of future horrors. What capability does the United States need for these unforeseeable wars of necessity? Is a force reconstituted at pre-Iraq levels (smaller, with less of a manpower issue than a larger force) adequate for these missions? Or, must the force be larger, making it more difficult to man? That depends on what the American people want it to be able to do. For instance, do the people of the United States want, or feel a need, to have the capability to engage in another long-term occupation in a place like Pakistan?

The point is that both those who propose that the United States should eschew future Iraq-style endeavors, and those who believe the United States needs increased capabilities that might include a capacity to deal better with such endeavors, have a burden to support their opinion. One way to engage such a discussion is through a framework, such as that suggested here, where military missions and capabilities are reconciled to one another. In a national security atmosphere where great threat is debated (the ongoing war on terror, for instance), the terms of the discussion will likely be tilted toward increased capability to deal with expanding, and expandable, missions, but that need not necessarily be the case. In the final chapter, some of the implications of getting out of Iraq for the strategic future will be examined.

SELECTED BIBLIOGRAPHY

Avant, Deborah D. "Contracting for Services in U.S. Military Operations." *PS: Political Science and Politics* XL, 3 (July 2007), 457–460.

———. *The Market for Force: The Consequences of Privatizing Security.* New York: Cambridge University Press, 2005.

Bacevich, Andrew J. "Who's Bearing the Burden? Iraq and the Demise of the All-Volunteer Force." *Commonweal* 132 (July 15, 2005), 13–15.

Baker, Fred W. III. "Chairman Supports All-Volunteer Force." *DefenseLink,* U. S. Department of Defense (online). October 25, 2007. (http://www. defenselink.mil/news/newsarticles.aspx?id=479thirty-five)

Clausewitz, Carl von. *On War.* Revised edition translated and edited by Michael Howard and Peter Paret. Princeton, NJ: Princeton University Press, 1984.

Clinton, Hillary. "Security and Opportunity for the Twenty-first Century." *Foreign Affairs* 86, 6 (November/December 2007), 2–18.

Dobbins, James. "Who Lost Iraq? Lessons from the Debacle." *Foreign Affairs* 86, 5 (September/October 2007), 61–74.

Edwards, John. "Reengaging with the World." *Foreign Affairs* 86, 5 (September/October 2007), 19–36.

Giuliani, Rudolph W. "Toward a Realistic Peace." *Foreign Affairs* 86, 5 (September/October 2007), 2–18.

Gordon, Michael R. and General Bernard E. Trainor. *Cobra II: The Inside Story of the Invasion and Occupation of Iraq.* New York: Pantheon Books, 2006.

Kagan, Frederick W. "The U.S. Military's Manpower Crisis." *Foreign Affairs* 85, 4 (July/August 2006), 97–110.

McCain John. "An Enduring Peace Built on Freedom. " *Foreign Affairs* 86, 6 (November/December 2007), 19–34.

Moskos, Charles. "What Ails the All-Volunteer Force: An Institutional Perspective." *Parameters* XXXI, 2 (Summer 2001), 29–47.

Obama, Barack. "Renewing American Leadership." *Foreign Affairs* 86, 4 (July/August 2007), 2–16.

RAND Corporation. "The Evolution of the All-Volunteer Force." *Research Brief: The Rand Corporation.* 2006 (http://www.rand.ord/pubs/research_ briefs/RB9195/index1.html)

Ricks, Thomas E. *Fiasco: The American Military Adventure in Iraq.* New York: The Penguin Press, 2006.

Romney, Mitt. "Rising to a New Generation of Global Consequences." *Foreign Affairs* 86, 4 (July/August 2007), 17–32.

Rostker, Bernard. *I Want You! The Evolution of the All-Volunteer Force*. Santa Monica, CA: RAND Corporation, 2006.

Rumsfeld, Donald H. "Transforming the Military." *Foreign Affairs* 81, 3 (May/June 2002), 20–32.

Scahill, Jeremy. "Bush's Shadow Army." *The Nation* 284, 13 (April 2, 2007), 11–16.

———."Making a Killing." *The Nation* 285, 11 (October 15, 2007), 21–23.

Shanker, Thom, and David S. Cloud. "Military Wants More Civilians to Help in Iraq." *New York Times* (online), February 7, 2007.

Snow, Donald M. *National Security for a New Era: Globalization and Geopolitics after Iraq* (Third Edition). New York: Pearson Longman, 2008.

Summer, Harry G. *On Strategy: A Critical Analysis of the Vietnam War*. Novato, CA: Presidio Press, 1982.

Chapter 7

Forecasting American Security

Once active participation in the Iraq War has ended, the problem of military manpower offers a parable of the broader issue of America's security role in the world. Because the extent of the manpower problem depends on the size of armed force the United States wants or needs in that future, the question of "manpower for what?" arises, and must be addressed before the manpower issue can even be defined. In turn, this means that some assessment of the post-Iraq future, and the demands it will place on the United States, is a necessary part of planning for the post-Iraq future.

The Iraq outcome will influence this assessment. In some ways, that outcome remains in doubt, but the broad outlines have already been suggested and can be reiterated as part of the context for the future. Two aspects of that outcome stand out, one of which has been argued consistently in these pages and one of which has been more implicit. The explicit aspect is that the United States will terminate its active combat participation in Iraq without any definitive end state having been reached. The policy of Iraqification will eventuate in a turnover of authority from American to Iraqi authorities, but whether the Iraqis can manage the transition to some peaceful, orderly future in the country remains problematical. For most Americans, the resulting level of orderliness, or disorder, will not likely be a major concern as long as there is a "decent interval" between the withdrawal of U.S. combat forces from the streets and the onset of any widespread disorder. The problems of Iraq, in other words, will not have been solved when the Americans withdraw.

The other, more implicit, aspect of the withdrawal is that it will not be complete—there will be a residual involvement of the United States in Iraq for the foreseeable future. The signs are clear. The current administration rarely even mentions a total military removal from the Persian Gulf area, but rather, discusses an over-the-horizon presence where American forces withdraw from the front line streets of Baghdad and other Iraqi cities. Various locations have been suggested for this residual presence, including surrounding countries like Kuwait and Dubai. Significantly, locations in Iraq, and especially Kurdistan, often make the list. To add substance to this intention, the United States is constructing bases around the country that appear too permanent to suggest an early abandonment, and which could house a large number of American military and civilian personnel (probably contractors). Additionally, the United States is constructing the largest American embassy complex in the world in Baghdad, further evidence of an intention to remain significantly far into the future.

There can be only one rational reason for this planning (which has received little attention and even less criticism from a public that says it "wants out" of Iraq). That reason, of course, is guaranteed access to Iraqi petroleum reserves. Although the United States would like to insure access for major American oil companies (mainly Exxon-Mobil and Chevron-Texaco) to all the vast reserves of Iraq, about half of these are in the Basra oil field of southern, Shiite Iraq, which will likely remain volatile and possibly anti-American. A likely fallback position is that the United States will instead concentrate its efforts on the Kurdish reserves, which, as noted earlier, comprise upward of half the known reserves, depending on what provinces are considered part of Kurdistan. Marrying American control of highly profitable upstream operations in Kurdistan to somewhat less profitable downstream activities centering on Ceyhan, Turkey could provide a powerful tool for the United States in the upcoming global energy competition. The degree to which the Kurds insist upon and receive greater levels of autonomy will be a fair indicator of the extent to which this possibility is being realized.

Whether oil or some other consideration provides the motivation (or at least public expression) for continuing American presence in Iraq, it will certainly exist and will be a factor in American security concerns more widely. The residues will continue to tie down American forces in the region, although undoubtedly in smaller numbers than is currently the case, but the result will be American forces unavailable for other missions. At the same time, however, the continued presence of the U.S. military in a highly visible manner in the region will likely affect other aspects of American interests as well.

One can assume without stretching credulity that American security interests will continue to be centered in the Middle East region. American ongoing addiction to petroleum dictates that the country cannot easily extricate itself from the region, and its residual interest in Iraqi oil guarantees that motivation will not disappear. In addition, it is clear that the struggle with Islamic religious extremists, a.k.a. terrorists, will remain a major priority after withdrawal from Iraq. Exactly what impact the end of the war will have on that part of the national security equation is not entirely certain, but if, as some suggest, American continuing presence in Iraq has actually stimulated anti-American terrorist sentiment in the region, a residual American presence will not diminish that dynamic noticeably.

The Iraq footprint on the future will also be influenced by the lessons both the United States and its potential adversaries take from the experience. From an American vantage point, Dobbins states both sides of the lesson for Americans. "It would be a mistake to employ Iraq as a yardstick by which [to] gauge the necessary future size and shape of the U.S. military, given that the war was probably unnecessary and the occupation mishandled from the outset," he argues. On the other hand, "The United States should certainly avoid invading large hostile countries on the basis of faulty intelligence and with the support of narrow, unrepresentative coalitions."

These observations bring the discussion back to the manpower parable. What the U.S. military should look like depends on the uses the United States has for the military in the future. Calling for a larger armed force, as essentially all presidential candidates have done, begs the question. The U.S. military was, after all, apparently large and capable enough to deal with the pre-Iraq environment, and the primary change the post-Iraq environment will feature will be the absence of a need for the large American occupation force currently deployed in Iraq. That being the case, why does the United States require additional forces? Presumably, the added capability being suggested would relieve the military of the onerous burden the Iraq occupation creates, which is another way of saying it would create the capacity for the United States to conduct another Iraq-style operation, including an occupation, without the strains that have been experienced. No one who has advocated an increase has put the need in terms of having the capability for another occupation, because it is not at all clear that the American public would support such a course of action. Indeed, a counter-argument can be made that denying the military added capabilities might be a way to prevent it from being used again in a way the American people will not support.

American public opinion is the trump card in all assessments about the post-Iraq future. If a lesson of the Iraq experience is "No More Iraqs," what constraints accompany that message? Does the American public want a military designed for rapid and decisive insertion and removal from trouble spots around the world, or one more suited for larger, more permanent intrusions where military action is followed by a sustained military commitment on the ground? Or does it want both? Or, for that matter, neither?

It is clear that the American people want the United States to end its involvement in Iraq and to remove its combat troops from that country. It is equally clear that mainstream American politicians have not wholeheartedly and in detail embraced that position. It is at least possible that the American people will also not be satisfied with a partial withdrawal that leaves a contingent of American forces, albeit probably in garrison at the new, permanent bases in the country or in over the horizon locations. The only rationale for keeping troops near the scene, after all, is so that they can rapidly be reinserted, a course that would almost certainly bring howls of public opposition. The United States will implement some form of Iraqification, in other words, but that will not necessarily be the same thing as removing Iraq from the American national security agenda. The extent, if any, of an "enduring presence" in Iraq has become a clear point of distinction between the Democrats (who oppose the idea) and the Republicans (who favor it) in the 2008 election campaign.

The post-Iraq missions of the United States are thus in a state of flux, which is natural under the circumstances, because they deal with a future that cannot be foreseen, and the uncertainty is exacerbated by the possible outcomes of Iraq. One lesson Iraq has taught globally is that the most effective way to deal with the U.S. Armed Forces is some variation of the way the Iraqi resistance groups have—through the use of asymmetrical warfare. Therefore, this discussion begins with a look at asymmetrical futures for the United States. It then moves to an examination of foreseeable missions in a post-Iraq world, emphasizing the continuing problem of terrorism, proliferation, and the specific problem posed by Iraq's neighbor (Iran), and oil. The discussion will conclude with the more difficult, unforeseeable problems, and the missions that arise from those.

ASYMMETRICAL FUTURES

From a military vantage point, the problem facing the United States in Iraq is not entirely unlike the problem faced by the British Army during the American Revolution. The British Army was, particularly in the terms of the time, a far superior armed force compared to the ragtag Continental Army commanded by General George Washington, and could defeat the colonials whenever the two armies met on the field of battle. Early in the war, after seeing his army nearly destroyed on several occasions,

Washington learned to avoid the kind of set piece linear battles that were the standard of the time (what is now called conventional or symmetrical warfare), even if he yearned for a decisive battle that was considered the apex of war fighting. Thereafter, the British had to chase the Americans through the countryside trying to engage and destroy the colonials, which they could never quite accomplish.

More to the point, the British Army also had to serve as an army of occupation, and this was ultimately its undoing. During the Revolution, the British Armed Forces in the colonies never exceeded about 35,000 troops, and their task was to subdue and repatriate a restless colonial population. To do this, the British needed to be present to repress the activities of any revolutionaries who opposed them, and there were simply not enough troops for the task. The best the British could do was to foray into hostile territory, suppress local revolutionaries, and move on. Except in the largest and most important places (cities like New York and Philadelphia), they could not leave behind enough troops to maintain an order loyal to the Crown, and when they left, the revolutionaries returned and the situation reverted.

The British thus had two missions: destroying the military aspects of the revolution as a way to defeat the political movement it represented, and a physical occupation of colonies that stretched over 1,300 miles north to south. They failed, both because they lacked the resources (manpower) to accomplish both tasks and because, eventually, British public opinion turned against what became an increasingly unpopular war at home. Part of the British problem was that the Americans adopted what is now called asymmetrical warfare as an important component of their resistance to the return of British rule.

The situation in Iraq is not identical, of course, but some of the military dynamics are similar. The superiority of American armed force in conventional warfare was easily established during the invasion and conquest phase of the war, and the Iraqis (at least partially from their earlier experience during the Persian Gulf War) put up only a token resistance before apparently dissolving in front of the American onslaught. Instead, many of them simply melted into the population, later to emerge as parts of the Iraqi resistance. That resistance has assiduously avoided direct contact with the Americans in the kind of concentrated, firepower-intensive warfare at which the American forces excel, and have instead adopted more indirect, unconventional tactics. In the face of the occupation, they are active where the Americans are not present, and fade away when the Americans arrive. They are asymmetrical warriors.

The analogy is particularly relevant in comparing the problem of occupation the British faced and that the Americans now face. There were simply not enough British troops to maintain control of the colonies in the late 1770s, and there are not enough Americans to pacify Iraq today. Like the British then, the Americans today are quite successful when they sweep into a particular location, brushing aside the opposition and establishing order. That order exists and can be maintained as long as the Americans remain physically present, but there are not enough troops to allow permanent occupation everywhere. The surge has made it possible to occupy more territory more of the time, but the net effect is not and cannot be comprehensive without the infusion of many more troops—levels like those proposed by General Shinseki and others before the war began. Eventually the Americans will leave any place they liberate, and the resistance will likely return.

Defining Asymmetrical Warfare

This dynamic helps fuel a confusion of achieving success with victory in the surge. The surge has indeed been quite successful in liberating and pacifying the places where it is applied, and enthusiasts for the war have conflated these successes into a projection of victory. The problem is that the successes are tactical and, since they are inevitably followed by the removal of American forces from the scenes of success, reversible. During the Revolutionary War, British successes in suppressing American patriots did not add up to victory, and the successes of the surge likely do not add up to victory in the current war.

It does not denigrate the efforts of American forces and individual soldiers to make this observation. It is undoubtedly true that many Iraqis appreciate the efforts Americans are making on their behalf. It is even possible that if the United States were to mount a comprehensive occupation, and it lasted long enough, victory might be possible, in the sense that Iraqis might overcome their differences and then embrace the American ideal of democracy that has been the publicized objective of the war. It is equally true that the American people will allow neither of these conditions to be met, because they represent long-term commitments with uncertain outcomes that the American public has rejected. To repeat an observation made in Chapter 3, political democracies do not like long wars, and the longer wars last, the more support will erode. The British learned this lesson in the American colonies, the United States learned it in Vietnam, and in both cases the occupiers withdrew eventually. The same dynamics are at work in Iraq, except the current administration has not accepted the likely consequences.

The problem for the United States is that the Iraq War has become an asymmetrical conflict, a conflict designed to frustrate the very kind of military force and political support base that the United States possesses. It is not a problem the United States has not confronted before: The underlying dynamics of Vietnam and Iraq are quite similar in this regard, as demonstrated in Chapter 2. Understanding and dealing with this form of warfare has been a difficult and reluctant mission for the military, especially the army, which bears the brunt of the mission. The efforts of General Petraeus and his acolytes is a step in the right direction, but his mission as surge commander is burdened by an albatross: running an occupation with insufficient forces. It is almost certainly a problem beyond even the most enlightened leadership. It is, however, absolutely incumbent on the military to learn how to better combat asymmetrical warfare in the future, because, as already mentioned, a major lesson of Iraq for America's opponents is that this form of resistance works.

What exactly is asymmetrical warfare? The name is much newer than the underlying phenomenon it represents. In asymmetrical warfare, one side fights using the prevailing "rules" of war whereas the opponent (the asymmetrical warrior) rejects those rules and refuses to abide by them. The asymmetrical warrior may or may not represent a government, might not organize its forces along conventional lines (use of military ranks, wearing of uniforms, for instance), and rejects the prevailing conventions about how war may be fought. The asymmetry flows from these differences. The American system of warfare is based on conventional, European-style warfare, in which everyone adopts the same rules and fights the same way (symmetrical warfare). The United States has had episodic experience with asymmetrical enemies (the Seminole Wars of the 1820s, and the Filipino Insurgency immediately after the Spanish-American War, for instance), but adapting to an enemy that does not fight the same way has always proven strategically and tactically difficult (see Drew and Snow), as Vietnam demonstrated and as Iraq also has shown.

Asymmetrical warfare poses a unique dilemma for the United States. During the years since the end of the Cold War, the United States indeed evolved as the most potent military power in the world. That status was, however, largely based in conventional measures of power: The United States has the world's overwhelmingly most powerful conventional (or symmetrical) forces, to the point that it is foolhardy for any opponent to challenge American armed forces on their own terms. As a result, two things have happened. First, since no country or movement can challenge the United States directly, the form of warfare at which the United States excels has become obsolete for the United States. No one will confront the Americans on American terms, because to do so is suicidal. Therefore, the United States will not be able to fight the way it wants to fight. Second, the consequence of this obsolescence is that, by definition, opponents will have to adopt asymmetrical measures to have a chance against the United States. American preeminence in conventional warfare has lead to its own irrelevance.

Asymmetrical warfare is as old as warfare itself. It is the approach of the disadvantaged, those who cannot compete successfully using the prevailing methods of warfare. Modern symmetrical warfare features large, heavily armored, and mobile armed forces that can concentrate extremely deadly firepower on another force. In cases like the Persian Gulf War, a conventional warrior like the United States may be able to rain devastation on a less well-equipped symmetrical enemy outside the range of that enemy's ability to retaliate, making the contest suicidal for the less powerful side, as the Iraqi Army learned in 1991. In circumstances where the symmetrical opponent is so overwhelmingly advantaged, fighting on those terms is suicidal for the weaker opponent. That opponent is left with three choices: compete under the prevailing rules (and lose); quit the contest and capitulate (and lose); or adapt the rules so that they have a chance to win. Stated this way, it is not a difficult decision.

The dynamics of modern asymmetrical warfare have evolved from practices that go back as far as Sun Tzu and come forward through the thinking and actions of leaders like Mao Dze-Dung and the Vietnamese leader Vo Nguyen Giap. It is a uniquely eastern form of warfare that does not emphasize so much the brutal clash of mass armies (more the western tradition), as much as it does indirection, maneuver, and outwitting the opponent. In *The Art of War*, his military manual written over 3,000 years ago, Sun Tzu captures the essence of the matter: "All warfare is based on deception. . . . To subdue the enemy without fighting is the acme of skill. Thus, what is of supreme importance is to attack the enemy's strategy." Luring isolated patrols into ambushes in heavy jungles in Vietnam is an example of this principle in action. Exploding improvised explosive devices (IEDs) in front of armored vehicles in Iraq is another.

In modern warfare, the asymmetrical warrior does not seek to defeat his opponent in the traditional sense, because he lacks the physical wherewithal to do so. The North Vietnamese Army could not defeat and force the American army from Vietnam, and the various forms of Iraqi resistance cannot physically force the United States to leave Iraq. What they can do is to avoid being decimated by the more powerful enemy and continue to act as an irritant, avoiding defeat and inflicting enough damage and suffering on the opponent that the opponent concludes continuing the contest is no longer worth the effort. The "weak link" of modern political democracies is public support for war efforts, and the asymmetrical warrior succeeds by "attacking" that soft underbelly. Knowing that democracies do not like long wars and dislike unneeded casualties, the dynamic for the asymmetrical warrior is to avoid his own defeat and provide just enough annoyance that the enemy eventually throws up its hands in figurative disgust and quits the field. Put a different way, it is in the interest of the asymmetrical warrior to nurture the instinct to cut and run.

Asymmetrical warfare is not a method or a set of doctrines, strategies, and tactics. Rather, it should be thought of primarily as an approach—a way of looking—at military situations. While all asymmetrical warriors face the same problem of facing and trying to figure out how to defeat (or avoid losing to) a militarily superior opponent, the ways they go about trying to accomplish this goal will vary considerably, depending on the circumstances that different asymmetrical warriors face.

William Lind (an aide to former Colorado Senator Gary Hart) and a group of others published a landmark study of this new kind of warfare in a 1989 *Marine Corps Gazette* article (summarized in Snow, *National Security for a New Era*, Second and Third Editions). They stated that what they called "fourth generation warfare" contains some common characteristics, some familiar, others not. The familiar elements (familiar in the sense they had been seen in other places like Vietnam) included the lack of distinction between civilian and military targets and between combatant and non-combatant zones, meaning everywhere is part of the war. In addition, the goal of war is not so much defeating an enemy's armed forces as causing the collapse of the enemy's will to resist—the enemy's political will—and that the target will be popular support for war.

Lind and his colleagues expand beyond these bases. They argue the explicitly non-Western, Asiatic (including Middle Eastern) tradition forms the core of this kind of warfare. Keegan applies this observation in an October 2001 description of 9/11: "The Oriental tradition . . . returned in an absolutely traditional form. Arabs, appearing suddenly out of empty space like their desert raider ancestors, assaulted the heartlands of Western power in a terrifying surprise raid and did appalling damage." In this same light, Lind and his colleagues believe that terror will be a standard tactic of asymmetrical warriors.

Afghanistan and Iraq

The American experiences in Afghanistan and Iraq offer two contrasting views of the variety and complexity of dealing with asymmetrical situations. American involvement in both began traditionally, through the use of conventional, symmetrical force, and that phase of the operations was quite successful. In both cases, however, the situation has become asymmetrical, with much less favorable outcomes.

The Afghanistan operation was directly related to the September 11, 2001, attacks, because Al Qaeda was housed in Afghanistan under the protection of the Afghan Taliban government. On September 12, 2001, the United Nations unanimously condemned the 9/11 attacks and authorized military operations against terrorists. After the Taliban chose not to honor an American request that the Al Qaeda leadership be arrested and turned over to them, the United States began a campaign that toppled the Taliban but did not secure the capture of the Al Qaeda leadership.

The Afghan war that brought the Taliban down was a conventional, symmetrical civil war between the government and a coalition of tribesmen and ethnic groups within Afghanistan, known collectively as the Northern Alliance. They had been waging an inconclusive civil war for some time, until the United States developed an interest in affecting the outcome. To this end, the United States infiltrated Special Forces into Afghanistan to coordinate activities with the Northern Alliance and to serve as spotters who could direct air strikes against Taliban positions. The air strikes began on October 7, 2001, and continued until the Taliban quit the field.

The campaign was successful because the Taliban had no choice but to mount a conventional—and entirely impossible—defense against the bombings. Prudence would have dictated that the Taliban quit the field in the face of American bombing, reverting to mountainous retreats (where they eventually went), but since they faced Northern Alliance forces, doing so meant quitting the field against their civil opponents. As a result, they remained in place and were inviting targets. In the end, the attacks caused the Taliban to flee and relinquish power, and the pro-American government of Hamid Karzai, who remains president of Afghanistan, replaced them. This phase was a clear victory for the Americans.

The Taliban were badly beaten, but they did not disappear. They and their Al Qaeda allies retreated to Waziristan, the mountainous border area between Afghanistan and Pakistan, where they regrouped. They have since returned to Afghanistan, where they are waging an asymmetrical, guerrilla-style war against the Karzai regime and its NATO allies. As of this writing, the Taliban "insurgency" controls about one-third of the country effectively, and has even formed alliances with local poppy growers, profiting from the opium and heroin trade that is centered in Afghanistan, which is the country's major source of foreign exchange. This asymmetrical campaign continues unabated and leaves the outcome in Afghanistan in considerably more doubt than it seemed to be not long ago (although administration spokesmen are reluctant to admit the peril in which the country exists).

The Iraq example has already been discussed thoroughly and needs little elaboration as an asymmetrical war. The major differences between Afghanistan and Iraq, of course, were that there was no ongoing war in Iraq before the American intervention, nor was there a demonstrable tie to terrorism, although some administration officials cling to the belief there was. The invasion and conquest was an entirely conventional affair, which the Iraqis hardly resisted at all, and some have suggested that their token resistance was cover for the onset of the Iraqi resistance that emerged with the occupation.

What has made dealing with the resistance so difficult in Iraq is that there is not *a* resistance, but rather, *several* forms of resistance that are at cross purposes; about all they share is a desire to see an end to the American occupation. Fortunately for the United States effort, they are sufficiently opposed to one another that they have been unable to form a common front against the occupation—which would multiply the American military problem considerably. Sunni resistance groups—which, if anyone, could have been part of a prewar resistance plan, since Sunnis ruled in Saddam Hussein's Iraq—are principally fighting to maintain control of traditional Sunni territories and to protect themselves from Shiites seeking revenge for their long-time suppression by the Sunnis. Shiite movements, such as the Mahdi army, promote Shiite control of as much of the country as possible. Al Qaeda in Iraq, established in 2004, as noted earlier, is the major foreign-based resistance movement, made up primarily of Saudis, Moroccans, and Egyptians, and is primarily dedicated to the expulsion of the Americans from the country. Meanwhile, Kurdish forces (the *pesh merga*) remain defiantly loyal to the idea of Kurdish autonomy or independence.

This highly differentiated nature of the resistance makes it hydra-headed and difficult to destroy. Tactical "alliances" have been made between American and Sunni elements in traditionally Sunni regions to deal with Al Qaeda, but even where these are successful, Al Qaeda retreats to territory controlled by Shiites or Kurds, and even successful actions against them do not deal with the problems associated with the other groups—sub-duing Al Qaeda in one part of the country does not help control the actions of the Shiite Mahdi army. The fact that even the communally based movements are fractured, especially the Shiites, only adds to the confusion and complexity of the situation.

American authorities rarely discuss this mosaic nature of the opposition, because it further confuses the equation of success and victory. Thus, alliances between the Americans and Sunni militias in Sunni areas against Al Qaeda help reinforce the appearance of pacification, but they effectively put the Americans in support of those Sunni groups, which is not necessarily their longer-term purpose. The only area where the Americans can consort with local forces without creating complicated intrigues is in the Kurdish North, since the Kurds are more united in their desire for autonomy than are factions in other communal movements (Shiites vs. other Shiites, for instance). Even at that, there is ongoing tension—some argue ethnic cleansing—by Kurds and Shiites in places like Kirkuk, and the Americans must tread carefully to avoid being swept into the intra-Iraqi squabble.

Asymmetry after Iraq

Other potential opponents of the United States in the Middle East and elsewhere are watching the American trauma in trying to accomplish its goals in that country, and the backlash that effort has had in the United States. Their circumstances may be less complicated than the ethnic and communal patchwork of Iraq, but they can also anticipate and plan for what might happen if the United States should attempt to impose something like the neoconservative dream of regime change and democratization on them. And they must be taking heart at what they see.

For other countries and movements, the lesson of Iraq has to be that asymmetrical approaches to warfare can blunt and negate the American military behemoth. The Persian Gulf War proved conclusively that it is masochistic to confront the Americans on their own terms—in symmetrical warfare. The Americans are simply too good at that form of warfare, and so they have indeed created the self-fulfilling prophecy of insuring they will not have to fight another conventional war. Since that possibility is precluded, the alternative is to change the rules and level the playing field by fighting unconventionally. The lesson of Iraq is that this works.

Iraq provides both strategic and tactical advice to future American opponents, and the United States needs to anticipate those lessons and take counteractions before the lessons can be applied. Strategically, it has to be clear to any future opponent that the way to "defeat" the Americans is to protract the conflict and make it as painful as possible for the Americans, who will eventually tire of the enterprise and leave. A strategy of attrition is the choice of the underdog, who must outlast his more powerful opponent. For the United States, the strategic imperative is to develop methods to shorten future conflicts so they can be concluded before public opinion turns on them. The only alternative may be to avoid such conflicts altogether. At the tactical level, asymmetrical wars are often distinguished by the new battlefield innovations they demonstrate, which frustrate the efforts of forces like those of the United States. In Iraq, the IED and the suicide bomber have been the primary tactical innovations, including experimentation with combining IED attacks with follow-on military attacks on helicopters seeking to rescue and evacuate the victims of IED attacks. It is a given that some form of IEDs will be part of the tactical repertoire of the next asymmetrical opponent. The trick will be in anticipating what innovation will be applied to make their use even more deadly, and to figure out and counter other tactical changes that future opponents bring to the fray.

Adjusting to the problems caused by asymmetrical opponents is not a new experience for the United States. Indeed, much of the soul-searching that surrounded the post-Vietnam period centered on this exact problem, and a good bit of time and energy was devoted to things like counterinsurgency (the topic of General Petraeus' *FM 3–24*). In the post-Vietnam environment, there was also a good deal of resistance to this topic, as its implications flew in the face of well-established doctrinal approaches that dominated the army and related services. The same dynamic and tension will be part of the post-Iraq debate over national security. Will the outcome be different?

FORESEEABLE MISSIONS

It is clear that the conclusion of active American combat participation in Iraq (the implementation of Iraqification) will neither conclude American presence in Iraq nor solve any of the problems that existed before, or emerged during the Iraq years. As already noted, the United States will likely have a residual involvement in Iraq for the foreseeable future that will include direct (bases in Iraq) and indirect (bases over the horizon in places like Kuwait) military components. Unlike Vietnam a generation ago, the Americans will not simply disappear from the Iraqi scene, unless the public—when it becomes fully cognizant of this planned residual presence—demands a more complete form of withdrawal. The Americans may retreat behind the walls of the its largest embassy within Baghdad's Green Zone, but they will be there, if for no other reason than to protect the upstream oil interests of American petroleum companies.

The American adventure in Iraq will also leave other security problems centering in the Middle East squarely on the table. Three will be examined in this section. One security problem is the continuing "war on terror," which formed part of the rationale for invading Iraq in the first place, and has certainly not abated as a result. If anything, the problem has been exacerbated by American presence in Iraq. The second problem, proliferation of weapons of mass destruction, another of the official reasons for attacking Iraq, has also not been solved by American intervention. In fact, it is arguable that a major lesson of Saddam Hussein's fate was that countries threatened by the United States need such weapons to prevent being attacked by the Americans: Weapons of mass destruction—especially nuclear weapons—may be needed to deter the Americans from attacking. Had Saddam Hussein in fact possessed WMD, some speculate, he might still be in power. This problem comes into focus on a single country, Iran, which has been the subject of speculation about potential military actions by the United States. Iran, which is the largest, most powerful, and potentially most important state in the Persian Gulf region, will continue to be a major source of concern for the United States. The primary reason the United States remains intimately engaged in the region is the need for Middle Eastern oil, and Iraq is important because it can provide a stable source for the United States, independent of places like Saudi Arabia. Securing that resource, without irritating the regional situation to the point of stimulating an increase in terrorism, represents the third great security problem for the United States.

Dealing with International Religious Terrorism

The current tone of national security began with 9/11, and the primary concern with terrorism will survive an Iraq War partly justified as an attack upon terrorism. Within days of the attacks in New York and Washington, the Bush administration had declared "war" on terrorism, an unfortunate designation that continues to overshadow efforts to come to grips with a phenomenon far more complex than the simple connotation of the GWOT engenders. Dealing with terrorism is a far more complicated matter than assigning it to the military realm, implicit in the war analogy, and the often-expressed idea that Iraq has somehow been a "theater" in the "war" further degrades the analogy. The GWOT as an acronym may be a welcome victim of the "end" of the Iraq War; the phenomenon of international religious terrorism will, however, remain as a focus of national security.

Terrorism and the Middle East are often equated in the public realm and by the administration, but the problem is broader than that. The U.S. State Department compiles an annual list of "designated foreign terrorist organizations." The 2006 list is representative, and it reveals that while a majority of the currently active terrorist groups are Muslim and Asian (including the Middle East), by no means are they all one or the other. Using additional analysis provided by *Infoplease*, an online publication of Pearson Education (the publisher of this book), the actual pattern is revealed in Table 7.1:

Table 7.1: Demographics of Terrorism

Location	Affiliation		
	Muslim	Non-Muslim	Total
Middle East (excluding Turkey and Pakistan)	13	4	17
Other Asia	6	6	12
Africa	4		4
South America		4	4
Europe		5	5
Total	23	19	42

One-quarter of the organizations are Middle Eastern and Muslim, with Al Qaeda and Al Qaeda in Iraq listed as separate organizations. That means, however, that three-quarters of the terrorist organizations do not share this combination of characteristics and are generally less interesting to the United States. A number of Islamic groups focus on establishing Islamist states in their own countries (groups in Egypt, Algeria, and the Philippines, for instance). Non-Muslim groups range from Jewish extremists in Israel (Kahane Chai) to separatist groups in Europe (factions of the

Irish Republican Army, the Basque Fatherland and Liberty—ETA), to Marxist organizations in the Philippines, to groups whose most prominent activities feature protecting South American drug smugglers from the authorities. Not all of these organizations oppose the United States or are of interest to the United States Government. The organizations that form the basis of an ongoing U.S. concern with international religious terrorism are, however, concentrated in Southwest Asia.

It is no longer surprising to say that the war effort in Iraq has not contributed to alleviating this problem. Figures like Vice President Cheney regularly assert that there is a connection between Iraq and religious terrorists, but they rarely cite convincing evidence to support their claims. Rather, it is more common to assert the opposite: that the war in Iraq has inhibited the effort to stifle terrorism emanating from the region. Two bases are often used to support these claims. First, it is widely asserted that the Iraq effort has diverted resources from the direct assault on terrorist organizations and terrorists—notably Usama bin Laden and his Al Qaeda structure—by taking resources that could have been used in Afghanistan and even along the Afghan-Pakistan border from that effort and redirecting them toward Iraq instead. Iraq was, before the toppling of Saddam Hussein, one of the most secular states in the Islamic world, and the idea that his regime would actively support religious terrorists, who, by and large, actively opposed his regime, has always been difficult—if not impossible—to sustain. Religious fanaticism has, if anything, been increased by the Iraq War, as particularly Shiite factions have been freed to practice their faith, sometimes violently. The second basis for these claims is that the American occupation of Iraq has unleashed its own terrorist opposition to the continuing American presence. Al Qaeda in Iraq, after all, which did not come into being until 2004, is the primary source of foreign fighters in the country, and resembles, in some ways, the foreign *mujahedin* who rallied to assist the Soviet expulsion from Afghanistan in the 1980s. Saddam Hussein would not have tolerated such an intrusion, and would almost certainly have suppressed it with his characteristic brutality. The fact that Sunni militias are cooperating with the United States to root out and destroy Al Qaeda in Iraq is evidence of the antipathy that exists between the terrorists and the Iraqis.

What happens to the GWOT after Iraq? An anti-terrorist emphasis by the United States Government will not disappear, because the threat of terrorism will remain. That effort will remain comprehensive but likely diffuse: part of it will concentrate on antiterrorist activity within the United States seeking to prevent terrorist attacks on American soil, and protecting

American borders from terrorist penetration will continue to be a major focus of U.S. agencies (principally Immigration and Customs Enforcement or ICE). These efforts represent the basically domestic aspects of the terrorism suppression effort and are also its least militarized parts. Neither should be affected physically much by the end of the Iraq War.

The end of the U.S. formal participation in Iraq is likely to affect the effort against terrorism in two ways. The first is conceptual. As noted, designating the effort as a war, GWOT has always been controversial, and this depiction could be a welcome victim of the end of the war. The effort has always been too multifaceted for the war analogy to cover very well—there are, for instance, large portions of the effort that can only be assigned to non-military entities like the intelligence community and law enforcement agencies. The war analogy is intended to amplify the importance of the enterprise but does not materially assist in focusing or directing non-military activities involved in fighting terrorism. Moreover, the depiction of Iraq as a GWOT theater further stigmatizes the GWOT enterprise, both because of the falseness of the connection between Iraq and terrorism and because the connection helped facilitate what many believe was the bad decision to invade Iraq.

More directly, an end to active combat operations in Iraq will allow the redeployment of American resources back to fighting terrorism in places like Afghanistan. Even if all American troops do not leave Iraq as part of the withdrawal, many will be redeployed, and some will go back to the *actual* war on terrorism in places like Afghanistan. The U.S. Marines keep volunteering for such a repositioning, but until they recently have been turned down in an atmosphere where there is the continued need in Iraq for active fighting forces in support of the surge. When whatever Americans are slated to remain in Iraq are safely ensconced in the "enduring" bases being built in that country, the remainder of forces will be available to fight terrorists. The most obvious location for that redirection of effort will be in Afghanistan, both to combat the resurgence of the Taliban and to help put pressure on Al Qaeda in Afghanistan and Pakistan.

The Pakistan connection has always been the most difficult part of this puzzle, and it was made even more so by the assassination of former prime minister and opposition leader Benazir Bhutto on December 27, 2007, less than two weeks before planned presidential elections in the country. Bhutto's death further destabilized internal Pakistani politics, which has been heavily divided over how aggressive the government should be in suppressing Al Qaeda in the lawless provinces of Northern Pakistan, notably Waziristan. Pakistani President Pervez Musharraf has tried to walk a thin line between American requests for very aggressive actions against Al Qaeda and violent resistance by the population in the region, which has been effectively ruled by tribal groups. Musharraf and Bhutto had reached a tentative compromise before her assassination; what will happen now is anyone's guess.

There is a conundrum that must be addressed and solved in these efforts. The puzzle, of course, is how best to control or eliminate religious terrorism directed at the United States. One solution is to attack it at its source, tracking down and eliminating terrorists and their organizations. That is clearly the approach that underlies the efforts in Afghanistan, and is the basis for the connection between Iraq and terrorism. The problem with this solution is that it has failed to eliminate the problem, most notably, capturing or killing bin Laden and his close coterie. It can also be argued that the effort is counterproductive. If the statements of international religious terrorists like bin Laden are to be believed, much of their objection to the United States is America's continued presence in Islam's sacred places (this was the basis of bin Laden's early *fatwas* against Americans). Iraq, of course, houses a number of the places holiest to Shi'a Islam, and while Al Qaeda is fundamentalist Sunni (Wahhabi), there is still a connection. The objection here is that American presence, including attempts to suppress terrorism, may actually stimulate terrorist activity by providing a recruiting device for terrorists. The Al Qaeda in Iraq phenomenon can be cited as some support for this thesis.

The polar opposite solution, deriving from the argument that American overt presence in the region is part of the irritant on which international religious terrorism is based, is that the United States should remove itself from the region, at least militarily. This possibility, however, is not given serious consideration because American interests in the area go beyond the suppression of terrorism. Two areas of interest stand out. One is the ongoing tension between the United States and Iran. The current emphasis of that tension is the alleged Iranian nuclear weapons program and Iran's resulting status as a potential nuclear proliferator. Can the United States leave the Persian Gulf region and maintain any leverage over events in Iran? The other reason the United States remains involved in the area is to guarantee its continuing access to Persian Gulf oil. Denials by the Bush administration officials notwithstanding, the United States would view the entire Persian Gulf littoral very differently if it had no petroleum. The United States is moving to lessen that dependency in a variety of ways: finding alternate sources of oil, including Iraq, developing new sources such as the Alaskan wildlife preserves, and conservation to reduce demand. None of these are short-term solutions, however, and in the short- and middle-terms (e.g., through 2020 or even beyond), the United States will need Persian Gulf oil, for which it will have to compete in an increasingly competitive world market. Physically abandoning the region during this period would be a potentially perilous step, to put it mildly. Invading Iraq may not have been a good idea; a precipitous total withdrawal might be a worse idea.

Iran and Proliferation

In an interview quoted by Nasr and Takeyh in a recent *Foreign Affairs*, Secretary of State Condoleezza Rice declared, "Iran constitutes the single most important single-country strategic challenge to the United States and to the kind of Middle East we want to see." Iran has been on the radar as one of American opponents since 1979 and the Iranian Revolution, it was one of the three countries identified as the "axis of evil" by President Bush in his 2002 State of the Union address, and more recently, there have been thinly veiled hints of military action against the largest and most powerful state in the Middle East because of proliferation concerns and alleged Iranian assistance to Shiite elements of the Iraqi resistance. Iran has also been one of the major neoconservative targets for "regime change," along with Syria, usually listed right after Iraq. Why?

The post-World War II relationship between the United States and Iran has been tumultuous. Between World War II and the Iranian Revolution of 1979, the United States developed and nurtured a close and enveloping relationship with the Iranians and particularly their leader, Shah Reza Pahlevi. During this period, the United States helped establish and sustain the Shah in power, providing massive assistance aimed at transforming Iran into a modern power that the Shah hoped would reestablish something like the old Peacock Empire. In return, Iran served as the surrogate for American interests in the region, using American-supplied military power to insure the free flow of oil from the region to the West. The United States, in turn, was not required to keep a visible military presence in the Middle East. All that changed in 1979, when the Iranian Revolution drove the Shah from Teheran and brought to power the fundamentalist Shiite religious regime of which the Ayatollah Ruhollah Khomeini was the most visible symbol, and which still dominates Iranian politics.

The current relationship between Iran and the United States can only be understood in the context of that history and evolution. The United

States was instrumental both in promoting the rise and power of the Shah, and in his demise. A strong, independent Iran was seen as a counterweight to potential Soviet intrusion into the oil-rich Persian Gulf areas after World War II, and after the Iranian people voted for a democratic government (Prime Minister Dr. Mohammed Mossadeqh) in 1951 that threw the Shah from power, the CIA helped organize a coup d'etat that put the Shah back in power in 1953. From that point until the Shah was overthrown in 1979, the two countries enjoyed extremely close relations. Most prominently, the United States was the leading force in assisting the Shah's White Revolution, a series of reforms intended to secularize and westernize the world's largest majority Shiite country.

The Shah-U.S. collaboration sowed the seeds of the current problems between the two countries, as well as providing a harbinger, had anyone drawn it, with parallel processes in Iraq. In retrospect, trying to westernize and secularize a Shiite state put the Shah and his American allies on a collision course with the sectarian, theocratic values of the Shiite majority and its leadership (unlike Sunni Islam, Shiites have a hierarchical arrangement of their religious leadership). The Shiite hierarchy was progressively displaced within the Iranian power structure and resented the fact. Resentment grew and centered about the exiled Ayatollah Khomeini. In the latter 1970s, the Carter administration withdrew some support for the Shah due to his abysmal human rights record, and the Shiite opposition strengthened. With the Shah debilitated by the cancer that would eventually kill him, the revolution began, and in February 1979 the Shah fled the country. American influence left with him and was replaced by the images of the Iran Hostage Crisis (the American embassy was occupied by Iranians and held until January 1981) and the depiction of the United States as the "Great Satan."

Geopolitically, the effect of the Iranian Revolution was to remove the Iranian surrogacy over U.S. oil interests. The Iranian military would no longer enforce American guaranteed access to regional petroleum, but would become a part of the ongoing threat to that access. The result was the need for an ongoing American military presence in the Persian Gulf that continues today. After the United States conquered Iraq, the geopolitical rivalry expanded, as the United States became the regional counterweight to Iran for the Sunni Islamic states in the region. As Nasr and Takeyh explain it, "For close to half a century, the Arab world saw Iraq's military as its bulwark in the Persian Gulf. Having dismantled that force in 2003, the United States is now the only power present in the Gulf that can contain Iran militarily." As Nasr and Takeyh point out, this dynamic alone will make American military withdrawal from the region more difficult than it might otherwise be.

Iran and the United States have thus gone from being close allies to being rivals, even enemies in some depictions. This evolution complicates the United States' role in the region. First and foremost, it puts the United States into competition with the largest, most powerful state in the Persian Gulf area. Iran is a very large state, with an area of 632,296 square miles (using *CIA World Factbook* data), slightly larger than Alaska and 3.75 times the size of Iraq. It has a population slightly over 65 million people (July 2007 estimate), which is about 2.4 times that of Iraq. According to the 2007 *Military Balance*, it also has the world's eighth largest army with 545,000 under arms. Its proven oil reserves stand at 138 billion barrels, and it exports 2.8 million barrels per day. Iran is a country of consequence, and one against which military action, as has recently been hinted, would not be an easy task. On the other hand, Persian, Shiite Iran and the Sunni Arab states of the region (virtually all the other Islamic states in the region) are rivals of Iran's. In fact, the only other major country in the region with a Shiite majority is Iraq, a fact that complicates the Iraq situation as well.

The United States and Iran are currently at odds over two primary issues. One of these is alleged Iranian assistance to elements of the Iraqi resistance. The Iranians, for instance, have been accused of providing the Iraqis with sophisticated IED devices (known as explosively formed penetrators or EFPs) capable of penetrating American armored vehicles. Because of this assistance, which the Iranians deny, the Iranian Revolutionary Guard's Quds Force, an element of the Iranian religious power structure, has been condemned by the United States.

The more consequential, and controversial, issue is the Iranian nuclear program. Iran has begun an aggressive program of nuclear power plant construction, which it maintains is for power generation. The United States has argued that the Iranians are actually engaged in a concerted effort to obtain nuclear weapons, which is much of the basis of Rice's statement about Iran, and adds to what Nasr and Takeyh refer to as Washington's "sense of urgency" about Iran. The December 2007 release of the U.S. National Intelligence Estimate (NIE, a CIA-produced compilation of data from the various intelligence agencies) indicated that Iran had abandoned its weapons program in 2003, setting off a fierce debate over exactly what the Iranian intent might be. If the NIE is accepted, Iran could probably not obtain nuclear weapons capability until into the 2010s even, with a concerted effort, but suspicious Bush administration officials continue to worry actively about the Iranians. As 2007 ended, however, the NIE had at least cooled active discussion about U.S. military actions against Iran.

There is general agreement, at least outside Iran, that a nuclear-armed Iran would be destabilizing. From a regional vantage point, Iranian possession of nuclear weapons would only exacerbate tensions between Sunni Arabs and Shiite Persians that go back centuries, even millennia, and could spur the Arab states to try to obtain nuclear weapons of their own to offset the Iranians. The United States joins Israel in fearing that the object of an Iranian nuclear capability would be the Jewish state, possibly prompting Israel to attack Iran preemptively, with uncertain consequences after such an attack occurred.

The Iranians, meanwhile, deny they have an interest in nuclear weapons but may be influenced, as suggested earlier, by their observation of a non-nuclear Iraq under Saddam Hussein. Although it sounds fanciful to Americans, the notion that a country might need nuclear weapons to avoid being attacked by the United States had circulated in the developing world (notably within axis of evil countries) before the American invasion, and gained credence when the United States, in fact, attacked a defenseless Iraq. Nuclear weapons possession, by that reasoning, injects an uncertainty into American calculations of the consequences of attacking a nuclear-armed state and may be decisive in avoiding that fate.

The fracas with Iran is exacerbated by two very different impacts. One surrounds the extremely combative style of Iranian President Mahmoud Ahmadinejad, who relishes challenging the Bush administration with a fervor approximating that of Venezuela's President Hugo Chavez. Ahmadinejad's actual political power within Iran is controversial, because he is the leader of the secular government that is overshadowed by the religious "shadow government" run by the Shiite hierarchy (the Revolutionary Guards, for instance, are loyal to the religious hierarchy, not the formal government). Thus, it is not clear how much weight can be attributed to his anti-American positions, and the Iranian government was actually quite helpful in the American action in Afghanistan in 2001 (before Ahmadinejad became president). His combativeness, however, has kept him at odds with the Bush administration that refuses to meet directly with him to discuss points of disagreement (some of the 2008 candidates, most specifically Obama, have suggested that meeting with Ahmadinejad would be an early priority).

The other complication is the military question: Should the United States decide it feels the need to take military action against Iran, what could it do? The first and easy answer is the use of air power, which is readily available (very little of U.S. bombing capability is being used in Iraq, for instance), against Iranian military targets, including nuclear facilities. The effectiveness of such actions is questionable and would almost certainly bring retaliation by Iranian ground forces, probably in Iraq. Beyond that, U.S. capabilities are suspect as long as the great bulk of American ground forces remain tied down in Iraq. At that, the Iranians present a military problem that is far more extensive and complex than Iraq. One can ask whether the United States is in any physical position to pick a fight with Iran, even if it wants to. Any Iraq hangover will also militate against military adventurism in Iran. Yet, Republican candidate Michael Huckabee still warned in a 2008 *Foreign Affairs* article that "Our failure to tackle Iran may be leading inexorably to attacking it" and that if all else fails, "a military strike may become the only viable" option. The Iranians presumably know and understand these inhibitions on the United States, one of the reasons they have not been overtly cooperative with the Americans.

The Oil Glue and "Enduring" American Presence in Iraq

Does the United States Government actually plan to leave Iraq altogether at any time in the near future? Public demands suggest that that should be the direction of policy, but it may be that policymakers and the public are at odds on this question, just as they are on the question of ending the war quickly. Although it has received little overt publicity and is denied when the subject comes up, it may well be that the United States does not plan a withdrawal from Iraq at all. The reason is oil.

Former President Jimmy Carter, in a widely quoted statement on Larry King's CNN broadcast of February 3, 2006, stated this assertion most bluntly: "There are people in Washington . . . who never intend to withdraw military forces from Iraq and they're looking for ten, 20, 50 years in the future. . . . The reason that we went into Iraq was to establish a permanent military base in the gulf region, and I have never heard any of our leaders say that they would commit themselves to the Iraqi people that ten years from now there will be no military bases of the United States in Iraq." (Quoted by Gerson.) When administration officials are asked about ongoing work on military bases in Iraq, they tend to talk about enduring bases. On May 31, 2007, Seale quotes Secretary of Defense Robert Gates as telling a U.S. Pacific Command group in Honolulu that the United States seeks a "long and enduring presence" in Iraq, and that the precedent already exists. "The Korea model is one," he said, "the security relationship we have with Japan is another."

The basis for this enduring presence has been on public display for most of the Iraq War. When the United States invaded the country, it occupied most of the existing Iraqi bases, and it has winnowed that number down, initially to about seventy-five bases that it has used for operational purposes. Of those, fourteen bases "in Northern Iraq (Kurdistan), Baghdad, Anbar Province (home of Sunni Fallujah, Ramadi, and Tikrit), and Shi'a-dominated southern approaches to Baghdad" are under renovation at a cost to American taxpayers of about $1 billion a year, according to Gerson. These bases, according to reports, have been designed and built for the long term, with well-developed infrastructures and amenities, and they could house thousands of American military and civilian personnel. When combined with the construction of the largest American embassy in the world in Baghdad, it is clear that the United States does not plan simply to pack up and leave Iraq when fighting has concluded.

The protection of American access to, or control of, Iraqi oil is the only plausible reason for maintaining such an "enduring" presence. The Korea and Japan analogies are appropriate as models for a lengthy stay, but the reasons are entirely different: Japan was a conquered country (which, of course, Iraq is, if for different reasons), and South Korea had been invaded and conquered, and it apparently needed continuing protection to avoid a repetition. That rationale does not apply in Iraq. There is some danger of interference by Iraq's Sunni (Saudi Arabia, Syria) and Shiite (Iran) neighbors in postwar Iraqi politics, but that is not enough provocation to justify an indefinite American presence.

Protecting the giant Iraqi oil and natural gas reserves from other countries is an adequate justification, but it is a two-step proposition. It first requires a government in Baghdad that will accept a continuing American military presence, which, if the earlier analysis is accurate, will not be easy for any regime that does not want to be labeled a quisling. The problem is particularly difficult if the Iraqis—Hamas-style, as in Palestine—should conduct free and open elections that produce a government that demands the United States leave entirely. In that case, the fallback position for the United States would likely be to advocate greater Kurdish autonomy that included American bases in Kurdistan and oil concessions for American oil companies, including use of the pipeline from Kurdistan to Ceyhan, Turkey. If, on the other hand, a government comes to power that will accept continued American presence, the second requirement would be the ability to exclude the oil interests of other countries, notably China, Russia, and possibly France, from exploiting the Iraqi reserves.

The protection of access to Iraqi oil makes geopolitical sense as an American long-term justification both for the war and for a prolonged presence beyond the current occupation. The geopolitics of energy over the coming decades has already been discussed, and controlling the Iraq oil production system provides at least a partial solution for the United States. Estimates of how much oil can be produced by Iraq vary, with most beginning at about one million barrels a day. That is clearly not enough to sate the American need for imported oil (nearly ten million barrels a day), but the flow can probably be expanded enough to allow the substitution of Iraqi oil for product from politically unreliable (e.g., Venezuela or Saudi Arabia) sources. It has even been suggested that the development of Iraqi reserves could allow the United States to wean itself away from the Saudis and the embarrassing position of supporting a regime that has ties to the terrorists who attacked the United States. Moreover, if the United States seriously follows a policy of reducing its dependence on fossil fuels over the next decade or two, as is widely advocated, having a secure source of petroleum as that dependence is decreased by strategies of alternate fuels, conservation, and the like, can ease that transition period. Control of upstream oil rights by American and British oil giants also contributes to their corporate well being.

If controlling Iraqi oil makes sense, why does the United States not admit that is the (or at least an) objective of the war? Many Iraqis, as noted earlier, by Record, are convinced this has been the motivation all along. Most of those Iraqis cite American oil control as a cynical plot to manipulate and bleed Iraq dry of its only major strategic asset. Admitting this would be tantamount to admitting an imperial motive similar to the secret Sykes-Picot Treaty after World War I that divided Middle Eastern oil resources between Britain and France. At the same time, admitting the oil motivation to the American public would also provoke predictable opposition and would be scandalized by what would be described as a cynical "American blood for oil" manipulation. Most Americans do not like to think of themselves as imperialists.

The plan to remain in Iraq with substantial numbers of troops (probably 50,000 or so, according to a figure endorsed by the Iraq Study Group) for the foreseeable future is inevitable if maintaining a finger on the pulse of Iraqi oil is part of the bedrock of American policy. It comes with costs. These include residual resentment of American military presence throughout the region that will contribute to the attractiveness of terrorism as a means to remove that presence, and tying down significant American military assets that will be unavailable for use elsewhere because they are in

Iraq. Maintaining a residual enduring American military presence in Iraq also makes calls for a larger post-Iraq military more sensible than they might otherwise be: such forces can compensate for forces that remain tied down in Iraq even after the war is over.

The oil-driven enduring presence of the United States after the war has been declared ended in Iraq complicates the question "What after Iraq?" by suggesting that, at one level, there is no "after Iraq" planned by political leaders. This is a prospect that has not been presented directly to the American public, and it is not clear that it is an option the public will embrace. If a sizable American garrison remains in Iraq indefinitely, it does moderate some of the concerns of those who fear a bloodbath after the United States leaves, because the Americans will not really leave, and will presumably remain available to quell such violence. On the other hand, that continuing presence may also provide a continuing shield behind which the Iraqis can avoid solving their political problems. Those prospects raise the question seldom asked, but which begs for an answer: Why is the United States *really* in Iraq, and what will it take to achieve that goal and allow the disengagement the American people have asserted they want? Or, is the pursuit of oil security in Iraq an adequate justification for an enduring presence?

UNFORESEEABLE MISSIONS

Foreseeable missions may be difficult, involve significant threats, and require considerable resources and ingenuity to thwart, but the parameters of the risks involved are at least known. At the same time, there are situations and threats that cannot be foreseen and which will, from time to time surface and require attention.

Unforeseeable problems, and the missions they create, are of a different order from foreseeable problems. Mostly, they thwart careful, purposive attempts to match resources to threats, and thus, to reduce risks. How can one prepare for something that cannot be conceptualized? By definition, one cannot prepare for that which one cannot anticipate, and the result is to maximize the amount of uncertainty with which one must deal.

Will there be unforeseeable missions in the post-Iraq future? Of course there will be, but the heart of the problem is that no one can predict them. One can extrapolate from the past into the future—for instance, there will be more asymmetrical challenges in the American future, and they will build upon, but likely not exactly replicate, what the United States faced in Iraq. As suggested earlier in the chapter, the United States can try to anticipate the vectors of change, but the times and places and exact outlines of the challenges are impossible to know in advance.

The historic military method for dealing with uncertain future events is through what is known as *worst case analysis*. The basic idea is to determine what is the worst possible threat that could face the country (the worst case) and then to plan to thwart that situation. The reasoning goes that if the worst case is effectively neutralized, then other, less dangerous possibilities (known as *lesser included cases*) will also be neutralized by the resources devoted to countering the worst case.

The Cold War was the midwife of worst case analysis and demonstrates the principle in action. During the confrontation with Soviet communism, the worst case was all-out war with the Soviet Union and its allies. That war would involve a massive conventional (symmetrical), World War II-style war in Europe and possibly a nuclear exchange between the superpowers. To neutralize this worst case, the United States and its NATO allies maintained large forces in Europe to dissuade a Soviet conventional invasion of Western Europe and massive nuclear forces threatening a cataclysmic retaliation, should the Soviets launch nuclear missiles against the American homeland or that of its allies. The lesser included case corollary suggested such preparations should deal with threats across the board.

The latter assumption was based on the idea that these lesser cases would be smaller microcosms of the worst case: that a non-Soviet threat elsewhere would also be conventional, and that the forces built to confront the Russians would also be capable of dealing with other contingencies. The flaw was that those lesser threats were *not* microcosms of the worst case. Rather, the lesser cases were quite different than the worst case; they were asymmetrical, with the asymmetry aimed at blunting forces built for conventional war. Thus, planning for the worst case did not necessarily prepare the United States for lesser contingencies. Vietnam is the clearest case in point.

Worst case analysis is difficult to apply in the contemporary, and especially post-Iraq, environment, for three reasons. First, there is no obvious worst case (certainly not one of the overarching presence of the Soviet threat) for which to prepare. The closest available paradigm is terrorism and the GWOT, but it is not an exact match. The terrorist threat is diffuse rather than centralized, its exact nature and structure are not a matter of universal agreement, and it is unclear how one confronts it. It is clearly more than a military threat, and were it adopted as the standard for military preparation for unforeseeable missions, military capability would be compromised. Moreover, any plan for dealing with terrorism is a response to an asymmetrical warfare threat, which is the very kind of problem from which the American military shies away.

The second reason worst case analysis might not be applicable is that the post-Iraq period is likely to be resource-constrained. The sources of this restraint are likely to come from two sources. One will be the impact of the Iraq hangover. There will be a reluctance to involve American forces in conflicts anywhere for fear that doing so might create another Iraq-style quagmire. In the 1980s, a popular bumper sticker read, "El Salvador is Spanish for Vietnam." An insurgency was being waged with the United States supporting the government's counterinsurgency efforts and this was an admonition against involving American forces in El Salvador. The next time the United States seems poised for another Third World intervention, will there be bumper stickers asserting that "X (the country) is Arabic (or whatever language is spoken there) for Iraq"? The public reaction to the rumors of military strikes against Iran suggests that there will be.

The other source of resource constraint is likely to be the competition for budgetary priorities within the United States. There will be economic repercussions of the war, which has been financed by deficit spending at record levels and the deferral of spending on domestic matters (children's health care, for instance). A post-Iraq administration is almost certainly going to have to adopt policies reducing or eliminating government deficits and funding neglected domestic programs, the State Children's Health Insurance Program (SCHIP), for example. There will almost certainly be less funds available for the large military funding that worst case analysis indicates.

The third reason that worst case analysis is difficult to apply is that there will be the residual commitment to Iraq. Once again, there is very little discussion of this prospect, and especially little debate about what it will cost. When Iraqification is declared a success and American combat troops are removed from the country or redeployed to the enduring bases in or around Iraq, the American financial commitment to Iraq is not going to end. There will be a continuing program of economic infrastructure rebuilding and developing (which the Bush administration has beggared, leaving much work to be done), and the forces that remain will not be without cost. Unless there is a sufficient public demand for removing *all* U.S. forces from Iraq, what is left behind could remain a Korea-like burden for years or even decades into the future.

It is impossible to know where and when contingencies may emerge that will cause the United States to feel the need to employ military forces in the near future. Some temptations can reasonably be anticipated, and most of these are in the Middle East. A rededication to Afghanistan is one such foreseeable mission, and the possibility of some form of military activity in Iran or even Pakistan cannot be ruled out altogether. Hopefully, one of the positive legacies of Iraq will be that either of those, or other, contingencies will receive a much more thorough vetting before it occurs than did the decision to invade Iraq.

And then there are the unforeseeable missions. It is a cautionary note that the American involvement with Iraq began as an unforeseen crisis: the invasion of Kuwait by the Iraqis in 1990. At the time, the attack was widely advertised as evidence of the need for vigilance and preparation. Who would have thought, in late spring or even early summer 1990, that the United States would be in a military confrontation with Iraq in September 1990? Yet it happened, and it is probably true that had it not, the whole sequence of events leading the United States to its current predicament would not have followed. What after Iraq? One can only hope that it will not be another Iraq.

SELECT BIBLIOGRAPHY

Betts, Richard K. "How to Think about Terrorism." *The Wilson Quarterly* 30 (Winter 2006). 44–49.

Boot, Max. "The Struggle to Transform the Military." *Foreign Affairs* 84, 2 (March/April 2005), 103–118.

Burke, Jason. "Think Again: Al Qaeda." *Foreign Policy* (May/June 2004), 18–26.

De Bellaigne, Christopher. "Think Again: Iran." *Foreign Policy* (May/June 2005), 18–26.

Dobbins, James. "Iraq: The Unwinnable War." *Foreign Affairs* 84, 1 (January/February 2005), 6–25.

———. "Who Lost Iraq? Lessons from the Debacle." *Foreign Affairs* 86, 5 (September/October 2007), 61–74.

Donovan, Michael. "Iran, Israel, and Nuclear Weapons in the Middle East." *CDI Terrorism Project* (online), February 4, 2002.

Gallagher, James J. *Low-Intensity Conflict: A Guide for Tactics, Techniques, and Procedures.* Mechanicburg, PA: Stackpole Books, 1992.

Gerson, Joseph. "'Enduring' U.S. Bases in Iraq." *CommonDreams.org*, March 19, 2007 (http://www.commondreams,org/views071319-26.htm)

Goulding, Vincent J. Jr. "Back to the Future with Asymmetrical Warfare." *Parameters* XXX, 4 (Winter 2000–2001), 21–30.

Haass, Richard N. "Regime Change and Its Limits." *Foreign Affairs* 84, 1 (January/February 2005), 66–78.

Hoffman, Bruce. *Inside Terrorism* (Second Ed.). New York: Columbia University Press, 2006.

Huckabee, Michael D. "America's Priorities in the War on Terror." *Foreign Affairs* 87, 1 (January/February 2008), 155–168.

Jenkins, Brian. "International Terrorism." Robert J. Art and Kenneth B. Waltz (eds.), *The Use of Force: Military Power and International Relations* (Sixth Ed.). New York: Rowman and Littlefield Publishers, 2004.

Keegan, John. *A History of Warfare*. London: Hutchison, 1991.

Lind, William S., Keith Nightengale, John F. Schmitt, Joseph W. Sutton, and Gary J. Wilson. "The Changing Face of War: Into the Fourth Generation." *Marine Corps Gazette*, October 1989, 21–26.

Mao tse-Tung. *Mao tse-Tung on Guerrilla Warfare* (Translated by Samuel B. Griffith). New York: Praeger, 1961.

Mueller, John. "Is There Still a Terrorist Threat?" *Foreign Affairs* 85, 5 (September/October 2006), 2–8.

Nacos, Brigette L. *Terrorism and Counterterrorism: Understanding Threats and Responses in the Post-9/11 World*. New York: Penguin Academics, 2006.

Nasr, Vali, and Ray Takeyh. "The Costs of Containing Iran." *Foreign Affairs* 87, 1 (January/February 2008), 85–94.

O'Hanlon, Michael E. *Defense Strategy for the Post-Saddam Era*. Washington, DC: The Brookings Institution Press, 2005.

Peters, Ralph. *Fighting for the Future: Will America Triumph?* Mechanicsburg, PA: Stackpole Books, 2001.

Pillar, Paul. "Counterterrorism after Al Qaeda." *Washington Quarterly* 27, 3 (Summer 2004), 101–113.

———. "Intelligence, Policy, and the War in Iraq." *Foreign Affairs* 85, 2 (March/April 2006), 15–28.

Reidel, Bruce. *Al Qaeda Strikes Back.*" *Foreign Affairs* 86, 3 (May/June 2007), 24–40.

Seale, Patrick. "U.S. Is Building Bases on Iraq." *Gulfnews.com*, June 4, 2007 (http://archive.gulfnews,com/articles/print_friendly_version.jsp?global_name=channels/g)

Sloan, Stephen. *Beating International Terrorism: An Action Strategy for Preemption and Punishment*. Montgomery, AL: Air University Press, 2000.

Snow, Donald M. *Distant Thunder: Patterns of Conflict in the Developing World* (Second Ed.). Armonk, NY: M. E. Sharpe, 1997.

————. *National Security for a New Era: Globalization and Geopolitics after Iraq* (Third Ed.). New York: Pearson Longman, 2008.

————. *September 11, 2001: The New Face of War?* New York: Longman, 2002.

Sun Tzu. *The Art of War* (Translated by Samuel B. Griffith). Oxford, UK: Oxford University Press, 1963.

Van Cleveld, Martin. *The Transformation of War*. New York: Free Press, 1991.